Praise for *Abraham Hanibal Prince of Logone*

Scholars in recent years have attained a more complex understanding of the facts of Pushkin's African heritage and a more sophisticated approach to its possible significance for both the poet and his readers in his own time and in ours. Ground-breaking works in this regard include Dieudonné Gnammankou's "Abraham Hanibal, l'aïeul noir de Pouchkine" (Paris, Présence Africaine, 1996).

Melissa Frazier, *North American Pushkin Review*

Abraham Petrovich Hanibal, the Russian African, was in every sense a man of extraordinary destiny. No other African in eighteenth century Russia, or for that matter anywhere else in Europe, received so many honours and distinctions.

Leonid Arinstein, Russian Cultural Foundation

Dieudonné Gnammankou's work on Gannibal, culminating in the publication of « Abraham Hanibal, l'aïeul noir de Pouchkine », ushered in a new era in the study of Pushkin's African ancestry. Gnammankou, a Beninese scholar, has definitively established that Gannibal came from an area in central Africa bordering Lake Chad (currently a part of North Cameroon) and not from Abyssinia or Ethiopia as scholars had earlier asserted. The interest (and in some cases scandal) that has ensued after this discovery is worthy of fiction. Rumours of a conflict between an Ethiopian « mafia » that has thrived for years off a generous fund devoted to Gannibal and Gnammankou as a result of his destruction of the Ethiopian version of Gannibal's origins circulated among Africans in Russia. There has been a flurry of new, largely academic works on Gannibal in the wake of Gnammankou's bombshell and in 1996 scholars celebrated the tricentennial of Abram Gannibal's birth, which served as an occasion for a revisiting and revision of the previous research on Gannibal's life; most likely the tricentennial, nourished by the new information provided by Gnammankou, generated a new focus on Gannibal.

Theimer Nepomnyashchy, Harriman Institute, Columbia University, *Under the skies of my Africa : Alexander Pushkin and Blackness*

Gannibal's roots in Africa, however, long remained vague. Russian biographers decided early on that he was Ethiopian, though the only known fact was that he himself wrote in a letter to Empress Elizabeth, Peter the Great's daughter, that he was from the town of "Lagon." Vladimir Nabokov, conducting research for his definitive translation of Pushkin's "Eugene Onegin," was the first to cast serious doubt on the Ethiopian angle. But it was Mr. Gnammankou who first made a strong case in 1995 that "Lagon" was Logone, the capital of the ancient Kotoko kingdom of Logone-Birni on the southern side of Lake Chad, now located in northern Cameroon.

Mr. Gnammankou's thesis caused something of a stir in Russia, where Pushkin has the status of a god. Roots in black Africa, Mr. Gnammankou suspects, seemed less acceptable than roots in the ancient Christian kingdom of Ethiopia. Nonetheless, his book on Gannibal was translated into Russian in 1999 and was judged the best book on Pushkin that year at the Moscow Book Fair. In 2000, a documentary about Gannibal shown on Russian television included scenes shot in Logone, as well as an interview with Mr. Gnammankou.

Serge Schmemann, The New York Times / International Herald Tribune

Gnammankou has written an insightful and detailed biography of Pushkin's Negro ancestor that works on two levels. On one level, it is a historical narrative that provides the reader with facts and dispels the misconceptions surrounding Pushkin's great-grandfather. On another level, the book reads like a good detective novel, where the author seeks to clear up the mystery of how and why this African ended up in Russia. Both levels are superbly handed,.. By writing such a book, Gnammankou has set the stage for future work on Blacks in the Diaspora.

Dwayne Woods, in Black Renaissance, New York University

ABRAHAM HANIBAL
Prince of Logone
PUSHKIN'S AFRICAN ANCESTOR

Dieudonné Gnammankou

Translated from the French by Edyth Watt

Publisher: Books of Africa Limited

16 Overhill Road

East Dulwich, London

SE22 0PH

United Kingdom

Web site: www.booksofafrica.com
Emails: admin@booksofafrica.com

sales@booksofafrica.com

Copyright : ©Books of Africa 2015

ISBN : 978-0-9566380-3-8

A CIP catalogue record for this book is available from the British Library.

Printed in India by Imprint Digital Ltd

First published in French by Présence Africaine under the title: Abraham Hanibal, l'Aïeul noir d'Alexandre Pouchkine

CONTENTS

PREFACE 9

FOREWORD 13

INTRODUCTION 17

CHAPTER I – From Logone to Constantinople 21

"Under my African skies" 21

Constantinople 26

CHAPTER II – The White Tsar's Black Godson 43

Ibrahim in the Kremlin 43

The school of war: an African witnesses
the Great Northern War 48

The Tsar's private secretary 55

CHAPTER III – In the land of Louis XV, KING OF FRANCE 60

The Journey to Europe 60

In France 63

Letters from Paris 66

The School of Artillery at La Fère 72

A victim of French financial reform 76

CHAPTER IV – Return to Russia 79

Peter I's African Disciple 79

Abraham's Library 84

The death of the Emperor and the accession of Catherine I ... 85

Mathematics tutor to the future Emperor 87

Abraham's manuscript 90

CHAPTER V – Exile in Siberia 92

The Friends of Princess Volkonskaya 92

Menshikov's Infamous Ukase 95

Hanibal! 100

CHAPTER VI – The first marriage 104

Under orders from Count von Münnich 104

The Baby Scandal and the Poison Affair 107

CHAPTER VII – A new life: 1733-1741 126

Retirement in the country 126

True Love 128

Reval's Black Lieutenant Colonel 132

Reval – 1741 134

CHAPTER VIII – Major General and statesman 1742-1752 139

The reign of Elizabeth 139

Reval – 1742 144

Hanibal – Defender of Russia's Interests 149

The von Tiren Affair 154

Holmer the Rebel 157

Mission to Finland 161

The Black Russian Nobleman 162

The Shadow of Eudoxia 164

CHAPTER IX – Chief engineer 1752-1762 168

    Hanibal, technical director of the Russian Imperial Army 168

    Director of Works on the Kronstadt Canal and Head
of the Engineering Corps 1755-1759 172

    Imperial Russia's first black General in Chief 179

CHAPTER X – The black lord 183

    Retirement in Suyda 183

    Reasons to be proud 186

    Hanibal's Will 189

    The death of the Patriarch 192

EPILOGUE 204

ENDNOTES 206

APPENDIX 1 220

    WHERE WAS IBRAHAM HANIBAL'S BIRTHPLACE? 220

APPENDIX 2 225

    REPORT BY IRINA YURIEVA 225

APPENDIX 3 229

    AUTOBIOGRAPHICAL NOTE BY HANIBAL'S SON,
PETER ABRAMOVICH HANIBAL (1742-1826) 229

APPENDIX 4 232

    THE FIRST PART OF ALEXANDER PUSHKIN'S
AUTOBIOGRAPHY 232

APPENDIX 5 237

    CHRONOLOGY 237

APPENDIX 6 243

GENEALOGY OF THE HANIBAL FAMILY
(1696-1906) 243

APPENDIX 7 245

GENEALOGICAL TREE: ABRAHAM HANIBAL TO PUSHKIN 245

APPENDIX 8 246

LIST OF EMPERORS OF RUSSIA IN THE XVIIIth CENTURY 246

APPENDIX 9 247

INVENTORY OF HANIBAL'S BOOKS 247

BIBLIOGRAPHY 251

LIST OF CAPTIONS 258

INDEX 261

PREFACE

Abraham Petrovich Hanibal, the Russian African, was in every sense a man of extraordinary destiny. No other African in eighteenth century Russia, or for that matter anywhere else in Europe, received so many honours and distinctions. He was the product of several civilizations – African Turkish-Islamic, Western Christian in the sophisticated French version and finally Russian-Orthodox. An exceptionally talented man, he was the only African ever to be made a general in the Russian army.

I have not yet touched upon one essential element in the story of this remarkable man – that is the intimate connection between him and two of the most outstanding personalities in Russian history: the greatest creative talent on the one hand and the greatest talent for destruction on the other, one a great poet and the other a great emperor, the Russian Christ and the Russian Anti-Christ. He was the great-great grandfather of the one and the godson of the other.

If for nothing else Hanibal would have been known and honoured in Russian history for those amazing connections. Peter the Great's reign in Russia was as illustrious as that of Louis XIV or Napoleon in France. Everyone in Peter I's entourage shares his fame – and Hanibal was not only his godson; he was also his close disciple and devoted companion-in-arms.

Peter I may be the equal of Louis XIV or Napoleon, but the reverence felt for Alexander Pushkin in the spiritual life of Russia is far greater than that for the great English, French or German poets and writers – Shakespeare, Molière, or Goethe in Western Europe.

The Russians' devotion to Pushkin is almost a religion and anyone connected with his divine person is naturally assumed to be a saint. No one who is unaware of this extraordinary phenomenon will be able to appreciate the esteem in which the Russians hold Abraham Petrovich Hanibal.

But what did Peter I destroy and what did Alexander Pushkin create?

Russia's history is a bitter tale. Like France and Germany, it has been shattered by constant wars with its neighbours and simultaneous internal unrest. It has won through, not by superior force of arms – arms were often lacking and were never more advanced than those of the enemy – but by sheer determination and the people's profound faith in their God and the Tsar, the chosen of God and the symbol of the Fatherland.

The Russian state's unique character was developed over the centuries through the mutual confidence in each other of the Tsar, the Church and the people. The Church made no claim to secular power and – at least until the rule of Peter I – the secular power made no claim to the spiritual. Regardless of the suffering imposed on them by both the Tsar and the Church the people never ceased to trust them piously and in times of danger rose as one to defend Russia from its enemies.

At the turn of the seventeenth and eighteenth centuries, this traditional harmony was disrupted by the celebrated reforms of Peter I. He sought to "catch up with Europe", and tried to re-direct Russia's social and economic culture towards speedy development of the country's industrial and commercial potential. In doing so, he crushed the power of the Church and made himself the sole arbiter of the fate and well-being of his subjects. The authority of the Church and the spiritual life of Russia were diminished.

During the years when the Church was weak the people's thirst for a religious dimension found expression in literature, endowed with the responsibility of defending and re-affirming fundamental Christian values. Hence its high spiritual content, the great beauty of its poetry and the brilliant tradition which gave us Pushkin, Gogol, Dostoyevsky, Blok, Pasternak, Akhmatova, and the Russian religious philosophers of the twentieth century.

Pushkin was the first: loved not only for his works, but because he gave his life in an honourable cause with the nobility of soul we associate with the great humanitarian spirit of Christianity.

Anything to do with Pushkin's life is sacred. That is why in Russia such an interest is taken in his forebears, though genealogy is not normally a subject which Russians find very absorbing. The name of his great-great grandfather – Abraham Hanibal – is the subject of legend and unsubstantiated "discoveries". One of these legends concerns the supposed Ethiopian origins of Hanibal. It appeared from nowhere but has proved surprisingly difficult to discredit, being passed on from one book to another and one scholarly work to the next, without being questioned...and there are many works on Hanibal in Russia!

What are the facts that the legend ignores?

There are two: Hanibal, by his own account, was born in the town of Lagon or Logone, the capital of a principality where his father was ruler. The town and the principality of the same name appear on eighteenth century maps of Africa in the area of Lake Chad, and there is no other town with the same name anywhere else on the continent. In complete disregard of the direct evidence, Hanibal's homeland has been sought everywhere but there – in the little village of Logo in the Hamassen region of Eritrea – in another little place called Logo on the bank of the Mareb River (Eritrea) – with no reservations about confusing these names with that given personally by Hanibal.

It has fallen to another African, a researcher into Slavonic studies, to reject all these preconceived notions, and to make a careful study of the map of his home continent in order to identify the town and principality of Logone.

The town of Logone is situated on the banks of the river Logone, known in the local language as Lagane. There is another circumstance, which for some unknown reason has escaped attention. Hanibal, recounting his abduction, remembered how his sister, Lagane(!) threw herself into the water and swam for a long time behind the boat carrying the boy into slavery...

Lagane: was it a name given to the sister in remembrance of the river, or was it a mixture of half-remembered words in Hanibal's

11

account? (The name of his sister, the word Lagane meaning the river and his people, the Laganie or Lagwanie). Whatever the case, one would have to be blind not to pick out the name.

I should like to add that I have not changed one word in the research paper produced by Dieudonné Gnammankou. There was no need to do so. Read it and judge for yourself.

Leonid Arinstein.[1]
Saint Petersburg, April 1995

---

[1] Professor of Russian and West European Literature (Moscow, St. Petersburg, Ivanovo, Cambridge, Birmingham, London…), formerly Dean of the Faculty of Modern Languages at the Institute of Civil Engineering, Leningrad. Dr. Arinstein is one of the most eminent Russian specialists on Pushkin. He is the author of over 100 articles and books and since his retirement has acted as consultant to the president of the Russian Cultural foundation, Nikita Mikhailkov, and as Coordinator of the Anglo-Russian project for the translation of Pushkin's complete works into English.

FOREWORD

The nature and depth of involvement of peoples of black African descent in the historical developments in early modern Europe attracted little scholarly interest before the late twentieth century. This neglect left intact the prevalent popular perception blatantly articulated by the eminent philosopher Immanuel Kant in his eighteenth-century essay on *Observations on the Feeling of the Beautiful and Sublime*, alleging that:

"...The African Negro by nature has no feelings which rise above the trifling not a single one was ever found who presented anything great in art or science or any other praise-worthy quality, even though among the whites some continually rise aloft from the lowest rabble, and through superior gifts earn respect in the world. So fundamental is the difference between these two races of man." [1]

The esteemed philosopher, who during his 80-years of life never ventured as far as a hundred miles from his native Königsberg [now Kaliningrad] on the Baltic Sea, apparently had missed the mid-eighteenth-century saga of the African general Abraham Hanibal, who commanded the Russian army governing Reval [now Tallinn], just some four hundred miles to the north on the Gulf of Finland. In retrospect Hanibal's fame derives mainly from the fact that he was to become the maternal great-grandfather of the single greatest Russian cultural icon, Alexander Pushkin. However, as Dieudonné Gnammankou richly details in the present splendid biography, here was an historical figure of singular accomplishments on his own merit. Demonstrating through meticulous detective work that Hanibal's most likely place of birth was in the region of present-day Cameroon, Gnammankou dispels the racist mythology popular until now even in Russia that made Alexander Pushkin's direct descent from a Black African unthinkable. With this biography Gnammankou joins a growing number of other scholars now reminding the broader public of just how long Blacks have been making a constructive contribution to European societies.[2]

The most famous of a corps of black court servants that would be brought to Russia in the period from the seventeenth century to the end of the tsarist regime, Hanibal was acquired in Constantinople for tsar Peter the Great at the age of 8. For years he bore only the names Abraham and Petrov, the latter of which he acquired when baptized in 1707 into the Orthodox Church at Vilnius, with Peter the Great as his godfather and the wife of the Polish King August II, Christina, as his godmother. He subsequently became the tsar's secretary, orderly and adjutant, serving him both at home and on travels and military campaigns, such as the Battle of Poltava in 1709 and the Russian victory at Hangö on the Baltic in 1714. In 1716 Peter sent him to France along with several other students to acquire a higher education to better serve the modernizing Russian state. He remained for six years, studying mathematics and military engineering. He returned to Russia from France with what was one of the largest and most up-to-date libraries in the empire, numbering some 400 volumes and including such authors as Euclid, Machiavelli, Racine and Corneille, in addition to the latest technical works. He himself authored a substantial book in two volumes entitled *Geometriia I fortifikatsiia*, published in 1725-1726, and dedicated to Empress Catherine I.[3] As a military engineer in the 1740s, he rose to the rank of full general and from then until 1751 he served as commandant of the city of Reval. He was granted a number of estates in Pskov and Petersburg provinces, with hundreds of serfs. Hanibal would also later direct major canal construction projects before his final retirement. He died in relative obscurity in 1781, leaving his estates to his children and his Swedish wife of 43 years, Christine von Sjöberg. All four of their sons, out of their seven children, also became military officers, with two of them, Ivan and Peter, also attaining the rank of general. Ivan gained special acclaim leading battles against the Turks and founded the town of Kherson in the Ukraine.[4]

Here it should be noted that there were also instances of Blacks rising to comparable prominence in other parts of Europe in the eighteenth century. An example in Kant's own German philosophical circles was Anton Wilhelm Amo (1700-1750), who entered the universities at Halle in 1727 and Wittenberg in 1730, where he became skilled in Latin, Greek, Hebrew, French, German and Dutch; earned a doctoral degree in philosophy from the University of Wittenberg; and became a lecturer at the University of Halle and later at the University of Jena. Nearby in the Netherlands the former slave Jacobus Capitein (1717-1747) also mastered several European languages and became a Dutch Reformed Church predicant after completing theological training at the University of Leiden in 1742. In England an eighteenth-century counterpart worth mentioning in this group for comparison is Ignatius Sancho (1729-1780), a former slave who became famous as a writer only after his letters were published posthumously in 1782 and became a best seller. Other prominent examples were the eighteenth-century black courtiers Angelo Soliman (1721-1796), at the royal court in Vienna, and Adolph Ludvig Couschi [called Badin] (1747?-182(2)) in Stockholm. There were as well illustrious contemporaries in France: the Chevalier de Saint-George (1745-1799) who excelled as a composer and performer of classical music, was a widely recognized master swordsman, and commanded a special black legion formed by the National Assembly during the French Revolution. One of his junior officers was Thomas Alexandre Dumas (1762-1806) who would later rise to the rank of general under Napoleon, and incidentally became the father of the great nineteenth-century novelist Alexandre Dumas père (1802-1870).

Yet, none of these elite figures matched Abraham Hanibal in terms of career achievements. Nevertheless, he remains little known outside of Russia. Even there his complete story only became available upon publication of the Russian version of Gnammankou's biography in 1999, which soon garnered the prestigious Moscow International Book Fair prize for the best Book on Pushkin for that year. The combination of the Russian edition, the original French edition published in 1996, and this first English edition finally provides the broader international public access to the full dimensions of this remarkable story. Furthermore, this is still very timely early in this new century that is witnessing an unprecedented level of Black population in both Russia and Europe in general, and where the old prejudices fostering racial and colour bias are still very much alive throughout the world.

Allison Blakely
Boston, Massachusetts
June 27, 2012

---

1. Kant, Immanuel. *Observations on the Feeling of the Beautiful and Sublime*. [1764] Trans. John T. Goldthwait. University of California Press, 1961, 2003.

2. Dmitri Anoutchine, "Alexandre Sergeevich Pouchkin: Esquisse anthropologique," *Ruskie Vedomosti* Moscow, 1899." Soloviev's comment appeared in *Vestnik Evropy* (September 1900), 305.

3. A recent biography persuasively locates his place of origin, consistent with his own account from archival documents, in the region of present-day Cameroon, rather than in Ethiopia as indicated by earlier biographers who were skeptical of Gannibal's version. Dieudonné Gnammankou, *Abram Gannibal* (Moscow: Molodaia Gvardia, 1999) 64-65. See also I.L. Feinberg, *Abram Petrovich Gannibal praded Pushkina*, ed., A.B. Davidson (Moscow: Nauka, 1983), 64-65.

4. M. Vegner, *Predki Pushkina* (Moscow: Sovietskii Pisatel', 1937), 210.

Introduction

by Dieudonné Gnammankou

"In Russia, where there is very little in the way of historical memoirs, famous men are quickly forgotten. Thus, the amazing life of Annibal[1] is known only through family tradition. In time I hope to be able to publish his complete biography." The writer of these lines is the great Russian poet, Pushkin. In 1825, he included this piece of information in a note to readers in the first edition of his celebrated verse novel, *Eugène Onegin*.

In August of the same year, Pushkin wrote in a letter to Madame P. Osipova: "I intend going to see that old Negro, my great-uncle, again. One of these days he will die on me, I suppose, and I must get from him some memories of my grandfather." The Negro great-uncle was Peter Abramovich Hanibal, an old man of 83, who died the following year. Who was his father, the man Pushkin referred to as his grandfather, in fact his great-great-grandfather?

The poet had received several written documents from his great-uncle and used them in 1827 as the basis for a historical novel (unfortunately incomplete) dedicated to his famous ancestor. This book, *The Negro Of Peter The Great,* is the first historical novel in Russian. It is also the first work of Russian literary fiction where the main protagonist is a black man. In Pushkin's works there are several references in to his Africa, and his black African ancestry. He always spoke with pride of the members of the Hanibal family who made up the African branch of his family tree.: "… my great-grandfather,

Abraham Petrovich Hannibal, the godson and pupil of Peter the Great, the confidant of the Tsar (witness a letter written in Catherine II's own hand), father of the Hannibal who took Navarino, general in chief of the Russian Army, etc. was a negro, the son of a minor African king."

Among the documents Pushkin received from Peter Hanibal was a petition made in 1742 in his ancestor's handwriting. The letter was addressed to the Senate and in it, his great-great-grandfather made an important statement on his African origins:

"I was born in Africa, of illustrious noble lineage, in the town of Lagon, in the territory of my father, who was the ruler of the town and two other cities.... In 1706 [2], while I was still a child, I agreed to go from Constantinople to Russia under the auspices of Count Savva Vladislavich. I was brought to Moscow and taken into the household of our sovereign of glorious and eternal memory, Peter the Great. I was baptised according to the rites of the Greek Orthodox religion and His Imperial Majesty graciously attended the ceremony in his august person, acting as my godfather. From that day on I was the constant companion of his Imperial Majesty."

The importance of this document is inestimable, for without it there would be no way of knowing the answer to the questions: Who was he? Where was he from? How did he come to be in Russia? Half the mystery is already solved.

Pushkin was killed in a duel in 1837 by Georges d'Anthès, a French officer in the Russian Imperial Guard. He was 38 years old. Long before his death he had won the hearts of his fellow Russians who called him "the sun of Russian poetry." Later Gorki was to write that Pushkin's contribution to Russian literature was as great as that of Leonardo da Vinci to European art. Pushkin's tragic death left unfinished a number of projects, one of which was the proposed complete biography of Abraham Hanibal. He had however immortalised him in his incomplete novel, *The Negro of Peter The Great*, some chapters of which had been published in 1829, 1830, and 1834, during his lifetime. Khmyrov, a Russian historian, writing a biography of Abraham Hanibal, in 1873, commented that Hanibal's memory should not rest in the shadows.

The events in the life of this man are the material for a real adventure story; his achievements in the realm of military science and technology were of a high order. To our knowledge, he is the only black man to have held such high office in eighteenth century Europe. He was the most powerful and gifted African in Europe during the Age of

Enlightenment... and a great humanitarian. A victim of the infamous slave trade, he was seized from his native land, (Logone, a principality in the heart of ancient Sudan, nowadays an area in northern Cameroon) and sold to the Ottoman Court in 1703. He arrived in Russia in 1704 at the age of eight, and became the godson and subsequently a close collaborator of the reforming Tsar Peter I, The Great. Hanibal was a man of great ability and a remarkable personality.

In the reign of the Empress Elisabeth (1741-1761) he became one of the leading figures in the Russian Empire. He spent several years in France studying warfare, becoming the Russian "Vauban" of his century. He was general in chief in the Imperial Russian Army, the Director General of Fortifications and Chief of the Engineering Corps. In 1726, he wrote a wide-ranging work on geometry and fortification for engineering students and he later introduced the study of civilian architecture into the curriculum of Russia's schools of military engineering.

Since Khmyrov's biography, Abraham Hanibal, the man called " the ancestral genius of the poetic genius" by the historian and publicist Nathan Eidelman, has been the subject of biographies by other Russian writers; Vegner in 1937, Leets in 1980 and Feinberg in 1983. In Russia during the nineteenth and twentieth centuries, there were dozens of articles about him, in the press, in encyclopedias and in biographical dictionaries. One mystery remained unsolved – the name of the African general's country of origin. "Ethiopian-Hamitic"(D. Anuchin,1899) was generally accepted, but Russian specialists in Pushkin's work claimed that did not match the poet's own view of his origins. Anuchin's analysis remained valid for a century, making nonsense of the poet's conviction that his mother's grandfather was a black African. In 1899 the anthropologist Anuchin, imbued with the racist prejudices of his time, had insisted on the age-old overworked theory that Ethiopians or Abyssinians, in spite of their black skin and tightly curled hair, were not Blacks or Negroes! However, research in Ethiopia failed to reconstruct the childhood of Hanibal... an important fact being that there was no town called Logone (or Lagone) where Pushkin's black ancestor could have been born. The mystery remained a mystery.

Today the riddle has been solved and Pushkin has been proved right. This book can be considered as the first complete biography of Abraham Hanibal, in the sense that previous publications missed out the chapter on Africa, which is at last available. We now have the full story of the African who became a Russian, lived briefly in Turkey, received his education in France, led a happy married life for half a century with a beautiful Swedish wife and gave Russia two generals and its greatest poet.

---

1. Pushkin wrote the name of his ancestor either as Annibal or as Hannibal, taking the latter from the conventional French spelling of the name of the famous Carthaginian general. Russian writers of the nineteenth and twentieth centuries did the same; we have chosen to use Hanibal as being closer to the man himself, who always used that spelling when writing or signing his name (cf. all the documents in his personal archive). The spelling Hannibal is of course retained in direct quotations from other sources.

2. The date is wrong. He was kidnapped in 1704.

CHAPTER I

From Logone to Constantinople

I was born in Africa,
of illustrious noble lineage,
in the town of Lagon,
in the territory of my father"

Abraham Hanibal, in a letter to the Russian Senate,

St. Petersburg, 1742.

"Under my African skies"

The town of Logone was a fine fortified city in central Africa, situated in the area which is now on the border between Chad and Cameroon, it lies on the banks of the river Logone, which is about 1,000 kilometers long. The city's population, the Laganie or Lagwanie, was made up of Kotoko, a people well known in African history for their clay figurines and their massive fortifications. Their capital was proudly named Logone Birni, Birni in the local language meaning a fortress or fortified city. Many a traveller passing through Logone was surprised by the beauty of the place. Giovanni Anania, an Italian who visited the region in the sixteenth century, speaks of Logone as one of the principal Kotoko capitals of the period.[1]

Denham, an English major passing through Logone in 1824, was granted an audience with the Miara (Prince) Salih V. Later, in 1852, the great explorer Heinrich Barth "stayed in Lagon in the reign of Yusuf... and finally, Nachtigal, in 1872, on his way to Bagirmi, had an audience in the same town with the Miara Marouf, the son of Salih V.[2]" Barth's description of the town is quite detailed. He writes: "We entered the capital of the Logone, called Logon-Birni, or Karnak Loggon by the Kanuri...the further we went the more attractive the town began to look. The streets became wider and I was particularly struck by the grandiose character of the buildings in the main street (*dendal*)...I was assigned lodgings in the palace of the Ibalaghuan and was surprised by its excellent architecture and grandiose style. It consisted of a large number of adjacent wings surrounding small courtyards, each supporting an upper storey with several large rooms...the Sultan's palace was a vast building surrounded by a 14 foot high wall...to my amazement I saw two iron cannons in the first courtyard. We were led through a series of long and scrupulously clean courtyards to the audience chamber containing the royal throne..."[3]

Logone was the capital of an African principality of the same name. At the end of the seventeenth century and the beginning of the eighteenth, the ruling prince of Logone was the sultan (*miara*) Brouha. He is regarded as the founder of the city, probably because he rebuilt it around 1700.[4]

It was in this city that the child who was to become Abraham Hanibal was born towards the end of the seventeenth century (1696). In a letter to the Russian Senate in 1742 he wrote: "I was born in Africa, of illustrious noble lineage, in the town of Logone, in the territory of my father, who was the ruler of the town and two other cities..."[5] Since the ruler of the little principality at that time was the Miara Brouha or Brouwa, we have every reason to think that he was the father of young Ibrahim. We also know from accounts by Hanibal's descendants, notably Pushkin, that he had a sister called Lagane.[6] The only two words of his maternal language that have come down to us from this great Russian-African himself are Logone or Lagon (the name of his native city) and Lagane (the name of his sister). Both of these words exist in the language of the inhabitants of the principality. The name of the local people, the Lagane or Lagwane, sounds strangely like the name of Hanibal's sister. Barth, in his report on his travels, even notes that the inhabitants of Logone called the "Logone river *laghame na logone*" (see accompanying map: *The principality of Logone and its neighbours in the 16th-18th centuries*). One of the princes who succeeded the Miara Lagwan Brouha was called Ana Logon.[7] Also the town of Logone was built on a river. This fits with the story told by one of Hanibal's sons that his father, the son of an African prince, had been kidnapped in (1703) on the banks of an African river. Pushkin adds that, at the time of the kidnapping, his ancestor's sister, Lagane, jumped into the water and swam desperately after the boat, which had carried off her brother...

A further point – Hanibal claimed that his father ruled over three cities, and it is known that in the eighteenth century the Kotoko people on the banks of the river Logone lived in three large cities, Goulfeil, Kussiri and Logone.[8]

The little kingdom of Logone was a monarchy with limited powers: the prince ruled with aid of a council led by the *Ibalaghuan*.

Most of the states in the region had long embraced Islam, but this African kingdom had remained faithful to the traditional religion, laying itself open to constant raids by the neighbouring Moslem sultans, Bagirmi in particular, in search of slaves.[9]

Logone's neighbours, Bornu and Bagirmi, had commercial links with the Ottoman Empire. Bornu was at the time considered to be the world's fourth most powerful Islamic state. One of its emperors, Ali Gaji, had been invested with the title of Caliph by the Abbassid Abd-al-Aziz ben Yacoub at Mecca in 1484. In 1555, after the conquest of the Fezzan by the Ottoman Turks, a treaty of trade and friendship was established between the Ottoman Empire and Bornu.[10] Bornu sold gold, perfumes, leather goods and slaves in exchange for firearms, paper, European imports and even from time to time European slaves. The Sultanate of Bagirimi exported numerous slaves and eunuchs to North Africa, then under Ottoman rule, and Turkey.

In the seventeenth and eighteenth centuries, many of the Moslem states of the central Sudan region were involved in the trade in slaves with the Arab world and the Ottoman Empire. The principal victims of the trade were the non-Moslem peoples. Any non-believer could be enslaved, whatever his origin or the colour of his skin. How was one to distinguish between a Moslem and a non-Moslem? "In practice it was not easy. After the famous battle of Tondibi, when the Moroccans defeated Songhai (western Sudan) they brought back to their country

40 camel-loads of gold dust and 1200 prisoners. One of them, Ahmed Baba, a well-known jurist from Timbuktu, invoked Islamic law, and boldly challenged the Sultan, who finally released him.

In 1611 Ahmed Baba was consulted by his admirers in Touat. They were appalled by the huge numbers of slaves or "black gold" who passed through their oasis. They asked whether anyone taking part in such trade endangered his immortal soul? Since, as everyone knew, there were many Moslems in the Sudan, was there no risk that some of those seized from their homeland might be "brothers"?

In response, Ahmed Baba wrote a brochure: *"Steps to raise the legal status of Sudanese slaves[11]."* He insisted that any Sudanese or black African who had "voluntarily embraced" Islam could not become a slave:

"Unbelief is the reason why an individual can be enslaved. The position of non-Moslem black Africans is the same as that of anyone else, Christians, Jews, Persians, Turks, etc."

However, could not any black African, even if Moslem, be enslaved "by invocation of the malediction of Ham?" (Gen.9:20-27) The jurist's answer to that question was unequivocal. No black Moslem could become a slave.

"On the contrary, any non-Moslem, whether or not he is a descendant of Ham, who refuses to accept the Moslem faith, can be enslaved. In this respect there is no difference between the races[12]."

He went on to state: "It is within the law to enslave non-Moslems if they have been taken as the result of a holy war – under certain conditions: pagans must first be called upon to accept the Moslem faith. If they refuse, they should be offered the option of paying a capitation tax, in which case they will be allowed to keep their own religion. Only when they have refused both options can they be reduced to slavery[13]."

When Abraham Hanibal was born, around 1680 and 1707, the principality of Logone and the other cities along the river were frequently attacked by the Sultan Abd El Kader of Bagirmi[14]. It is likely that the son of the Miara Brouha and other inhabitants of the city would have been captured in 1703 during one of these attacks on Logone and then sold as slaves to the Ottoman Turks, a common practice at that time in the area. There were trade routes linking the states of the central Sudan with the cities of North Africa. In Libya towns like Benghazi and Tripoli were veritable slave markets[15](See accompanying map: *Trade routes linking central Sudan with North Africa and the valley of the Nile*).

Most of the victims of the slave trade in these regions were children of both sexes, between seven and sixteen years old. They were exchanged for horses, firearms and white slaves. At the time there was a brisk trade in European slaves between the territories of the Ottoman Empire and the Moslem Arab world. A Russian historian writes: "For 400 years from the fifteenth century onwards including the eighteenth century Great Russia (Russia), Little Russia (the Ukraine) and Poland lost between three and five million inhabitants of both sexes. They were seized to live in servitude in Turkey and sold as slaves[16]." That is why certain African sultans in ancient Sudan had dozens of white servants in their palaces and fair-haired concubines in their harems...

The child of Logone was seven years old when he became the victim of the trade in slaves with the Ottoman Empire and was taken in 1703 from Africa to Constantinople.

Constantinople

In the summer of 1703, a major political event took place in Constantinople: the revolt of the janissaries, which led to the abdication of the Sultan Mustapha II in favour of his brother, who, on assuming power, took the name of Ahmed III. Ahmed III was no sooner installed than he set about re-establishing *"dev<u>sh</u>irme"*, a system whereby 1,000 Christian children were abducted from European territories under Ottoman rule and forced to serve in the army and the royal palaces. These children were brought as slaves to Constantinople where they were converted to Islam and educated to serve either as the Sultan's pages or as soldiers with the janissaries

There were thousands of black and Arab African soldiers, pages and eunuchs in the Ottoman army and at the court in Constantinople. The strong African presence was particularly visible in the first quarter of the eighteenth century among the troops raised in 1717 to "fight against His Imperial Majesty in Hungary, and also against the Venetians [which consisted of] cavalry and infantry from East, West, South and North[17]." Of a total of 534,100 soldiers in the two armies, 103,000 were Africans, one fifth of the total!

Black Africans were employed in the palaces and in various other positions in the Ottoman State from the sixteenth to the eighteenth century. The sultans brought both eunuchs and children to work at different levels in the administration. They came mostly from Ethiopia and the area around Lake Chad[18]. In 1587, the commander of the palace halberdiers (*baltaci*) and chief of the numerous high functionaries of the Ottoman Empire, including the supervisor of the Treasury, was an African known as Kizlar Aghâsi or the Grand Eunuch. He had immense authority in religious matters; he was in charge of the imperial mosques and the religious foundations of Mecca and Medina; he was the only person privileged to approach the Sultan at any hour of the day or night[19]...

It seems probable that the advent of the new Sultan would have given renewed impetus to the slave trade in both the Ottoman Europe and Africa. When the children arrived in Istanbul (Constantinople) they underwent a series of tests to determine their physique and

4. Sign in present day Logone celebrating the birth of Pushkin's ancestor.

5. Map of the Kotoko country in northern Cameroon.

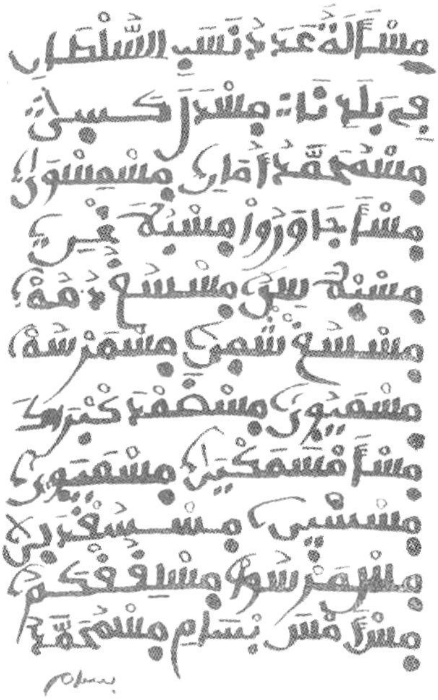

Fig. 2. — Type de manuscrit en langue arabe.

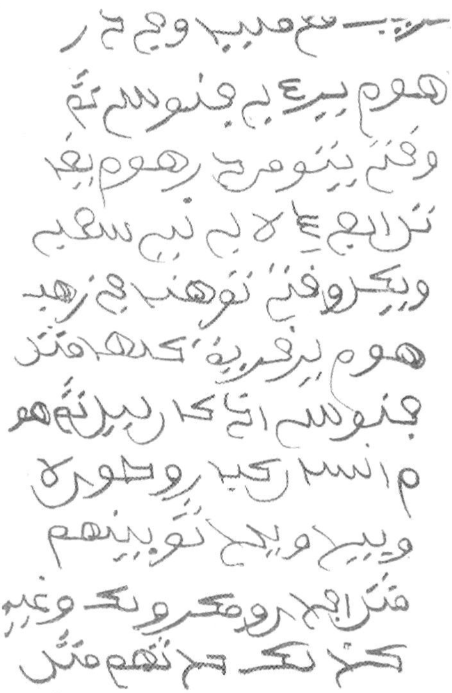

Fig. 3. — Type de manuscrit en dialecte kotoko et en caractères arabes.

6. Ancient manuscripts in Arabic and in the local Kotoko language, using Arabic letters.

بسم الله الرحمن الرحيم وصلى الله على سيد نا محمد وآله الأكرمين
الحمد لله الذي رضينا

Photographie du manuscrit original de la
Généalogie Royale de Logone-Birni

7. The royal genealogy of the Logone-Birni kingdom. According
to this document, the first Miarré, ruler of Logone was Mra Amana.

8. Abraham Petrov aged 12 drummer boy at the battle of Lesnaya (1708).

9. (Detail of No. 1)

17/18. The Sultan's palace, Logone (1940s). Lebeuf A. & J.P.

19/20/21. Inauguration of the plaque commemorating Hanibal's stay in La Fère, France. 2010.

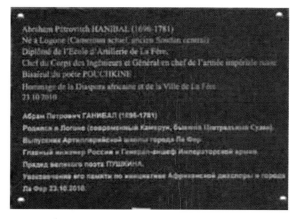

22. Mahamat Bahar Maruf, Sultan of Logone-Birni since 1965.

23. The Queen of Logone, mother of the young Brouha (the future Hanibal), painting by Jeki Esso, 2010.

CHAPTER II

The White Tsar's Black Godson

The Emperor Peter the Great
In the year 1705 heard
The Te Deum in commemoration
Of the victory over
The armies of Charles XII
And offered to the church the standard
Captured from the Swedes
In the course of the battle
And in this place he had baptized
The African Hannibal
The ancestor of our illustrious poet

A.S. Pushkin

(Engraved inscription on a marble plaque in the church of Parakseva in Vilnius)

Ibrahim in the Kremlin

On 13 November 1704, Andre Vasiliev and Constantin Yanov arrived in Moscow with the three children entrusted to their care by the rich merchant, Savva Raguzinski. Immediately on arrival they went to the Chancellery to give an account of their journey.

The Tsar was away from the capital. Two of the three children were taken to the home of Count Golovin, head of the Chancellery. They were Abraham and Abdul. According to Raguzinsky's servants they

43

were brothers. One of them had been baptised during the journey which explains why he had a Christian name.

Chancellor Golovin was a close friend of the Russian Tsar. On his return to Moscow on 19 December 1704, after the victorious campaigns against the Swedes at Dorpat and Narva, the Tsar stayed in the Chancellor's house. It must have been there that he first set eyes on Abraham and Abdul. The Tsar had a very precise idea of what he wanted. He had ordered Golovin to bring him some black children, and Golovin had approached Savva Raguzinski as he was about to visit the Sublime Porte, the name by which the Ottoman Empire was then known. Raguzinski travelled regularly to Constantinople to buy cotton, cloth and other merchandise unobtainable in Russia to sell on his return.

Golovin had received a letter from Ambassador Tolstoy explaining the decisions concerning the children's travel and was able to give a full account to the Tsar. It seems that the Tsar's plan was to take an African child and educate him at his court in order to prove that people of all races had the same intellectual aptitudes. This was a period when many conservative Russian nobles refused to send their children to school; some even claiming that the new sciences that the Tsar wanted to introduce were not suitable for Russians.

Peter I was obsessed by the idea that his immense empire could not progress in the modern world without a competent, educated ruling class. Until the last twenty-five years of the seventeenth century there were very few schools in Russia. The few educated civil servants there were had passed through the Slavonic-Greek-Latin Academy where most of what they learnt from the priests was about the Gospels. Then around 1700 the Tsar decreed the creation of the first modern Russian schools. To staff them he brought to Moscow the best foreign teachers; one was the Englishman, Farquharson, who set up the first school of mathematics and navigation in Moscow in 1701.

The younger members of the nobility, however, showed no inclination to do anything other than make a career in the army or stay at home to administer their vast inherited estates. They saw no reason to study sciences with barbaric names like geography, geometry, arithmetic and grammar. The Tsar then decreed that "all young nobles from the age of five years to their entry into his service five years later should study grammar, arithmetic and geometry". The number of pupils did not increase, however. Quite the opposite. The dislike of schooling was so intense that "many young men went into hiding to escape from school which bore an uncanny resemblance to a prison. One example is enough. In the naval academy old soldiers stood by each classroom door, riding-crop in hand, ready to 'restore order when necessary'."

In the face of such reluctance Peter I took it into his own hands to arrange the future of the sons of his highest dignitaries. The children of the Tsar's two great chancellors and those of Count Musin-Pushkin, for example, were sent by him to study science and the arts with the Jesuit fathers.

Peter I had a profound knowledge of men. When the children were presented to him he immediately chose Abraham, the younger one. No one knows what the Tsar had in mind for the little stranger from a distant land, but it is not difficult to imagine that he hoped the child would flourish in Russia. Perhaps he wanted to use him as an example to those who persisted in the belief that no Russian could be a good engineer. The Russian historian, Eidelman, is in no doubt that the Tsar's intention was educational when he secretly instructed the ambassador in Constantinople to find highly intelligent black children. Peter I had no time for any form of prejudice and valued his subjects simply for their abilities. He would have found ridiculous the idea that a man's intelligence depended on the colour of his skin or his place of birth.

The merchant, Savva Raguzinsky, returned from Turkey on 30 January 1705. He was received by the Tsar who wanted information about the Ottoman Empire. On this occasion it seems likely that the two men would also have spoken about the black children the merchant had sent from the Ottoman capital.

Peter I took good care of his young protégé. In the Imperial archives, there is a record, dated 15 February 1705, that over fifteen roubles had been allocated for the purchase of a tunic for Abraham. He was taught the Russian language as soon as he arrived in Moscow.

In the same month, February, the Tsar left for Voronezh to supervise the naval shipyards under construction. He stayed there two months, working long hours with the help of Count Apraksin.

He returned to Moscow at the end of April, intending to set off immediately for Polotsk where his elite troops were stationed for the winter. He was not able to go as he caught a severe fever and had to remain in bed for three weeks. One of the aides who attended the Tsar was the young African, Abraham, who had been attached to the Tsar's personal household.

There are many indications of the growing affection of the lord of the Kremlin for his young protégé. In the spring of 1705 he commissioned his chief engraver, the Dutch artist Schoenebeck, to portray him with Abraham. In the very rare engraving, 'Peter the Great and the little Negro', Schoenebeck shows Peter I as the conqueror of the Swedes. The black child whose head appears behind the Tsar is almost certainly the one who would come to be known in Russia as Abraham Hanibal. In this first portrait Abraham is just nine years old.

Another mark of Peter I's attachment to the African child lies in his decision to arrange a re-baptism, enabling him to stand as Abraham's official godfather and distinguish him by giving him his own name. Abraham had in fact already been baptised on the journey from Constantinople to Moscow, when the name Ibrahim, given him on his conversion to Islam by the Ottoman Turks, had been replaced by the Christian equivalent, Abraham. The new baptism was not to take place in Moscow. The Tsar wanted to make it a very solemn occasion. In the meantime he ordered that the boy be part of his entourage and accompany him everywhere. The first journey in the company of his powerful patron took place at the beginning of summer 1705. He was in the Tsar's entourage when he went to Polotsk and Vilnius in the north of the country. From that time on Abraham was never parted from Peter I. They were inseparable. It would be difficult to find anyone during the reign of the Tsar whose life was more intimately connected with his own – not even that of his son, the Grand Duke Alexis Petrovich, who found his father far too demanding and preferred not to be under his constant surveillance.

Abraham, however, owed his entire upbringing to Peter I. We shall see how he remained loyal to him, even half a century after his death. The first journey with the Tsar was one of the most memorable experiences of his new life in Russia. In the second week of July, when the Tsar was in Vilnius, news of a great military victory reached him. Bauer, the

Russian general, had defeated the Swedes at Mitawa (Gemäuerthof). The Tsar was handed a trophy of the war and he ordered that the great event be celebrated with pomp and ceremony. On 13 July at the Parakseva church in Vilnius there was a great gathering : the Tsar and his entourage, his generals and the populace. To this day one can still see in the church the marble memorial tablet with the posthumous inscription quoted at the beginning of this chapter.

It was not only the victorious General Bauer who was honoured on that memorable day. His triumph was shared with a young African called Abraham. The baptism was not a simple religious formality. It was the coming together of two destinies, two men; one the ever-attentive father, the other the son always ready to listen. It was also the union of two peoples, two continents, an extraordinary liaison between a powerful European king and a boy from deepest Africa. Ties of ancestry were established that day of which the participants were totally unaware. Peter would never have thought that by adopting this African child he was relating himself to the most illustrious poet in the history of his people.

As for Abraham, now to be known as Peter Petrovich Petrov (three times Peter and son of Peter), he could never have imagined the long and amazing life he would lead in the immense, unknown country which was his second home.

The date, 13 July 1705, was celebrated as Abraham Petrov's birthday[29]. He settled down happily as the godson of the young and powerful king who showed him so much affection and was fortunate to be able to persuade the Tsar to allow him to continue to be called Abraham instead of Peter, his new baptismal name. He did not want to lose Abraham, which reminded him of his original African name (Brouha?). The little nine-year old boy clung to the only thing that connected him to Africa, Logone his native city, his father, his mother and his ancestors.

The school of war:
an African witnesses the Great Northern War

It was a time of dark trouble,
Calamities unending,
Russia, beset on all sides,
Tried out its youthful energy;
Peter's sparkling genius
Set it on its way:
He was the most notorious master;
She learnt her lessons
In unforgiving battles.
In the tortures of Calvary
Inflicted by the Swedes
Our nation was forged:
The hammer breaks glass
But forges the steel of war.

Pushkin, extract from "Poltava", 1828

Translated into French by Vardan Tchimichkian.

On 18 August 1700, a peace treaty had been signed between Russia and the Ottoman Empire. The following day Russia declared war on Sweden and its young king, Charles XII. Peter I's calculation was quite simple: his country could not afford to fight two great military powers at the same time. Lacking allies, he decided his crusade against the Turks must wait until later. Sweden, however, was a very tough opponent, as Peter was to realise in the course of his many battles with its powerful army.

The war was to last over twenty years. History books call it the Great Northern War. Russian historians divide it into three phases: the first is from 1700-1706, the period of the coalition and the triumph of the Swedish forces (Narva, Fraustadt). The second is shorter (1707-1709) when Russia gained some decisive victories (Poltava). The third is the longest (1710-1721) and was ended by the Peace of Nystadt in 1721.

The Great Northern War brought into conflict two major powers; Sweden, which was known throughout Europe for having the strongest army on the continent, and Russia, a gigantic country determined to affirm its new found strength. It was equally remarkable that nearly three hundred years ago an adolescent African was to be a witness and later an actor in the Great Northern War.

When the war began in 1700, Abraham was still a child in Africa. He was four years old. He would only hear of Narva many years later: Narva, "the cruelest military defeat in the Russian army's entire history". In November 1700, eight thousand Swedish soldiers crushed a Russian army of over forty thousand. It was a catastrophe, but the Tsar did not lose heart. He believed in his people and their powers of regeneration. He reorganised the army. "His energies seemed to be stimulated by the disaster. Two weeks after the battle he wrote to Boris Sheremetev: "One must not lose one's head in misfortune. I command that we continue the work we have begun. We shall not lack men...' "

One year later, in December 1701, the Russian army led by Sheremetev won its first victory over the Swedes near Erastfehr, on the Livonian border. The Tsar exclaimed: "Thanks to God, we can now beat the Swedes!" Other victories followed. The frontier town of Nöteburg on the banks of Lake Ladoga and Nienschantz on the Neva fell into Russian hands. On 16 May 1704, Peter I made the decision to found his new capital, St. Petersburg, at Nienschantz. At last, his dream of opening a Russian 'window onto Europe' was to be realised.

In the summer of 1704, when Tolstoy, the Russian Ambassador to Constantinople, and Savva Raguzinski, his commercial agent, were organising the clandestine transfer of the three black children to Russia, Peter I was taking his revenge on Charles XII, King of Sweden. The re-taking of Narva followed the Russian general Sheremetev's conquest of the town of Dorpat. The Tsar celebrated the event with all his people: "In the very place where four years ago God inflicted on us the most terrible defeat, He has now made us joyful conquerors: sword in hand, I seized this fortress in three quarters of an hour."

Shortly after his baptism at Vilnius Abraham Petrov became a drummer-boy in the most prestigious regiment of the Russian army, the Preobrazhensky. He was not yet ten years old. From now on, he would follow his adoptive father wherever he went and be present in all his military campaigns.

His baptism of fire came at the age of twelve in the second phase of the Great Northern War. On 30 August 1708, he was at Peter I's side at Dobroe for his first victory over a Swedish detachment of six thousand men led by General Roos. One month later the drummer-boy Abraham Petrov was one of the twelve thousand men led by Peter I to inflict a heavy defeat on General Löwenhaupt's fifteen thousand men near Lesnaya. The African child's presence at this battle has been immortalised by the French painter, Pierre Denis Martin (1660-1742). The French engraver, Nicolas de Larmessin, used his canvas (1684-1755). Larmessin's engraving (see illustration no.2) depicts the battle of Lesnaya and shows the Tsar, Peter I, at the head of his cavalry. On the right at the bottom of the engraving, four young pages are standing behind Prince Menshikov on his white horse. One of them is black, wearing a white turban. He is the drummer-boy of the Preobazhensky regiment, Abraham Petrov.

The life of a regimental drummer-boy is not without risk. In war no-one takes into consideration the age or function of an enemy soldier. Many a drummer-boy has been killed on the battlefield. The African godson of Peter the Great received his first experience of military training in the heat of war. At Lesnaya even in the ranks of the victorious Russians more than a thousand men were killed and almost three thousand others wounded. Abraham discovered the horror of war at Lesnaya.

Less than a year later Abraham was again present; this time at the famous battle of Poltava, known to Russian military historians as the "mother of all battles". In the two armies, Russian and Swedish, a total of seventy thousand men were assembled on the battlefield. Here is the description by Constantin de Grunwald in his book *The Russia of Peter the Great*: "On 27 June 1709, the armies finally met for a pitched battle. n front of the walls of Poltava which had already been subjected to a series of assaults from the Swedes, there were fifty infantry battalions and eleven regiments of dragoons and Cossacks under the command of Sheremetev. Facing them were the troops of Charles XII. Numerically the forces were more or less equal; thirty thousand men on each side entered the battle. The Swedish camp had already given up hope. The Swedish king had placed his trust in the Ukrainians, who had disappointed him; the Turks had fled. The expected arrival of Stanislas

Leszczynski had been delayed. Peter's attacks on their flanks during their march across the devastated countryside had exhausted the Swedes; it was not only beer and brandy that were missing; they were also short of bread and ammunition. To add to their troubles Charles XII had been hit in the leg by an enemy bullet and had to conduct the battle from a camp bed.

Russian morale on the other hand was high. They had a reserve force of ten thousand men behind the lines...they had learnt to construct redoubts, which were scarcely known in the West, and their courage had been roused by their tsar's address, subsequently to become famous. 'The hour has come when the destiny of our fatherland will be decided. Think of her, fight for her...as for Peter – life is nothing to him, if only Russia can live on in glory and prosperity'[30]."

At Poltava, the Swedes were totally crushed by the Russians. Their army was decimated and King was obliged to flee to Turkey. Their 27 June 1709 was Russia's greatest day of victory. In the nine years of the Great Northern War the Russian army had become one of the most feared in Europe. Peter I was overjoyed. He proudly congratulated all his generals, his officers, his soldiers; he visited the injured and promised military decorations to all. Beside him rode his favourite, Menshikov who, as the head of the cavalry, had played an important role in sending the Swedish forces into disarray.

Some days later, the victorious Tsar went to Kiev, the capital of Little Russia, to give thanks for the victory in the cathedral of Saint Sophia. In his entourage was young Abraham, now thirteen years old. The Tsar was overwhelmed by the beautiful words and clarity of thought of the orator, Theophane Prokopovich. "He had never heard anything so wonderful. The Tsar ordered that the eulogy should be printed alongside a Latin translation, so that all Europe might read it." There is also an allegorical painting of the Tsar and a black adolescent showing Peter as the conqueror of the Turks at Azov and the Swedes at Poltava (see illustration no.3). To all appearances, the young black boy is Abraham Petrov, the only African to be constantly in Peter I's company[31].

In a short time, the Russians had learnt a great deal about the art of warfare. The army's strength was confirmed by a series of victories in the following year. In 1710, the Swedes lost Riga and Pernov. The Russians also took Vyborg on the Finnish peninsular and Keksholm on Lake Ladoga, thus ensuring the security of Petersburg. In September, they took Reval (now Talinn in Estonia). Among the Swedish prisoners taken in this town was a certain Captain Mathias von Sjöberg. This enemy officer would later be responsible for integrating the Russian army with many others. We have another reason to be interested in Captain Sjöberg: twenty-five years later he would come across a young black officer in the Russian army...

Meanwhile the Great Northern War was far from over. "The thunderbolt that was Poltova was heard all over Europe. Russia's prestige had grown enormously. She had upset the balance of power of the whole continent by destroying two of France's external bastions, Poland and Sweden; now it was up to her to 'keep order in the North'. One final bastion of 'Richelieu's system' remained intact, however, and the enemies of the Tsar, led by Charles XII, were eagerly persuading Turkey to enter the war[32].

In 1710, the Sublime Porte declared war on Russia. Ambassador Tolstoy was incarcerated in the "Castle of Seven Towers" in Constantinople. Abraham Petrov, still a drummer, was once again engaged with the troops in the newest phase of the Great Northern War. On this occasion, fortune smiled on the enemy. The Ottoman army, led by the Grand Vizier Baltaci Pasha, had vastly superior numbers. Peter I and his forces soon found themselves surrounded and at the mercy of the Grand Vizier on the banks of the Pruth River.

The Russian army was so helpless that the Tsar made what he imagined was his last ukase to the Senate: "If I am taken prisoner consider that I am no longer sovereign. Disobey any orders purporting to come from me in prison".

Then a miracle occurred: the Grand Vizier agreed to negotiate rather than crush the Russians completely. Why the Ottoman leader should have shown such magnanimity remains a mystery to this day. Did he succumb to the precious jewels sent to him by Catherine, Peter I's Livonian mistress – or did the janissaries force him to negotiate for peace?

These events all had their effect on the developing personality of young Abraham. He was in the very best of school of warfare. At the end of 1712 and the beginning of 1713, the Tsar was once again engaged in military operations against the Swedes, but it was not until the following year that the two countries clashed in a major sea battle on the waters of Cape Hangö.

The 1714 archives relating to Russia's military campaigns include some indications of the presence of Abraham Petrov in the Tsar's entourage. On 31 May 1714, Abraham Petrov went on board ship with the Tsar. The next day, 1 June, Peter I transferred to the ship 'Pernov' and then onto an English merchant ship. He was accompanied by Abraham, Bitka, a priest who was his inseparable chess partner, and others. On 2 June 1714, "His Excellency dined on the warship, and then transferred to a Danish boat and from there to Prince Basil Dolgoruky's warship 'Victory'. His Excellency was accompanied by Bitka, Abraham and Shemiakin[33]."

One month before the battle, Abraham was by now a tall young man of eighteen and probably part of the Tsar's general staff. On 27 July, two weeks after celebrating his eighteenth birthday, Abraham joined him when ten Swedish galleys and a frigate were taken at Cape Hangö. The commander of the frigate Erenchild put up fierce resistance and when all was lost threw himself into the sea. He was rescued and taken prisoner. The Tsar honoured him and praised his bravery. The naval victory gave the young Russian fleet control of the Baltic Sea.

The archives of ship's captain, Siniavin, note that a few days after the battle of Hangö: "10 August 1714 the negro Abraham came to Reval on a Russian brig". Unfortunately, we do not know the purpose of the mission. The Russian writer Malevanov suggests that Abraham may have been sent by the Tsar to deliver a message informing the inhabitants of the town of the naval victory at Hangö. It is a likely explanation since Abraham only stayed a few hours in Reval. He went back the same day on the brig to Helsingfors (Helsinki).

On the way back to Petersburg, the Tsar's ship was caught in a severe storm. In the general panic "only Peter knew what to do: he ordered the captain not to lower the mast but to try to advance in the direction of the wind. Meanwhile he and a few of the crew leapt into a small boat and at the risk of their lives tried to reach the shore. It was a long and desperate struggle against the currents, the wind and the waves but by great good fortune they reached land." Once there they lit an huge fire to guide the other ships safely along the coast. Abraham was almost certainly with his adoptive father on this terrible occasion. He would have been one of those who boarded the small boat. The memory of the danger he had lived through never left him; he retained such a violent dislike of the sea that ten years later he refused to go on board ship.

The Tsar's private secretary

My grandfather, so cheaply bought,
The Tsar himself treated with trust
And gave him welcome at his court.
Black but never again a slave.

Pushkin, extract from "My Genealogy"

When he became the godson of the Tsar of Russia at Vilnius in 1705, Abraham can have had little idea that he would become one of the great man's most intimate friends. For twelve long years, from 1705 to 1717, his whole life was lived at the pace of his powerful patron. Peter I was a man of boundless energy, obsessed with the future of his country. He had decided on the modernisation of his vast empire and the task took all his intelligence, all his power, and all his time. He soon realised that it could not be done in one man's lifetime. Therefore, the Great Russian patriot put his efforts into ensuring that the next generation would be better educated, more competent, more daring and free from the old attitudes. His dream came true: twenty-five years later, in every Russian province, there were thousands of young intellectuals and technicians waiting to take over. Abraham was to be one of them...but before we reach that point, let us see how he fared at the Kremlin, the Imperial Court.

There is every indication that the African child quickly learnt the language of his newly adopted country, thus overcoming the first obstacle to his integration at Court. He joined the young Russian nobles, "Orlov and Rumiantsev, among others," reports Pushkin , who were in the Tsar's personal service. As we saw in the previous passage, he received a sound military training during his many years on the battlefield. His position as drummer to a company of bombardiers in the most prestigious regiment of the Russian army, the Imperial Guard, did not prevent him from being attached also to the Tsar's personal entourage, since the Tsar was its commander in chief.

The Tsar often had occasion to assess the personality of his young protégé. He authorised him to sleep in the room adjoining his own. At times, he even had a little bed in the Tsar's own room. This was the case in the small house built for the Tsar in the Ekaterinental park at Reval where Peter I sometimes stayed in 1714-1715. "In the bedroom of this house there can still be seen two ordinary beds; the bigger one, behind a curtain, was Peter's; the other smaller one was probably kept for his personal attendant. It is reasonable to assume that in 1714 and 1715 the attendant would have been his pupil and favourite – the future general and commander in chief of the city of Reval, Abraham Petrov Hanibal[34]."

Abraham Petrov was easily the Tsar's greatest favourite among the young nobles in his service. It is no exaggeration to say that he loved him as if he were his own son. All his contemporaries at Court in the first quarter of the eighteenth century testify to the great affection of the emperor for the "little negro, Abraham".

A revealing anecdote is told about them: "One day, when the little black boy was out on a walk with Peter, he stopped to satisfy an urgent need. Suddenly he shouted in terror, 'Sire! Sire! My intestines are coming out!' Peter walked back to see and realised what had happened. He said, 'You're wrong, that's not your intestines, that's a worm!' – and he pulled it out with his fingers[35]." The story shows "the level of intimacy between Peter and his little black boy".

However amiable the Tsar might be with those he approved of he could react cruelly if the conduct of those same people was not to his liking. His big walking stick became famous in Russian history. Very few of his intimates, ministers or senators, boyars, generals, even foreign ambassadors escaped without having felt at some point a blow from this famous stick. Abraham fared no better in spite of his impeccable behaviour. He had often witnessed the harsh punishment the Tsar inflicted on those whose attitude displeased him, but on one occasion, he too fell victim. It so happened that one day Peter, who liked to have a siesta and could not bear to be disturbed at that time of day, had fallen asleep after lunch in his cabin after spending the morning at work on board ship. Some members of his suite, including the royal doctor, Lestocq, (who subsequently became a Count and the Tsar's secret counsellor) and Johnson, the chamberlain, were sharing a joke on the deck not far from the Tsar's cabin. The noise woke Peter and he rushed out onto the deck in a fury. The guilty ones heard him coming and hid, so that the first person the Tsar set eyes on was Abraham, who received a real beating...when the Tsar learnt that Abraham was innocent he smiled and said: "I hurt you for no reason, so some day when you do something wrong, remind me, and I will let you off[36]."

Abraham slept lightly. He could wake at any hour of the night and be in full possession of his faculties. It was a quality that the Tsar required of his close associates. Peter's brain did not rest while he was asleep. He used to wake up regularly to jot down on paper all the ideas that came to him. His wisest decisions on the administration of the country were made in his sleep. It was essential for him to have a night secretary to make accurate notes of all his thoughts, but most of those who offered themselves for the task disappointed him. Abraham therefore had the dual role of aide and night secretary to the Tsar. The Russian historian, Golikov (1735-1801) wrote about this period in Abraham's life in volume XV of his book, *The Acts of Peter the Great, Russia's Wise Reformer...*: "this Russian Hanibal had among his other gifts, the ability to sleep exceptionally lightly; he might appear to be sound asleep but would wake at the first call and respond immediately. This was the reason the Tsar made him his personal attendant and ordered him to spend the night in the room adjoining his and even, on occasion, in his own bedchamber.

"Hanibal himself told the following story, always with tears in his eyes. Not one night passed without the monarch waking up, sometimes more than once. As soon as he woke the great lord would call, 'Arap[37]! And he would reply immediately, 'Sire, what can I do for you?' 'Bring me the lamp and the slate.' (A slate and a writing implement hung at the head of the Tsar's bed.) He would fetch it and the Tsar would either make a note himself of the thought he had just had, or ask Abraham to do so, after which he would say gently, 'Put it back and lie down again.' In the morning the Tsar, who was punctilious in such matters, would re-write the notes or, according to their importance, transfer them to a notebook if he was not going to act on them immediately[38].

As time passed, Abraham became the Tsar's confidant. The Tsar might ask him occasionally to make a neat copy of a decision that had come to him in the night. When he had settled on it and the Tsar had signed it, Abraham was the one to carry it to the Chancellery concerned. As we have seen, after the naval battle of Hangö in 1714, he had been sent on a mission to Reval. The young African became the courier for secret dispatches. The monarch could not help but be impressed by his high intelligence, his fine feelings, his unfailing courtesy, his discretion and his dynamism. The entire Imperial family took him to their hearts. He was a particular favourite with Catherine Alekseevna, the Tsar's second wife whom he had married in 1711, shortly before the tragedy of Pruth River. The Tsar's children also held their black 'brother' in great affection. We shall see shortly how fully Abraham was accepted as a member of the Russian imperial family.

Peter placed much responsibility on the shoulders of his young African pupil, but he did not forget to supervise his education closely. Abraham developed a remarkable liking for mathematics and as soon as the Tsar noticed this, he sent him to the best teachers, and ordered for him the most recent books from abroad. To cite but one example, Willem Bartjens published *Arithmetic* in Amsterdam in 1708 and Abraham had it in his possession as early as 1711. He inscribed his name in it when it arrived, "Abraham Petrov, Moscow 1711." Abraham carefully preserved this mathematics textbook and, still in good condition, it can be seen to this day in the Hanibal Museum in Russia. It is also worth noting that the book was written in Dutch, which must mean that Abraham also had to learn that language.

The Russian monarch was exercised more than ever at this time by the question of education for his people. Progress was far too slow for his liking. He sought the best methods of diffusing knowledge of the sciences throughout Russia. In 1711, he left for a rest cure in Bohemia at the spa of Karlsbad (known today as Karlovy Vary in the Czech Republic). He took the opportunity to visit Dresden and study the process of silver mining in Freiburg. On 14 October, he went to Torgau on the Elbe to preside at the marriage of his son Alexis to Princess Charlotte of Brunswick. The Queen of Poland was also present on this happy occasion. Abraham Petrov, of course, was part of the Tsar's entourage...the Tsar used his time in Torgau to meet the German philosopher, Leibnitz, and discussed with him ways of spreading more effectively the knowledge of science and the arts in Russia. The Tsar was very appreciative of the great philosopher's advice and had recourse to him again later on. In recognition of his services, Peter I nominated him Confidential Counsellor for Justice and awarded him a pension for life.

How could Russia become a modern state if the great majority of her people remained ignorant? The Russian historian, Chistiakov, illustrates the Tsar's obsession in his book, *The History of Peter the Great*:-

"Peter found it agonising to meet subjects of his who were ignorant and uneducated; he knew he could not bring (from abroad) enough people to meet every need and for this reason a major preoccupation was education. He began with his own family; he made sure that his daughters, Anna and Elisabeth, learnt not only Russian but also French and German. He sent young people to study abroad; he also sent qualified Russians to other countries to discover useful new ideas, study them and put them into practice in Russia on their return. For example, he entrusted the mining engineer, Tatischev, with the task of selecting likely boys from Russian schools to send to various mining companies in Germany to learn about the mining industry." The brilliant Abraham Petrov in turn would be sent away to study engineering.

CHAPTER III

In the land of Louis XV, King of France

*"Here money can buy you
a great deal of knowledge"*

Abraham Hanibal, in Letter to Makarov, February 1722

The Journey to Europe

In 1716 the Tsar undertook his second journey to western Europe. On this occasion Abraham Petrov was one of the members of the Russian Imperial entourage. He was put in charge of the books selected for the journey. Two of the titles were *The Chronicler of Kiev* and *The History of Troy*.

The Tsar's retinue reached Dutch soil in early December 1716, and by 6 December was in Amsterdam. Three days later, he gave orders to pay Abraham some of his allowance for the coming year, slightly more than seven *livres*. His annual salary was then one hundred roubles, a considerable sum at the time. On 11 December Peter gave him money to buy new clothes and shoes for Christmas.

On 15 January Abraham received half of his allowance for the new year, fifty roubles in Dutch currency, and in January the Tsar spent more money on his beloved godson, immortalising him with a wax statuette, ordered on a visit to the studio of the Dutch master, Johann Kalm. It was intended for the Tsar's Cabinet of Curiosities: "In one of his letters from Holland Peter had announced that he was putting together a

Cabinet of Curiosities and that he was ordering and buying all sorts of rare objects for it. It seems that Peter ordered these wax figures, which were expensive, for his Cabinet (*Kunstkamera*)...but the Cabinet went up in flames on 5 December 1747 and one can only assume that the statuette of the African went with it[39]."

The Tsar continued to govern the Russian Empire, even from Amsterdam. Instructions were sent to the Senate and to his generals. In Amsterdam, he took the opportunity to meet the young Russians he had sent to study abroad some years previously. He personally checked on their progress and arranged for them to study with reputable teachers in various scientific disciplines. He even ordered that he should be sent "every new book published in Russia" during his absence[40]. In Holland the Tsar went to see everything of interest, especially if it was unknown in his country. As well as paintings he bought Professor Ruysch's anatomical cabinet and museum collection ...

The Tsar left Holland for France on 24 March 1717. In April the Russian Imperial retinue was in Antwerp. It then went on to Brussels. In Antwerp, where they arrived on 2 April, Abraham went with the Tsar to see the Cathedral Tower and Peter asked him to buy some *ficelles* (breadsticks). On 6 April, in Brussels, the Emperor's Treasury reimbursed Abraham for the purchase of the bread. The following day they went on to Bruges, then to Dunkirk. There the trunk in which Abraham transported the Tsar's books was found to be in poor condition. Abraham had it repaired and on 16 April was paid ten roubles for his outlay. Shortly after this, the Imperial retinue reached the Pas de Calais. There the Tsar found two more 'curiosities' which he bought, a French dwarf and a giant. The giant's name was Nicolas and he became part of Peter I's entourage; the French dwarf was sent to Peter's wife, Catherine, as a present, together with the message: "Look after him and make sure he wants for nothing[41]."

On 18 April, the Tsar sent Abraham with six men ahead of the retinue to Paris. That he should be entrusted with this mission is further evidence of his adoptive father's great confidence in him. Peter's archives record the names of three of the six members: Lacosta, Cherkasov and Ovsianikov. The three others were sergeants. They left with Peter's assurance that all their expenses for food and lodging would be met from his private purse. The journey through France took them eight days, passing through Boulogne, Montreuil, Abbeville, Beauvais and Beaumont. They arrived outside Saint Denis on 18 April, and were joined the same day by the Tsar. An account of the arrival of the Tsar in Saint Denis appeared in No.1, 1717, of the Russian paper "News":

"Paris, 26 April. His Majesty the Tsar arrived here, safe and sound, by the grace of God. The following arrangements were made for his reception: eight miles from Paris, at Saint Denis, His Majesty was welcomed by the French Marshal de Tessé. His Majesty reached Paris at dusk when it was already very dark."

In France

The Tsar and his entourage were lodged at the Hotel Lesdiguières, although the French authorities had arranged for him to stay in the sumptuous apartments of the Old Louvre. Peter I declined the invitation and asked his hosts for more modest accommodation.

France was at the time under the Regency of the Duke of Orleans. The great "Sun King" of France, Louis XIV, had died two years previously, leaving his very young heir, Louis XV, on the throne. The Sun King had allegedly said to the boy: "My dear child, you will be the greatest king in the world." In 1717, Louis was a boy of seven. He would not come into his own until the age of fourteen. Meanwhile the Duke of Orleans was in charge.

The Regent came in person to greet the Tsar the day after his arrival. The boy king, Louis XV, visited him on 29 April. In the royal delegation was the Duc de Maine, Louis XIV's illegitimate son, who had been recognised as a prince of the blood. He was the Grand Master of the Artillery and, for a time, supervised Louis XV's education. The Tsar had previously decided he would leave Abraham in France to study artillery and engineering, and he naturally entrusted his African godson to the care of the Duc de Maine. Here is Abraham's own account of this momentous event in his life at the time when he was no more than a junior officer: "…in 1717 the Tsar, a man of unfailing kindness, thought it advisable to leave me in France to pursue my military studies. With this in mind, the monarch, the Great Father of Our Country, graciously recommended me in conversation to the Duc de Maine, Prince of Dombes, Grand Master of the Artillery, and the natural son of the famous French King, Louis XIV…"

A personal recommendation of this kind is a further indication of the father-son relationship between the Tsar and his protégé, who was 21 years old in 1717. Peter found it very hard to leave his young black disciple, as he had grown very fond of him. The arrangement for Abraham to study in Paris for several years would have been made by the Tsar solely in the interest of the Russian state, which desperately needed competent administrators with the best possible education.

The French had a high reputation in the rest of Europe for their military training, not surprisingly only two years after the death of Louis XIV, whose reign had been made famous by "the military triumphs of Turenne, Berwick, Villiard, Vendôme" and "Vauban, the greatest and most brilliant engineer of our times[42]."

We can be sure that Abraham too wept bitter tears at the painful separation, although the prospect of receiving military training in France would give him a bright future on his return to Russia.

The Tsar, for his part, loaded him with gifts before leaving Paris: on 14 May, the Tsar spent over three hundred livres on new clothes for his godson. On 23 May, he bought him a hat; on 30 May, a week later, he bought cloth and brocade to make other outfits for him; on 8 June, the Emperor ordered the payment of fifteen ducats to Abraham Petrov, his allowance for the rest of the year 1717.

At last, on 9 June the Tsar made ready to leave France. He sent for Abraham and Alexis Yurov, another young nobleman from his entourage staying behind to study in Paris, and gave them his last pieces of advice: "If you become spendthrifts or land in prison, do not expect me to help you out; if you are studious and live within the law I shall never abandon you."

The Tsar had every reason to deliver such a warning to his protégés. The reports he usually received on the behaviour of Russian students abroad did not inspire confidence. "In England 'Russian navigators' created endless problems for the Tsar's diplomats. Scarcely had a certain Prince Saltykov landed in London when he organised a banquet for prostitutes. Later he took a mistress who cost him three times the amount of his allowance. Several other students were imprisoned for debts[43]."

Parisian life was full of temptations and Peter I could not bear public money to be wasted. He returned to Russia saddened by the separation, trusting that his godson would be able to avoid the pitfalls in his new independence. Abraham Petrov, after all, had no experience of living independently. He was twenty-one years old and had never been out of Peter's company, having passed the last twelve years exclusively in the service of his adoptive father. Peter's plans for the modernisation of the Empire could not be realised without a young, highly qualified administrative force. It was essential that Abraham, whom he had intended to use as an example, should study at the highest level. In Paris, he would become an expert in fortifications and artillery, "above all in engineering studies"[44].

For the first nine months, Abraham Petrov lived in Paris in the happiest of circumstances. During this period, we have little evidence about the life of this African pioneer from the vast and snowy wastes of Imperial Russia. We can imagine, however, how happy and carefree Abraham must have felt to find himself in Paris and under the protection of a powerful patron. There are rich and highly coloured accounts in Russian literature of the early days of the African student's life there, not least from Pushkin, the most famous of his descendants. No doubt, the patronage of the Duc du Maine would have made it easy for "the Tsar's negro" to be admitted into Parisian society. A few years earlier most of the people at court would have heard of or seen another black man, Captain Aniaba, who had been the godson of Louis XIV. Everyone had wanted to see the Sun King's 'Moor[45]' with their own eyes. Abraham, from distant Russia, must have been even more of a wonder.

As a first step, Abraham paid private tutors for lessons in French and mathematics. He had been in Paris two months, when, a mere thirty days after the departure of Peter, political events in France lost him his powerful royal patron. The Duc de Maine was accused on 1 July 1717 of plotting against the Regent and was deprived of his title as prince of the blood. The summer of 1717 brought an event that was to have further repercussions on the life of the African student: Spain invaded Italy and this was to lead to war with France.

Until the end of the first year, Abraham had no financial worries. He had plenty of money and a well-stocked wardrobe. From the first weeks, he was already buying books for his library. He probably even managed to save a little from his 1717 allowance since, when his salary did not arrive, he did not complain for the first two months of 1718. By March, however, the first signs of financial difficulties appear.

Letters from Paris

There are in existence twelve letters from Paris, written by Abraham to Makarov, cabinet secretary to the Tsar, and to the Tsar himself. Thanks to the work of the Russian academic, Pekarski, and Anna Semionovna, Abraham's great-great grand-daughter, we have a clear idea of the conditions in which Abraham lived during the years 1718-1722. The letters also give us historical insights into the academic courses of the time and the effect of France's financial crisis on foreign students.

Abraham and his colleague, Alexis Yurov, a student of political and civil science, were quickly reduced from a life of ease to total poverty. On 5 March, they wrote together to the Russian Emperor.

> *"Most dear Sir,*
>
> *We wish to assure Your Majesty that we are applying ourselves faithfully to the fulfilment of your wishes, as required by our duty to you if we are to continue to be honoured with your servants, We beg you most humbly to end our poverty and provide us with an allowance that will enable us to live here without incurring debt.*
>
> *As God is our witness, it is quite impossible to live in this country on two hundred roubles. Reassure us of your continuing benevolence, Sovereign. Do not leave us in despair as we try to accomplish the task you have set us, which we hope and pray to complete.*
>
> *We do not presume to name a sum of money; we are confident of your generosity as our Tsar and Father. The report of Lieutenant Captain Konon Zotov will make our position clear. In the expectation of your assistance we remain Your Majesty's very devoted and humble servants.*
>
> *Alexis Yurov, Abraham*
> *From Paris, 5 March 1718[46]"*

The two young students hoped that the Tsar would increase their allowance in view of the high cost of living in Paris. They did not 'name a sum' but relied on Peter's generosity. Less than a week later Abraham sent a second letter, this time to Makarov, the Tsar's cabinet secretary, whom he knew well. He wrote thus:

My dear Sir, Alexis Vasilievich,

I implore you, sir, not to leave us in such poverty. Show us your good will by interceding on our behalf with His Majesty – please forget all the foolish behaviour of my youth.

We are your children, be kind to us as a father would be, do not let us sink into total poverty in this place. Believe us, my Lord, the two hundred and forty roubles we are allowed do not even buy us food. We nhave written to His Majesty, and we rely on your good will.

Your servant Abraham.
Paris, 11 March 1718[47]."

There was no reply to the students from Moscow. The Tsar was preoccupied. One of the most serious disputes in the history of the Russian royal family had just begun. Peter I found himself in conflict with his only son and heir to the throne, the Grand Duke Alexis Petrovich. The disagreement was essentially political. "One faction was intent on creating a new Russia, making enormous demands on the nation's strength; the other supported the old Muscovite Russia, its idleness, indifference, and horror of innovation...Without any premeditated plotting the Tsarevich became the focus for all the malcontents of the Empire. The Tsarevich was incarcerated in the Peter and Paul Fortress on 14 June 1718[48]." The Tsar summoned the Supreme Court to judge his son and on 24 June 1718, the judges unanimously sentenced him to death. However, Prince Alexis died in prison two days later before he could be executed!

In view of these distressing events it is easy to understand why the difficulties of the students in France were forgotten. Only the Tsar could make decisions about them and he had no time for any minor problems. By October 1718, there had been no improvement in their situation, and Alexis and Abraham again took up their pens and wrote to Makarov. They were adamant that they were in urgent need; their teachers had agreed to take them on credit and they had no money to pay them. The authorities remained silent and Alexis wrote comparing himself dramatically to a sick man calling for a doctor. He ended his letter with the words:

"We are not being deceitful in our request; we are in genuine need and rely totally on your great munificence."

Your very humble servant, Alexis Yurov.
Paris, 1 November 1718[49].

Alexis' use of the word deceitful is understandable if we remember that there were many Russian students abroad at the time and that some of them, like Prince Saltykov, quite happily threw money about and then, on false pretexts, made constant demands on the Tsar for financial assistance. Alexis had to prove that their claims were well founded. That was the reason they had referred in their first letter to Captain Zotov who had been sent to France in 1715 to "oversee everything that was necessary for the fleet, in port and at sea", and to supervise Russian students. Zotov reported to Makarov in 1717 on "the Russian marine guards studying the maritime arts in France" and asserted that the later were living in extreme poverty. The Treasury should send them 300 ecus per person per year so that they "could live in a decent manner."

When, a few weeks later, the Russian ambassador finally did pay their allowances for 1718 the students received no extra money. Abraham and Alexis sent their last letter to the Tsar on Christmas Eve:

> *"Our very dear Sovereign Lord,*
>
> *…We are suffering serious torments of conscience as we try to lose no time (from study) in spite of our great poverty. Dearest Sovereign, reassure us of your great kindness so that not everything we are undertaking is wasted. We know that a million souls depend on Your Majesty's munificent assistance, and that they all are as happy as we ourselves who grew up surrounded by your kindness. Make us glad, dearest Sovereign, we are truly suffering. Command that our allowance be increased. Savva Raguzinski has only sent us 200 roubles through his agent here and that is not enough to feed us and save us from getting into debt.*
>
> *Your very humble servants*
> *Alexis Yurov, Abraham*
> *24 December 1718, from Paris*

Once again, Abraham's and Savva Raguzinski's paths had crossed. The same man who had been the Tsar's agent in Constantinople was now Russia's representative in Paris. There were yet other surprises for them, thousands of miles away…

The second stage of Abraham Petrov's stay in Paris was in great contrast to the first, as we have seen in the first group of letters. The letters and appeals must have gone unanswered since the allowance of two hundred roubles was not increased. The question was how to survive and be respectable as well as continuing to study. The teachers in France would not continue to teach on credit for ever. Zotov's report for the preceding year warns that a number of Russian naval students, unable to bear their miserable living conditions, had told the Tsar's emissary that they intended to enter bonded service with rich French people. Zotov says that he "threatened them with terrible punishment" if they did so.

Abraham was not long in finding a way out of the difficulties he had experienced in 1718. He decided to take advantage of the French politico-military situation. France declared war on Spain in the year. Spain had violated the Treaty of Utrecht by attacking Italy the previous year. Britain, allied to France, also declared war. In the summer of 1718, the British Admiral Bing had defeated the Spanish fleet. Abraham knew about the progress of the war through reading the Paris press and in 1719, he decided to volunteer to join the French army in the field.

The Russian historian Khmyrov describes this episode in Abraham's life as follows: "Marshal Berwick led the French army to the Spanish frontier and Hanibal entered its ranks as a trainee engineer. He took part in the capture of Fontarabie and San Sebastian by the French. He was wounded in the 'underground war' (in the trenches) and was promoted on merit to the rank of lieutenant engineer."

The Tsar's black godson had made a very wise choice when he volunteered to join the French army at war. He was twenty-three years old and the dangers of the battlefield held no terrors for him. For a man of his calibre who had been initiated into warfare at the age of eleven and who had been present at every battle of the Great Northern War from 1707 to 1717 including the Russian army's most glorious victories at Lesnaia, Poltava and Hangö, the risk of death did not worry him. In 1709, the drummer boy, Abraham Petrov, "did not carry arms. He was very young, at the battle of Poltava he was thirteen, at the naval battle of Hangö he was an adolescent of eighteen". If we take into account his personal services to the Tsar, "he would have been part of Peter's general staff. Since Peter I always placed of fire of the enemy artillery: thus Abraham was in a situation of immediate danger. To be present in such circumstances was counted as active military service in the army's regulations...[50]".

In the Spanish war Abraham was to learn that even those who survive the bloodiest wars could still be killed on much less dangerous battlefields. No one is safe from a stray bullet and the head wound he received remained as a permanent proof of his vulnerability..

There may well have been other reasons for Abraham to join the French army. He was a foreigner and this was the best way to make sure he received the training he dreamed of as an engineer. He had promised the Tsar that he would return to Russia a fully qualified engineer. In 1717 and 1718, he had paid teachers in Paris for instruction in a series of subjects without which he could not hope to be accepted to train in military engineering. The selection of candidates was rigorous. A high level of technical and intellectual ability was demanded. Anne Blanchard, the French military historian, in her excellent book *Les Ingénieurs du "Roy" de Louis XIV à Louis XVI* writes, "young men who wished to gain entry to work on fortification as engineers" had to take a public examination to test their knowledge "not only of geometry and measurement, but also other essential areas of mathematics, trigonometry, mechanics, arithmetic, geography, civil architecture and even drawing".

The number of places available was also very limited. According to A. Blanchard's paper only one candidate in three was admitted between 1716 and 1739. It was not enough to have mastered the "copious programme of advanced scientific and technical knowledge" for "the rules of admission were based on additional criteria, not least of which was the essential role played by influential patrons. Most candidates were supported by either the Comte de Toulouse or the dowager Princess Conti, others by being related to an officer in the King's army."

The Duc de Maine, to whose care Peter had confided his African godson, had fallen from favour in the summer of 1717. Abraham could not, therefore, logically expect to have the patronage of the former Grand Master of the Artillery. What is more, between 1716 and 1718 the French authorities decreed that it was not necessary "for the present, to train new engineers". When Abraham learnt that he could enlist as a trainee engineer in the French army he wasted no time in doing so. He took part in the Spanish War as a member of the French engineering corps. His bravery in battle earned him promotion to the rank of lieutenant engineer, and his achievements in the war enabled him to gain admission to a military school normally closed to foreigners. His acquired status as a veteran of the war and volunteer in the service of France, together with his new rank, combined to open to him the doors of the military school which Louis XV had recently founded at La Fère.

Three years later Abraham was to write a letter describing how he came to be admitted to La Fère:

"P.S. Please inform His Majesty the Tsar that I have served in the army here (in France) as lieutenant-engineer; I served one and a half years as trainee engineer. A new school for young engineers was set up here in 1720. No foreigners were admitted who had not served in the French army. I hope His Majesty will not be displeased to know that by joining the army I have gained admission to the best training."

The School of Artillery at La Fère

The new school created by command of the King was a school of artillery intended to produce the first officers of the Regiment of Engineers. "It is the oldest of the many that existed in France and produced generations of distinguished officers, among them Vallières, Gribeauvel, Drouot and even foreigners such as George Elliott, the English general whose skill defended Gibraltar in 1782. At first courses were given in a building in the grounds of the arsenal (built by the Duc de Mazarin in 1666); later on, after its acquisition by the state, in the town's castle. Once the School of Artillery had been established barracks had to be built." But "the work, begun in 1720, was held up by a lack of funds..."[51] Consequently, the then mayor of La Fère, M. Heebourg, and the citizens, the *Laférois* were obliged to lodge the new students in their own homes. Abraham, who was the first black officer to train at the school, almost certainly stayed in a private house in La Fère for two years, from 1720 to 1722.

Lieutenant engineer Abraham Petrov received a solid grounding in military engineering at La Fère, and went on to become the most brilliant military engineer of his generation in Russia. One of his teachers was a young academic called Bernard Forest de Bélidor. He had just published his *Sommaire d'un cours d'architecture militaire et hydraulique* (Paris, 1720). The Duc d'Orléans in person had nominated him for the teaching post in the new school. It is clear that the highest French authorities intended the school to give its students the best possible training in science and technology. According to Abraham the first two years of the course were largely theory: mathematics, fortification, artillery etc. followed by practical work in the final year. The practical work included experience with mines, conducting sieges on polygon models and the construction of fortifications.

At the beginning of 1722 the Tsar's ambassador to Paris, Prince Dolgoruky, sent for Abraham and informed him that the Tsar had ordered all the Russian students in France to return to Petersburg. Abraham was faced with two problems. First, he had not completed his studies at the school of La Fère. Several months of practical work lay ahead and they were indispensable if he was to distinguish himself, as he hoped, in engineering. Secondly, the Russian students were supposed to return by sea and Abraham had had a horror of sea voyages ever since the terrible events in the Baltic in 1714 after the naval battle of Hangö when he had narrowly escaped death with the Tsar in violently stormy seas and had sworn never again to set foot in a boat. He immediately sent two letters to Peter I's cabinet secretary, Makarov.

" Paris, 5 February 1722,

My Dear Sir,

The Prince has just announced to everyone here the ukase of His Imperial Majesty ordering our return to Petersburg this spring. I am ready to comply with His Majesty's will, but I would ask you to mention to His Majesty that I am not a seaman. You yourself know, Sir, how brave I have been at sea, but I am no longer accustomed to it. I shall die if I am not granted this favour. The Prince has said we must all travel by sea. If his Imperial Majesty does not wish to pay our travel overland to Petersburg I shall be quite content to come on foot.

P.S...may it be possible for His Majesty to give the order for me to stay this year for my studies. We have built a "town" without our teachers' help where we can practise various forms of attack and lay explosives.

If you think my request is justified and that H. M. will not be against it, I beg you, my dear Sir and Father, to pass it on to him. If you think that it will displease him I would be glad if you did not mention it. I am prepared to return with as much as I have already learned; I just pray to Christ and the Holy Virgin that I will not have to travel by sea.

The school I mentioned is not here near Paris, but about one hundred miles away. I received a letter telling me to come to Paris and I arrived here today.

The Prince announced the ukase about our return to Petersburg. I hope he will write to the Court on the matter of my staying another year. If in your opinion this matter will displease His Imperial Majesty, have the fatherly kindness to spare me his anger and say nothing about my wish to stay here.

Dear Sir, dear Father Alexis Vasilievich,

Please send a reply here to the right authority, even if it is an ukase of just one line, so that I do not leave later than the others.

Your faithful and devoted servant

Abraham."[52]

Letter of 16 February 1722

"May His Imperial Majesty be pleased to command that I stay here one more year so that I can do my practical training. In the engineering school we have constructed a city of sand where we are going to carry out attacks,…build trenches, lay explosives etc…I beg you, Sir, send me a reply soon, so that I do not waste time here. I have come to Paris from my garrison which is one hundred miles away.

…and I have no hope except in His Majesty. As for my studies and my way of life, all the Russians here, especially Zotov and Tuvolkov, who have been in Paris, know that for one or two weeks I have not been out of the house and that I was doing my best to continue to study. There are things that I have not been able to learn, but it is not because I did not care to or because I was not intelligent enough, but through lack of money. Here money can buy one a great deal of knowledge."[53]

Abraham's request was supported as he had hoped by Prince B.L.Dolgoruky, the Ambassador who sent a letter, dated 9 March 1722, to Makarov, making the following observations: "First of all let me thank you for graciously informing me that the various people sent here to be taught science should now return home. On careful reflection I have decided to let you know my thoughts on the matter. In the case of those studying theology…it seems to me that they could just as well study that in Russia without the expense of keeping them here and I shall of course send them home this spring. As for those studying the other sciences: we have kept them here for many years and paid their expenses. To send them home now before they have completed their studies would reduce them to a status where they were neither pupils nor masters, and our expenditure would have been wasted. Should His Imperial Majesty not command that they be given time to finish their studies? Abraham tells me that he needs one more year to do intensive practical work."[54]

A few weeks later Abraham's wish was granted. He was to be allowed to stay in Paris till the end of the year and he would not have to return by sea. He was authorised to join Prince Dolgoruky's party on his return to Petersburg overland in January 1723.

A victim of French financial reform

In the first term of 1722 the material conditions of students in France deteriorated to the point where a new spate of letters begging for financial assistance arrived in Petersburg. Abraham sent three in March informing Makarov that *"all the Russian students are in debt, not because they have been extravagant, but because of the French currency"*. The Scottish financier, John Law, had instituted radical reforms in the banking system, provoking a serious crisis from December 1720 onwards. Money lost value and many people were impoverished as a result: *"...prices are rising. Inflation is ravaging the country. Bread, eggs and meat are reaching record prices. Law was caught in a vicious circle of inflation. Prices were frozen, people refused to sell... coins were not accepted and the use of bank notes became obligatory, salaries went up, the demand for bank notes increased. Soon the bank itself was under siege. Repayments in cash were at first made only under certain conditions but later in practice refused altogether. There were riots. Panic broke out on 21 March 1720 when an edict was published proclaiming the devaluation of the currency and action designed to delay payments till the following September, when they would be honoured at half their value. That was the final blow to the system...*

In Paris, where, it is said, everything ends in song, they were singing 'Mr. John Law's Week'.

On Monday I bought shares,
On Tuesday I made millions,
On Wednesday I bought some gear,
On Thursday I furnished my house,
On Friday I danced at the ball,
On Saturday I was in hospital."[55]

The poverty overwhelming France seriously affected the lives of the Russian students who suddenly found themselves without resources and heavily in debt. Abraham's report on the situation was alarming: *"Here we are all in debt, not because we have been extravagant, but because of the paper money; I hope that Count Musin-Pushkin has kept you informed...if Platon Ivanovich (*Musin-Pushkin*) had not been here I should have died of starvation...".* He goes on to remind Makarov of the promise the Tsar made to Yurov and himself in 1717 promising that he would not abandon them in misfortune if they proved themselves to be serious students. He calls on all the Russians in Paris to be his witnesses: *"all the Russians know how hard I have always worked; I have looked for the best way to gain good training; I volunteered as a soldier in order to gain admission to one of the best schools, not normally open to foreigners unless they had served in the French army...."*

To underline the injustice of his sad situation he challenges Makarov, the cabinet secretary, asking him if it is fair that someone like himself, Abraham, *"who has spent seventeen years close to His Majesty, should now be chased away from here like a dog, without money".* All the Russian students were living on credit for food and lodging, since the allowances for 1721 were worthless. He promises to show them the money, unspent, when he returns to Russia. In the next letter, written on 24 March, he asks the Tsar to order Prince Dolgoruky to meet his expenses until he returns to Russia, adding: *"I do not want to be like Mitshurin and Lachinsky in England."* He informs Makarov that he has debts of two hundred and fifty roubles to pay.

A little later, on 11 April, the Imperial Cabinet sent him four hundred roubles. His other companions in poverty, Yurov, Resanov and Korovin also received money from Petersburg. Abraham was able to return to La Fère to finish his training.

Some months later and thousands of miles away from Paris came orders from the Emperor of all the Russias, who had not, after all, forgotten his young protégés in far countries. On 16 October 1722 Peter was on the shores of the Caspian Sea with his troops, having occupied the whole of Northern Persia (three provinces and the towns of Baku, Derbent, Astrabad, and Rasht[56]) which was to become Russian territory from then on. He gave the following instructions to his Chancellor, Count Gabriel Ivanovich Golovin:

" Abraham the Black, Gabriel Resanov and Stefan Korovin have written from Paris to say that in accordance with the *ukase* they are ready to leave Paris, but that they each have debts to pay of 200 écus; they also need 300 écus each for the journey. I wish you to send the Ambassador in Paris, Prince Dolgoruky, the money they need to pay their debts and the cost of their journey. Enclosed is a mandate drawn on the Treasury. If Dolgoruky has already left, send it to Prince Alexander Kuriakin and tell him to send them to Petersburg."[57]

At last, all Abraham's financial difficulties were over. He had enough money to pay the family where he was lodging in La Fère, buy himself new equipment and complete the extensive library of books he had been collecting continuously since 1717. He had his Diploma of the King's Engineers, signed by Louis XV, and the rank of Captain in the French army. It was with a light heart that he presented himself to Monsieur Tuffereau, the commander in chief of the School of Artillery of La Fère, to take his leave. When Prince Dolgoruky and his retinue left the French capital for Russia in early January 1723 one of his travelling companions was "the former captain of the French army, Abraham Petrov."[58]

CHAPTER IV

Return to Russia

---

*"Great and glorious Catherine, may your Majesty
grant your favour to this book, 'Practical Geometry and Fortification'
for it may be of service both to young people wishing to study these
sciences and to experienced engineers in the field."*

Hanibal, dedication to Catherine I
23 November 1726

Peter I's African Disciple

The Russian historian, Eidelman, vividly describes the political situation in Russia and the mood of the Emperor at the beginning of 1723: "...Shortly before the return of Prince Dolgoruky and Abraham, Peter I came back to Moscow from his campaign in Persia and found that all was not well in his country...

The Emperor was tired – he had exactly two years to live – and he had a presentiment that only a few of his projects would be successful; when his plans were thwarted, he flew into terrible rages.

Peter knew perfectly well that Menshikov[51], his second-in-command, was guilty of gross embezzlement of state funds; so were many, many others. At the very time that Dolgoruky's ambassadorial retinue set out for the old capital, Moscow, Peter decided, for the edification of his closest collaborators, to make an example of one of the most favoured of 'the eaglets in the Tsar's nest[52]'.

Baron Peter Shapirov, an experienced diplomat...had been accused of abuse of his powers and intrigue. A commission of ten senators had arraigned him, stripped him of his titles, his rank, his estates and condemned him to death.

His head was already on the scaffold; the executioner had raised his axe, but then lowered it. The Tsar had commuted the sentence to exile...

Moscow held its breath, expecting other executions; Basil Lukich Dolgoruky and another diplomat, Golovkin, (from Berlin) who had returned at the same time, were waiting their turn to be received and interviewed by the Tsar."

Abraham Petrov, with his new diploma in engineering, was also a member of Ambassador Dolgoruky's delegation and anxiously looking forward to seeing the Emperor.

To continue Eidelman's account: "...the Tsar received them, spoke at length with the new arrivals, exchanged a few words with Abraham Petrov and relaxed; convinced that after all he still had faithful adherents; reports from Paris and Berlin were better than he had expected in his overwrought, nervous and hypercritical state of mind..."

Reassured, the Tsar decided to arrange a triumphant welcome in St. Petersburg for the two delegations. He left Moscow for "Paradise[53]" on 1 March 1723, arrived on 3 March and on the agreed date rode out to meet them "...a few *versts* from the town, in a richly appointed coach, accompanied by a detachment of the Imperial Guard. They were given special honours."

Abraham was also honoured: "..the Tsar, having come to meet them, embraced them, invoked blessings on them all – including his godson – by presenting them with icons of Saints Peter and Paul[54]."

The African officer took great care of the holy image, and it was passed on from generation to generation in his family.

After six years in France Abraham was back in St. Petersburg, Peter's new town on the Neva. It had been greatly improved, with more beautiful streets, more inhabitants and a brilliant social life.

On his return, he again took up his duties as the Emperor's personal secretary. He was put in charge of the library and the office of plans and drawings and worked as consultant engineer, notably on the site at Kronstadt (Kotlin Island).

The Tsar had several vast building projects: the Ladoga canal (1719) under the supervision of von Münnich and another at Kronstadt. In the same year, he had founded the town of Ekaterinburg in honour of the Empress Catherine. To carry out all his plans the Tsar had had to bring civil engineers from abroad, but now, fortunately, many newly qualified young Russians were returning from their studies abroad. There were carpenters, engravers, sailors, fitters, setters and smiths.

The Emperor received them all personally and checked their qualifications. "Capable fellows, like the naval man Nepluev, were given immediate promotion, leading to a brilliant career". Everyone who proved himself fully competent in the practice of his new trade remained under the Tsar's orders and was lodged free of charge by the state. "For two years they received a living allowance". During this period they were supposed to tackle any difficulties associated with their work and gain experience. "Then each one would be given enough money to set up a workshop and make his own living. He would be expected to take apprentices and teach them his trade, but would receive no further public subsidy."

This method of integrating the newly qualified experts and craftsmen into Russian society had spectacular results. In a few years the Russian navy, which had not even existed at the beginning of Peter I's reign, was the envy of Europe: "at one point the Court of St. James (England) became worried about the rapid development of the Russian navy and demanded that all (Russian) students in the country be recalled[55]."

As for Abraham, a few months practical work on the site at Kronstadt were enough to convince the Tsar of the solid achievement of his years in France. Exactly one year after his return Peter I gave Field Marshal Prince Menshikov the following instructions:

" ...to His Excellency the Prince,

Abraham, (the Black), has served in France with the rank of captain and returned with certification. He should therefore be designated Lieutenant in the Company of Bombardiers in the Engineering Corps...

Petersburg
4 February 1724
Peter"

The company of bombardiers in question was that of the Preobrazhensky regiment, the most prestigious regiment in Russian history. The Emperor himself was its captain and Abraham's designation put him at the heart of the military elite. The young African officer was charged with the duty of "training new leaders for the Engineering Brigades…" and "teaching mathematics and fortification to guards intending to become military engineers."

The Imperial *ukase* made Lieutenant Bombardier Abraham Petrov head of the School of Engineering in the capital. There are several testimonies to the work of Lieutenant Abraham at this stage; for example the *Notes* of the well known eighteenth century Russian memoir writer, A. Bolotov, contain the following information: "at my uncle's house I also found mathematics books, some printed, some handwritten, and a particularly fine notebook on geometry and fortification with drawings and text from the time when he studied these subjects with Hannibal[56]."

As an officer in the Russian Imperial Guard Abraham was the Tsar's aide in several different areas. S. Geyshenko, an eminent Russian authority on Pushkin, asserts that the Tsar also made him "translator-in-chief of all foreign language books acquired by the Imperial Court[57]". He had come back from France with an excellent command of French, in addition to German, Dutch and of course, Russian, which he had learnt much earlier. He was called upon "to provide translations". When Peter I entrusted to Konon Zotov the translation of two French books into Russian, he wrote, "in books where you do not know the terminology, please call upon Abraham Petrov for advice[58]." To this day it is possible to consult works in the library of The Academy of Sciences in Russia including "the manuscript translations made by Hanibal of works in French on fortification; also a map drawn by him of the area of the river Vegmas (in Karelia) where mineral springs were discovered[59]."{See map, *Plan of the ferruginous waters of the river Vegmas in Karelia near the White Sea, drawn by Abraham Hanibal. Autographed by Hanibal, 1724*}.

Abraham enjoyed the Tsar's complete confidence and continued to live at his side as he had done in his early years. The Tsar rose early. At four o'clock in the morning, he rose to copy out his notes and read state documents. At five o'clock, he received his ministers and heard their reports. At six o'clock, he had breakfast and then began his work outside the palace. He went to debates in the Senate and the College of War, and then inspected the progress on the building sites in town. If he was not to be found on a building site, he was working on one of his shipbuilding projects, tools in hand like an ordinary workman. At midday, he took lunch and then had a siesta. It had been during one of his siestas ten years previously that Abraham had been punished so unjustly for a disturbance caused by Lestocq and Johnson. Such recollections must have made him smile, since now, at the age of twenty-eight, he was "one of the most highly qualified members" of the Russian administration.

Abraham's Library

Abraham Petrov, who had been a captain in the French army, had brought back from Paris one of the most prestigious private book collections in the Russian Empire. His library was one of the ten best belonging to Russian intellectuals of the period[60], and contained nearly four hundred volumes. He had books on mathematics, military science, architecture, history, geography, philosophy, literature, etc.

Luppov has made an exhaustive study of the private libraries of the first quarter of the eighteenth century and makes the following comment: "In Hanibal's library, books on mathematics, fortification, artillery, geography, history and literature were well represented. Among the works on mathematics was *Cours de Mathématiques* in five volumes by Ozanam (1693), *Nouvelle Géometrie Pratique* by the same author (1693), *Eléments d'Euclide* (1709) and a whole series of other books.

Luppov writes: "He not only bought books on fortification, artillery and other branches of the art of warfare, which would be closely connected with the exercise of his profession. He also had a great liking for historical literature and geography. His books include works on the history of Europe and other countries, memoirs, biographies of great historical figures. Hanibal was interested in the English revolution and the life of Cromwell. The geography collection contained such books as *Géographie Universelle* in five volumes and various accounts of travels. Also, like other intellectuals of his time, he possessed various dictionaries.

In his (literature) collection, there were several works by French writers as well as the classics of antiquity: Corneille, Racine, Molière, Homer, and a series of popular novels of his period. Interestingly he also owned a copy of the book of Mohammed, the *Koran*[61]."

It is appropriate to mention that some of the books in Abraham's private library are among the rarest to be found in our day. Geyshenko, the former Director of the Hanibal Museum in Petrovskoe (Russia) cites the 1687 edition of G. Grocius' book, *Sur la guerre et la paix* (Paris)" with Mazarin's autograph and seal" (See Appendix 11)

The death of the Emperor and the accession of Catherine I

The Great Northern War had ended in 1721 with the Peace of Nystadt. Peter I's sworn enemy, Charles XII, had died two years previously and his sister Eleanora had become Queen of Sweden. The Tsar had consequently been able to assemble enough men to win in his Persian campaign in 1722.

Peter I had other problems – not the least important being the question of his successor. The death of Prince Alexis in 1718 had been followed by the death in the next year of the young Prince Peter, the Tsar's other son, who should have inherited the throne. "The Romanovs[62] then had only one male descendant, the son of Alexis." In 1721 Peter introduced a reform of the rules of succession, giving the ruling Tsar the right to choose his own successor. The Viennese Court was concerned that the young Prince Peter Alexeevich, the son of Alexis and on his mother's side a cousin of the Austrian Emperor[63], would be debarred from the inheritance. It was thought that the Tsar intended to hand power to one of his two daughters, the Grand Duchesses Anna and Elisabeth Petrovna.

At this point, in November 1723, Peter decided to crown his wife, Catherine, as Empress. The ceremony took place on 15 March 1724 when Peter's health was already failing.

In the summer, the Tsar visited the work sites at Kronstadt, Peterhof and Ladoga. In 1723, the technical direction of the works on the Ladoga canal had been entrusted to General von Münnich. Peter was very pleased with the progress and quality of the work and warmly congratulated von Münnich saying, "that he was the hardest working foreigner he had ever known".

The Emperor's health later gave further cause for concern and his doctors, Blumenstrot, Bodlov and the English surgeon Horn attended him with some success.

Towards the end of the year several cases of corruption, involving some of the highest dignitaries in the land, came to light. Menshikov, the powerful president of the College of War, was not exempt. Greatly disillusioned, Peter nominated Repnin to replace him.

Abraham Petrov had been sent to Riga at the beginning of 1725. The Tsar had commissioned him to "plan and carry out new fortifications at the fortress of Riga[64]". He was there when the news of the Emperor's death reached him.

Peter died on 28 January 1725. He had not had time to nominate his successor. The Senate met to decide whether the Emperor's wife, Catherine, or the Emperor's grandson, the Grand Duke Peter Alekseevich (aged 10), should rule the greatest Empire in Europe.

The debate was stormy. The Senators quickly divided into two opposing groups: the Princes Dolgoruky, Golitsyn and Repnin were for the young prince; Menshikov, Count Tolstoy and the High Admiral Apraksin were in favour of Catherine and obtained the support of the Imperial Guard. After much deliberation, the Senate appointed Catherine Alexeevna as the new Empress of Russia.

Catherine, born in 1684, was from Livonia (Latvia and Estonia today). She was of humble origin and her story reads like a fairy tale. "At the age of four, she lost her mother and was taken in by a charitable institution. Her birthplace, Livonia, was laid waste and she was taken prisoner by the Russians (1702). She was passed from General Bauer to Field-Marshal Sheremetev and then to Prince Menshikov, in whose house she came to the notice of Peter I. She found favour with the Tsar, converted to the Greek religion, married the Emperor, was proclaimed Empress, and saved the honour of Russia by her actions at the disastrous battle of Pruth River (1711). She was Peter's inseparable companion in his travels and was crowned by him in 1724. She succeeded him as the first woman ruler of Russia to wield absolute power[65].

In Catherine's reign, Menshikov became all-powerful. He had, after all, played a key role in the Senate's decision in favour of Peter I's widow and she was aware she needed his help to rule. Menshikov loaded himself with titles and became known as the Generalissimo of the Empire.

Mathematics tutor to the future Emperor

Abraham was deeply upset when his powerful protector and adoptive father died at the age of fifty-three. He himself was twenty-nine years old that year. He probably wondered what future he had in Russia. He did not feel totally abandoned, however, as the Empress Catherine was well disposed towards him. All his old friends, who had been reunited with him on his return from France, were full of kindness and concern.

His best friend was Semion Maurin, formerly one of the Empress's pages. Ivan Cherkasov was another intimate whom he had known from his very early youth. All three were the rising stars of the new generation. Semion was the tutor of the Grand Duke Peter Alexeevich. Ivan was Secretary to the Imperial Cabinet.

Abraham was given another task. On her accession in 1725, the Empress engaged him "to teach mathematics to the heir to the throne, the Grand Duke Peter Alexeevich". In fact Abraham had always been a confidant of Catherine I, his adoptive mother. Certain of those present at Peter I's deathbed claimed that he had made his wife and daughter Elisabeth swear to look after and protect his black godson. "Catherine I", says G. Leets, "had known Abraham from the first day of his arrival at Peter's Court in 1705. She was fully aware of his devotion to the Tsar's family, and recognised his ability and erudition."

His appointment as tutor suggests that the African engineer was the best mathematics master in Russia. He proved to be an excellent teacher and the future emperor became very attached to him. Abraham, as one of the Tsarevich's tutors, was constantly in his company.

Abraham and Maurin were brought together on frequent occasions by their duties as the Grand Duke's tutors and they were party to many of the secrets of the Court. "They met often in the home of the Princess Agraphene Petrovna Volkonskaya, whom Abraham had known from childhood and for whom he felt the most sincere respect. Their time was passed meeting friends at the Princess's house, working at their appointed tasks and getting involved in amorous intrigues", writes Choubinski.

Thanks to two "letters" from Kronstadt, where he was working on an engineering project, we know the names of three of the favourites among Abraham's female acquaintance in the first years after his return from France: the Assechka Ivanovna, Philipievna and a certain Princess Daria Yakovlevna.[66] ".

Here is one of the letters:-

Love letter to a Petersburg coquette

"Dear Madame Assecha Ivanovna!

I thank you, my dear, for your good wishes regarding my person. You saw fit to mention in your letter that you would not deign to talk about affairs in your correspondence with me, and I am heartily sorry for that; however, what are you up to, my darling scamps, my little clowns, what is all this mischievous talk about your poor friend, black Abraham, being guilty of every misdemeanor in Kronstadt? I spend every day God gives on my knees in the mud, for no better reason than that that is my profession. You talk about kissing my knees, but that shows how little respect you have for me. My adorable little teases, what do you mean by saying that work is bad for my health? It is not true, here the weather prevents anything happening at all; I have been here a week, and not one day has passed without rain; kindly agree, my dear friends, that there is no need to worry about my taking time off. What are you alluding to when you hope I shall not lose my love of life? I do all I can to make sure I do not, but what can one do when one's friends are so unstable, one is tossed about like a ship in a storm, at the mercy of the winds and waves. The only solution is to make sure one has a solid, well-built ship and I do have a wonderful anchor, which will hold me in place if that is what pleases you. I will let you know when I am due to arrive so that my dears will wait patiently; I should like my friends to be as patient as I am – that is, I should like my friends to be less fickle and more considerate...

My shy little darlings, how dull you've grown while I've been away; you ask when I shall return; I don't know myself yet. I should love to see my saucy little friends again even though you say you do not really expect me. I regret that from the bottom of my heart, and I pray that God will grant your every wish. I will stop here.

I remain, dear Madam,
Your faithful servant, Abraham.

The amorous dalliance that this letter indicates took place some years before the death of Peter I, at the time when the African engineer was working on the site of the Kronstadt canal (1723-1724). In spite of the many and varied tasks he was allotted at the Emperor's side it seems that he did have enough time for a few flirtations. Life in the vicinity of Peter I, the "eternal labourer on the throne of Russia" to use an expression from Pushkin, demanded "devoting of all one's energies to work". Constantin de Grunwald describes him well when he writes that Peter I had "military discipline in his blood: the concept of duty is the one he would most readily have accepted and demanded of his entourage." In the last years of his life he tried to strengthen the sense of duty in the offices of his administration and inculcate in his staff the principles of honesty and civic responsibility. He tried to make them understand that the least infringement was the equivalent of treason and that a chief who was at fault would never be able to command the respect of his subordinates[67].

Abraham had been subjected to this discipline for over two decades. He had "little time for affairs of the heart".

Abraham's manuscript

On 23 November 1726, Catherine I gave an audience to the Grand Duke Peter Alexeevich's mathematics tutor. It had been requested by engineer Abraham Petrov himself. He handed the Empress the manuscript of a book in two volumes which he had just finished writing. It was an imposing document of seven hundred pages, richly bound, and dedicated to the Empress. Volume I was entitled: *"Practical Geometry"* and Volume II *"Fortification"*. The dedication itself is a mine of information on the writer. He outlines his autobiography: recalls that he was baptised in Lithuania at Vilnius in 1705, that His Majesty the Tsar was his godparent and that

> *"in 1717 {the Tsar}, a man of incomparable goodness, judged me worthy to stay in France to do military studies. To this end the monarch, the great Father of his Country, deigned to recommend me personally to the Duc de Maine, Prince of Dombes and Grand Master of the French Artillery, the natural son of the great King Louis of France. I had the honour of serving in the French army from 1717, and reached the rank of captain, for which I hold a certificate signed by His Royal Majesty, Louis XV...*

> *I then received the ukase of His Majesty the Tsar demanding my return; I obtained a formal release from the service of the French King and returned to Russia with the intention of devoting myself entirely to the service of my sovereign, who had given me life and learning...*

> *On my return in 1723, I had the honour of kissing Your Highness' feet, and His Imperial Majesty, out of his bountiful kindness to all orphans, was graciously pleased to nominate me for a position in his regiment of bombardiers. I received verbal instructions to teach military architecture to the junior officers and soldiers of the Imperial Guard. His Majesty, the father of the Russian Empire, desired above all to spread the knowledge of science throughout his lands and he pursued his aim with passion, determination and almost religious fervour. Peter the Great was preoccupied night and day with this idea. His personal love of his people was manifest in his decree that all the sciences should be taught in the academies, and also to the members of the army. Accordingly, he ordered that schools of certain branches of engineering should be formed for the regiments.*

> *...To this end, this book, Fortification and Practical Geometry contains passages on engineering translated from French into Russian. They have been selected from various well known writers and academics. They cover every question on geometry and fortification with graphic illustrations of*

circular processes, and sections on the special measurements used in the construction of fortifications and on other geometric proportions...

...To this end, I, your very humble subject, offer my modest efforts under the august protection of your Imperial Majesty, in the hope that Your Majesty will follow in every way in the steps of your glorious husband, Peter the Great.Great and glorious Catherine, may Your Majesty grant your favour to this book, for it may be of service both to young people wishing to study these sciences and to experienced engineers in the field.

Your Imperial Majesty's very humble servant
Abraham Petrov[68].

The black mathematician was thirty years old at the time. The manuscript he handed to the Empress was "the outcome of many years of work. It is a digest of teaching texts, sketches and technical drawings". He probably intended it for his adoptive father, who, sadly, had died before he could appreciate Abraham's work. Feinberg makes the following commentary on the quality of the work by the African engineer and mathematician.

"The text is handwritten, there are superb technical drawings, very finely executed, done by the Negro {Abraham} himself, and a dedication that serves as a preface to the book. The manuscript figures in the historical catalogue of the library of the Academy of Sciences, but with a very brief accompanying note[69]."

S. Luppov in his book: *Books in Russia in the first Quarter of the Eighteenth Century* (Leningrad, 1973) writes:

"the manuscript of this major work entitled *Geometry and Fortification* is preserved in the Library of the Academy of Sciences in the USSR. The first volume is a course on geometry and trigonometry, the second – a course on fortification."

Abraham's pioneering book was one of the first of its kind to appear in Russia. In 1724, the Tsar Peter I had created the Academy of Sciences and it was in this library that the two volumes of the book written by Abraham would be deposited.

To Abraham's great sorrow, the Empress Catherine, Peter the Great's widow, died a few months later, on 6 May 1727.

CHAPTER V

Exile in Siberia

"I am confident that I am guilty of no offence…
this is perhaps the last time I shall write to you;
they may send me off to some desert spot to die."

Hanibal, Letter from exile, 1727

The Friends of Princess Volkonskaya

During Catherine I's short reign (1725-1727) real power passed into the hands of one man, Menshikov, Peter I's former favourite and companion-in-arms who had enormous influence on the Empress.

Having assumed wide powers on Catherine's behalf, Menshikov, as Chubinsky describes him, became arrogant, brutal, overbearing, and hated by all. "Abraham Petrovich's position became difficult – he had known Menshikov intimately for a long time. Well before he went to France, Abraham, who was constantly in Peter's company from 1716 onwards, knew all the vices and inadequacies of the man. It had been under his care that "little Alexis" (Menshikov) had metamorphosed into a respected prince. Abraham knew of the link between Catherine[70] and Menshikov and on his return to Russia in 1723, his friends had informed him of Menshikov's malpractices…Menshikov for his part was aware how much Abraham Petrovich knew about him…and disliked him. He did not act against him immediately on Peter's death, deciding out of respect for the sovereign's memory to do him no harm, though he made no attempt to use his powerful position at Court to make Abraham's life easier[71]".

Abraham began to take an interest in politics. He joined "Princess A. Volkonskaya's circle of friends" and actively opposed the 'generalissimo'. The young black intellectual, the spiritual heir of the late Emperor, found there friends who shared his outlook. There were six people in the group:

− Princess Volkonskaya at whose house the group met. Born Bestuzhev, she was the wife of Prince Volkonsky and the Empress Catherine's lady-in-waiting and confidante.

− Ivan Cherkasov, the clerk to the Imperial Cabinet who had been promoted to the position of Cabinet Secretary in succession to Makarov (the same Makarov who had been the recipient of Abraham's youthful letters from France).

− Igor Pachkov, a member of the powerful College of War.

− Alexander Burtulin, favourite of the Grand Duchess Elisabeth, Peter I's daughter.

− Semion Maurin, tutor to the Grand Duke and to the future Emperor, Peter Alexeevich.

And Abraham Petrovich, Peter I's godson, tutor in geometry and fortification to the future Emperor.

They had all known each other well for a long time and were linked by a common "devotion to the Tsar's family", their love for all things Russian and their "hatred of Menshikov". Each of them had a particular reason to hate the 'Generalissimo'. Menshikov had wronged Princess Volkonskaya's father; his arrogance towards Ivan Cherkasov when he was clerk to the Cabinet had made him feel vulnerable; Burtulin was angry with him for not supporting Elisabeth rather than Catherine at the time of Peter I's death; Pachkov witnessed Menshikov's regular abuse of his position at the College of War; Maurin "detested him for his perfidy[72]".

When the health of the Empress began to fail it was rumoured that Menshikov wanted the Grand Duke Peter Alexeevich to succeed. Count Tolstoy went to the Princess Volkonskaya to ask her for confirmation of the rumour. There were two opposing factions in the Court; those who favoured Peter I's grandson, Peter Alexeevich and those who hoped that Peter I's daughter, Elisabeth Petrovna, would come to the throne.

Count Tolstoy and his party did not want the Grand Duke Peter to inherit, as they feared reprisals. Peter Tolstoy had been one of those to bring accusations against Peter I's son, the Tsarevich Alexis, who had died in prison in 1718. Their reasoning was simple. The Grand Duke was the son of Alexis and some day he might decide to avenge his father's death on those he held responsible. To be safe they had to make sure he did not become Emperor on Catherine's death. Intrigue was rife in the Petersburg Court. Certain foreign powers, most importantly the Austrians, were ready to intervene. The young prince's late mother had been an Austrian princess, related to the Austrian Emperor. The latter wasted no time in sending one of his ministers, Count Rabutin, as ambassador to Moscow with orders to support the heir apparent.

In this tremendous struggle for influence, Abraham did not remain inactive. He became the secretary of Princess Volkonskaya's circle. When they realised they needed the good will of Count Rabutin it was to Abraham that they turned. He made the acquaintance of the Austrian minister and they became good friends.

Abraham was very fond of the Grand Duchess Elisabeth, his adoptive sister, but equally attached to his pupil, Peter Alexeevich, the other possible heir. In his position as tutor he could have exerted considerable influence on the prince. In theory, he had nothing to fear from either of the presumed heirs to the Russian throne. Then events took a sudden turn. The Empress Catherine told Princess Volkonskaya, Abraham's friend, of Menshikov's secret plan. He had suggested to the Empress, who was gravely ill, that she should make a will in which she would name "the Grand Duke Peter Alexeevich as her heir, on condition that he married his (Menshikov's) daughter[73]".

As soon as this highly secret information reached the ears of the Princess's friends they decided to act. Menshikov, however, was too quick for them. He "was informed of his enemies' plans, arrested them immediately, and forced Catherine, a few hours before she died, to sign a warrant for the exile and execution of those involved[74]".

Menshikov's Infamous *Ukase*

" 8 May 1727. On the *ukase* of Her Imperial Majesty the Military College of the State orders:

> *Lieutenant Bombardier Abraham Petrov of the Preobrazhensky Regiment of Guards to be sent immediately to Kazan, to inspect the local fort and assess its need for restoration; or if in his judgement a citadel is indispensable, to provide a plan and projection for its construction; on termination of the inspection the details of the plan and projection to be sent by post to the College of War. To forward by post the expenses of his travel, comprising four post-coaches, from the Offices of the Treasury; to send to the Treasury an order to release the money for travel; to address an order to the Chancellery of Posts concerning the route to be taken; also to address an order to the Governor of Kazan for the direction of the operation and the provision of funds.*
>
> *Alexander Menshikov"*

On the original of this decree can be read the annotation in Abraham's hand :

"On the receipt of this I left Petersburg for Kazan where I spent 25 days; I then received another order sending me to Tobolsk."

The above commission, signed by Menshikov, was the first stage of Abraham's unofficial exile. Abraham was close to the young Emperor, Peter II, and Menshikov's first concern was the amount of influence the African might have over him. The mathematics tutor "knew all Menshikov's sins" and could undermine him by revealing them to Peter. For his own safety, Menshikov had to remove him from the company of the young Emperor, but he could not issue an order for his arrest when he was accused of nothing. Princess Volkonskaya's house had been searched but Menshikov had found nothing in her letters and papers to incriminate Abraham in any way. Also he could not issue any decree without informing the Emperor and would have had to justify any punitive action taken against Abraham. In order to separate

Peter and Abraham he had to act without arousing the suspicion of either, for if the latter were to seek to defend himself he would reveal Menshikov's duplicity to Peter I's grandson.

Accordingly Menshikov chose to post him to Kazan with a commission which seemed to involve serious responsibility. Abraham apparently suspected nothing, and obeyed without delay. He scarcely had the time to entrust his savings to the care of Cherkasov...

In Kazan he received another ukase from Menshikov:

> *"Honourable Sir, Lieutenant Bombardier of the Imperial Guard, Abraham Petrov!*
>
> *His Imperial Majesty orders that you go to Tobolsk, there to erect a fort on the instructions of the Governor, Prince Dolgoruky...to this end and on the instructions of His Imperial Majesty we suggest that in view of the urgent need for the construction of this fort you should leave immediately; the plan will be sent you by the next mail. Inform us without delay of the date of receipt of this order and the date of your departure.*
>
> *Peterhof, 28 May 1727. Alexander Menshikov[75]."*

On the original of this document, there is also a note in Abraham Petrov's hand:

"Upon which I went to Tobolsk[76]."

On receiving the second order, there was no doubt in Abraham's mind that his presence in Petersburg was not welcome and that he was in unofficial exile. The town of Tobolsk where he was to be sent on this urgent mission was in the heart of Siberia, thousands of kilometres from the capital.

On the same date, Menshikov sent a letter to Prince Dolgoruky, the Governor of Siberia, ordering that on arrival the African engineer should be sent yet further, to the Chinese frontier, to construct fortifications there. He adds:

"since he is a foreigner and it would be dangerous if he were to flee the country, he must be kept under strict surveillance; as for the

work on the fort, you must give him instructions; the plan will follow later".

We can infer that Menshikov hoped never to see the "dangerous" foreigner at court again. From the 25 March, his position at the heart of the regime was strengthened. As he had so ardently wished, his sixteen-year-old daughter, Maria Alexandrovna Menshikova, became officially engaged to the young Emperor.

Abraham remained at Kazan for another month. He *"was greatly in need of money"* as he wrote in a letter to his friend Princess Volkonskaya. He begged her to contact *"Ivan Antonovich Cherkasov, so that he can send the money that I left with him to Siberia as soon as possible."* Abraham knew that he was at the mercy of his powerful enemy, and in fact under sentence of death:

> *"I must inform you", he wrote to the Princess, "that I have received another order from Petersburg from M.[77] I enclose a copy of it. I am leaving today for Siberia, for Tobolsk, and it is possible that once there I shall receive a third order, sending me even further away; it is as they wish, I shall go anywhere without the least regret, apart from that of being separated from my friends; I am confident that I am guilty of no offence...this is perhaps the last time I shall write to you; they may send me to some desert spot to die. Lastly may I beg you to inform our friends in Petersburg and elsewhere that I have been sent to Siberia, to Tobolsk... and I would ask you especially to try to send on the copy of the enclosed ukase to Clochette[78], or Ivanovich the Chatterbox[79], or the Billy Goat[80] and Pantaloon[81]..."*

Abraham's suspicions were fully justified, as we have seen, by the letter from Menshikov to the Governor of Siberia (quoted above), though he, of course, did not know of its existence. He was also unaware that his friends had been scattered to the four corners of the immense Russian Empire. Princess Volkonskaya was under house arrest in a little village several hundred miles from the capital. Menshikov had also sent Maurin on a special mission to Tobolsk in Siberia. Cherkasov had been transferred to the secretariat of the Moscow Synod to "make an inventory of the Patriarch's sacristy"! The two other members of the group were not affected by Menshikov's repression – it is not clear why not.

On 29 June 1727 Abraham felt so near death that he wrote an appeal to the all-powerful Menshikov himself, addressing him as "the defender of widows and orphans" but received no response. At the end of the month, he finally left Kazan, arriving in Tobolsk on 30 July. In the meantime a third Imperial ukase, signed by Menshikov on 28 July, had reached him. He was to go to the Chinese frontier to construct fortifications. He stayed one month in Tobolsk and Governor Dolgoruky gave him one hundred roubles for subsistence, as by then he had nothing left to live on. He was informed that Semion Maurin had been appointed commander of the garrison and would shortly be arriving in Tobolsk. Towards the end of August, the Governor sent him to Tomsk in accordance with the Imperial decree, and he remained there until November. That is where he wrote his fourth letter to Princess Volkonskaya, as he still had no news of her. He also wrote to the Grand Duchess Anna Petrovna, Peter I's elder daughter, to ask her to intervene in his favour, and to his friends Alexander Burtulin and Peter Sumarokov. Menshikov, however, had sent the Grand Duchess out of the country to join her husband, the Duke of Holstein-Gottorp, and had thus successfully put another claimant to the throne at a safe distance.

Those of Abraham's friends who were still at liberty used all their influence to try to obtain his return from exile. From Copenhagen, Moscow and Petersburg they did all they could, but in vain.

Then on 8 September events took a totally unforeseen turn. The all-powerful 'Generalissimo', the very man whose daughter was engaged to marry Peter II, fell from favour. On 10 September he was "exiled to Ranenburg and deprived of his rank, his decorations and his title of prince". When Abraham's friends heard the news, they wept for joy. The faithful Major-General Pachkov, a member of the College of War, gave them the information; in an exultant letter to Cherkasov, the principal secretary to the Synod of Moscow, also in unofficial exile. He wrote: "With God's help everything is going well; we no longer have anyone to fear as much as Prince Menshikov. We are overwhelmed with joy at the fall of that vainglorious and haughty Goliath crushed by the strong right arm of God."

Pachkov and the Bestuzhev brothers were sure they would now be able to obtain the recall of the exiles. They were quickly disillusioned.

On 24 October Major General Pachkov wrote bitterly to Princess Volkonskaya: "Yes, I am working hard for the return of Semion Maurin and Abraham, but no-one is interested; people curse them, and intend them to suffer like dogs…"

The new faction in power, that of the Dolgoruky princes, was opposed to the return of the exiles. The correspondence between the friends was seized and they were overtaken by a new wave of repression.

Hanibal!

The African exile was in Tomsk, far away in Siberia in November 1727 and had heard nothing of the events at court since his banishment in May. He did not know that the saying "he who lives by the sword shall die by the sword" had already been fulfilled and that Prince Menshikov in turn had been sent away from the capital into exile. He did not know that the Dolgoruky princes were now masters of Russia. A few months earlier Menshikov had succeeded in distancing Peter II from serious affairs of state, causing him to forget "the friends of his youth"; now it was the turn of the new strong men of the court to continue on the same path for as long as they could. "The young Emperor may well have remembered his old friends, but he was trapped by the intrigues of the various factions at court. Levenvold and Anna Kramer were the most violently opposed to the "company" [Princess Volkonskaya's group of friends]. They had been devoted to Menshikov during the lifetime of Peter and Catherine; now they clung to the Dolgorukys and Lopukhin and used their influence to make sure that no one reminded the young prince about Maurin or Hanibal[82]."

By the last months of the dreadful year of 1727, Abraham had begun to think that the mission he had entrusted to his friend, Gregory V. Bozhinski, whom he had sent to visit Princess Volkonskaya in Moscow, might bear fruit. This time he had decided to play all his cards. In his letter to the princess he asked her to contact a large number of people who had influence at the Imperial Court. He knew that the coronation of the young Emperor would soon take place and he suggested ways and means of approaching the Grand Duchess Anna Petrovna to present his case. The letter is undeniable proof that "Abraham Petrovich was very close to court circles and knew its members well; he was familiar with all the secret channels of communication giving access to them[83].

His objective was to obtain a decree to be sent to the Russian Ambassador in China, Savva Raguzinski, whom he was due to meet at the Mongolian frontier, authorising him to return to Moscow in the Ambassador's company. The list of people he knew at Court and who might intercede for him is impressive: Alexander Burtulin, the Grand

Duchess Elisabeth Petrovna's favourite; Peter Sumarokov, a gentleman at the court of the Grand Duchess Anna Petrovna; the two princesses, Elisabeth and Anna, Peter I's daughters; Pachkov, a general and member of the College of War; Cherkasov, one of his close friends; Lestocq, a Count and the personal doctor of Elisabeth, Peter I's daughter; Grand Duchess Nathalie Alexeevna, daughter of the Tsarevich Alexis; Prince Dimitri M. Golitsyn; Alexis Volkov, Menshikov's secretary; Pantaloon, Billy Goat, Beluga and Makava (the nicknames of his friends); Prince Mikhail Vladimirovich Dolgorukov; Prince Sergey Dolgorukov; Prince Basil Vladimirovich Dolgorukov; Prince Dimitri Mikhailovich; Prince Nikita Feodorovich; Grand Duchess Anna Ivanovna; Rabutin, Minister and Austrian Ambassador to the Russian Court; Admiral Stefan F. Apraxin; Pavel Ivanovich, one of Apraxin's intimates; Matthew, Princess Volkonskaya's right-hand man; the Bestuzhev brothers, one the ambassador to Denmark, the other the ambassador to Poland...

Abraham had ceased to think he was under sentence of death. He believed he had a good chance of escaping from the horrors of Siberia if his friends followed his instructions to the letter. Besides on re-reading Menshikov's order sending him into exile he realised that he had not been deprived of his rank as officer of the Imperial Guard. He was still Abraham Petrov, Lieutenant Bombardier of the Preobrazhensky Regiment.

Since the death of his powerful protector and in the depths of his Siberian exile Abraham may have felt that the name Petrov no longer held any meaning for him. Perhaps that is why he chose a name that linked him more closely to Africa, a name that also had associations with his military career: Hanibal.

The name is that of the most famous African general in ancient history, Hannibal of Carthage, conqueror of the Romans; it is also close to that of another African who served in the French army and whose life story bore a certain resemblance to Abraham's own: Aniaba.

Aniaba was the son of King Zenan of Assini (in modern Ivory Coast) and was adopted by Louis XIV, the French King, in 1701. He was baptised in the cathedral of Notre Dame in Paris by (évêque) Bossuet in the presence of Louis XIV. The young black prince was given the name Louis Jean Aniaba. He lived in France for sixteen years, was given military training and became the captain of a cavalry regiment. When Abraham arrived in Paris with his adoptive father, Peter I, in 1717, Aniaba had already returned to Africa. When Abraham lived in Paris for six years and served as a captain in the French army, he would certainly have heard the story of Louis XIV's black godson, Aniaba. It is not impossible that those officers who had known Aniaba used to call the black Russian soldier by his name and that it became his nickname during his service with the French. "Hanibal" could well be a version of "Aniaba"[84].

The fact remains that at the end of 1727 the man who had been tutor in geometry and mathematics to the Russian Emperor, Peter II, changed his name to Abraham Hanibal (with a single 'n', not two as in Hannibal of Carthage). The first official document that mentions the changed name is an extract from the archives of the distant Siberian town of Irkutsk for the year 1727, in which the arrival of the engineer is registered. "December (1727) the lieutenant of the Imperial Guard's regiment of bombardiers, the negro, Hanibal Abraham Petrov, arrived from Tobolsk to erect the fort at Selenginsk."

It was at Selenginsk that the African engineer met Savva Raguzinski once again. Peter I's former secret agent in Constantinople was now the Russian Ambassador to China. Their paths had crossed in the Turkish capital, in Moscow, at Pruth River, in Paris and now they met again.

Abraham inspected the fortifications at the little settlement of Selenginsk and sent a report to the authorities on 15 January 1728. In Petersburg his friends were still having no success in changing the attitude of the new favourites. Unfortunately Count Rabutin had died, a sad blow for Princess Volkonskaya's clan. The Princess herself was still under house arrest.

A few months later, in April 1728, the Princess and her friends were victims of further oppression. This time she was denounced by her servants and arrested. Her home was searched and all her correspondence was confiscated. Cherkasov and Talysin, her cousin, were imprisoned and other members of the clan were harassed. The Supreme Privy Council was summoned in May to try the Princess and her friends; they were accused of creating a faction at court, trying to destabilise the government and "seeking the help of the Viennese court through the person of the

Minister, Count Rabutin...", consequently having "attempted to involve a foreign personage in the internal affairs of His Imperial Majesty".

Princess Volkonskaya was exiled to the distant monastery of Tikhvin, Senator Yuri Neledinsky was dismissed from the Senate, General Pachkov was dismissed from the College of War, Vsevolovsky was exiled to Guilian, Timothy Kutuzov was sentenced to a month in prison and stripped of his rank, Cherkasov was exiled to Astrakhan...[85].

On 17 July, the Supreme Privy Council sent an order to the administration of Tobolsk to keep Abraham Petrov at the Chinese frontier until his work there was finished. A whole year passed. By this time, Abraham could no longer bear to live in such difficult conditions six thousand *versts* from Petersburg. On 31 August 1729, he wrote a personal letter to Peter II. He asked the Emperor to allow him either to return to his regiment or to go to Tobolsk. He also asked for the payment of his arrears of salary, presenting himself as the victim of the personal scheming of Menshikov and his 'creatures'.

At the beginning of January, Abraham's house in Selenginsk was searched on the orders of the Supreme Council. All his correspondence was put under seal and sent to the capital and he himself was arrested. At the same time in Petersburg all his books were confiscated and deposited in the library of the Academy of Sciences.

Then, suddenly, the fortunes of the black prisoner of Tobolsk changed. On 19 January 1730, Peter II died at the age of fifteen, having reigned for only three years. Anna Ivanovna, his successor, was Peter I's niece. She "had known Abraham from his earliest years and was well disposed towards him". About a month after her accession, the new Empress acted to reprieve the exiled engineer; on 25 February, she ordered his release from prison, and the return of his correspondence. She then awarded him the rank of major at the garrison of Tobolsk.

There Major Hanibal was reunited with his great friend, Semion Maurin, the commander of the garrison. It must be said, however, "that even in these new conditions our African was less than enthusiastic[86]".

He did not smile again until he received a *ukase* from the Empress Anna Ivanovna a few months later. In September, he was ordered to return to the capital, given a posting to Estonia and transferred to the Engineering Corps.

CHAPTER VI

The first marriage

"Since the Tsar's Negro has decided to marry
The black man gravitates to the ladies
The black man's eyes wander over
the young women..."

Pushkin, October 1824

Under orders from Count von Münnich

On 25 September 1730, the Public Prosecutor Yaguginski read to the Russian Senate the Empress Anna's ukase concerning Abraham Petrov:

"To be assigned to the Count von Münnich's team in the Department of Engineering and Fortifications, according to his rank, Lieutenant Bombardier of the Imperial Guard, Abraham Petrov, nominated major at the garrison of Tobolsk."

The new posting, finally allowing the officer Abraham to leave Siberia after his three years of unofficial exile, was not due to anyone's wish to end his total boredom and frustration. He owed his liberation to the support "of another engineer, better known and highly influential at Court – B. C. von Münnich. He was able to plead for Abraham because the need for qualified engineers was so great that a special decree had been issued, inviting foreigners to come to von Münnich's aid. Anna Ivanovna's reign began with plans to continue the grandiose projects of her uncle, Peter I[87]".

104

Count von Münnich was now one of the most influential people in the Empire. He was the Governor of Petersburg, a member of the College of War, and Director of Works and Fortifications at Kronstadt. From May 1727, he was also General in Chief and Master of Russian Fortifications, and from May 1729 Grand Master of the Artillery. The great engineering expert had come to know and appreciate the young and talented Abraham Petrovich when working with him on various sites in 1723 and 1724, while Peter I was still alive.

The old Emperor's African godson was in fact the first fully qualified military engineer of his generation. At the time, almost every engineer of whatever grade was a foreigner and a Russian with Abraham's qualifications was a rarity. In his *Historical, Political and Military Memoirs of Russia from 1727 to 1744* General Manstein, who worked for many years in the country, notes: "The Russians are less inclined to take up engineering than artillery, and so there are very few who have succeeded in the former profession; most of the officers in the Engineering Corps are foreigners".

In 1730, Abraham made the long journey, taking several weeks in the depth of the Siberian winter, and returned to Petersburg in December 1730. His future seemed assured. In the same year, the Empress, probably on von Münnich's recommendation, promoted him to Captain of Engineers

During the first few days in Petersburg, he made the acquaintance of Captain Andrew Dioper. Dioper was Greek by origin, but had lived in Russia for more than thirty years. He had been recruited in Amsterdam in 1698, when he was living there, and had served in the Russian Navy ever since. He was married with two daughters and seemed to get on well with the young African.

Eyewitnesses of the period claim that Eudoxia Dioper, the daughter of the naval officer, was an outstandingly beautiful young woman. Abraham was dazzled by her and wanted her for his wife. Unfortunately, the fair Eudoxia was secretly in love with Kayserov, a lieutenant in the navy whom she hoped to marry. When Abraham told Dioper that he loved his daughter Eudoxia he raised no objection to their marriage. It is not known why Eudoxia and Kayserov did not tell the captain of their plans. Even when her father told her of the black officer's proposal, Eudoxia's reason for strongly rejecting it was simply that "he is not of our race". The Greek captain was not interested in his daughter's thoughts and feelings, being of the opinion that the African engineer was a good match for her. He accepted Abraham's proposal. Overjoyed, the black fiancé did not stop to consider the state of mind of his bride-to-be.

The marriage was arranged for 17 January 1731. Eudoxia, in no position to defy her father's wishes openly, found consolation in giving herself to her lover a few days before the wedding. In the evening of 17 January Captain Abraham Petrovich Hanibal and his beautiful bride, Eudoxia Dioper, were married in the church of Saint Simeon in Petersburg[88]. A few weeks later, the couple left for the town of Pernov (Pyarnu in Estonia today) on the shores of the Baltic. The unfortunate Lieutenant Kayserov, unable to bear the loss of his beautiful Eudoxia, arranged to leave the capital and on 15 March was transferred to Astrakhan on the other side of Russia.

The Baby Scandal and the Poison Affair

Pernov was a little provincial town with a garrison and a training school for junior military engineers. Abraham's new post was to train sub-officers for the Engineering Corps. He was to teach mathematics, fortification and technical drawing.

After three long years of exile in Siberia, far from the court and society, it would certainly have pleased Abraham better to have remained in Petersburg. The political situation, however, was not particularly favourable to him. Menshikov was experiencing the rigours of exile in Siberia in his turn, and even the powerful Dolgorukov princes had fallen from favour, but there was still a favourite at court. He was a certain Biren. "Haughty, ignorant and cruel," writes Khmyrov, "Biren was unfortunately the man who inspired the most confidence in the sovereign, and he manipulated her dishonestly and impudently... Levenvold, Mengdel, Keyzerling and innumerable other nobles from Courland...established themselves in Russia, seized the highest posts and greatest responsibilities, invading every aspect of the administration... expropriations were carried out to the letter; legal cases pursued without mercy. There was no region of Russia, however remote, where the name of Biren was not heard with dread...

The famous black, Hanibal, the godson of Peter the Great and the ancestor of the celebrated writer Pushkin, fled from the persecution of the terrible favourite (Biren), and hid himself away in a distant province... executions had become so common that they attracted little attention from the public, and often the executioners flayed someone alive or beheaded an individual with no one to watch but two or three poverty-stricken little old women and a few gaping boys[89]."

1731 was also the year in which Abraham's great friend, Princess Volkonskaya, died in the monastery where she had been sequestered. It was a sad blow for him and her circle of friends, some of whom were still in exile. It was better to remain anonymous in times of such severe repression. Feinberg speculates with some justification that it was quite likely that "the Grand Master of the Artillery, B. von Münnich, realised that the current political situation was unfavourable to Peter I's godson and thought it advisable as a temporary measure to give him a secondary position in Pernov, a little town far from the capital[90].

Captain Abraham Petrovich, lecturer in Military Engineering, was soon to experience another kind of upset in his peaceful provincial existence. A mere three months after their arrival in Pernov, in April 1731, Eudoxia Hanibal, who missed the constant activity of life in the capital, began an extra-marital liaison to relieve her boredom. The 'Don Juan' of Pernov was a certain Jacob Chichkov, a mechanical engineer and one of her husband's pupils.

At first Eudoxia and Jacob met to play cards at the house of a mutual friend, Madame Moor, a member of Pernov's lower middle class. Since her husband was often absent, Eudoxia had no compunction in inviting her new lover into the family home. The Town Clerk, a certain Timothy, acted as their intermediary. The affair had lasted several months before persistent rumours reached the ears of the wronged husband.

Pernov's residents were quick to notice what was happening. Madame Hanibal made the mistake of not realising how much interest the town'speople took in the black officer's marriage. The news quickly spread among the German population that the captain's beautiful wife had fallen for the charms of their local 'Lovelace'. The Captain himself had no evidence of his wife's adultery with one of his subalterns until February 1732.

A previous scandal had already made history in the little town. A few months earlier, at the end of September or the beginning of October 1731, Abraham's eyes had been opened: Eudoxia, who had become pregnant a few days after their marriage, gave birth to an unmistakably white child. The news went round the town like wildfire. "Although the date [of the pregnancy] was consistent with Hanibal being the father, the real state of affairs must have been quite clear to him. The scandal that the birth of the 'Ethiopian's' white daughter caused in Pernov society and among the officers of his garrison must have been a very unpleasant experience for him[91]."

Of course, the black officer knew perfectly well that the baby was not his, and that his beautiful wife had been deceiving him on the very eve of their marriage. They had not arrived in Pernov till March. However, he accepted the child, maybe in a spirit of tolerance, maybe to quell rumours, and she was given her mother's name, Eudoxia. He knew from other sources that his wife had never loved him and everything points to the fact that he did his best to adjust to the situation.

Life at Pernov became intolerable, no doubt because of the hurtful remarks, mocking smiles and questioning looks. Hanibal was not only captain of the garrison, he also lectured in the School of Engineering. In an attempt to escape from the painful situation, Abraham sent a report to his chief, Field-Marshal von Münnich, in which he asked for premature release from the army… for health reasons.

Count von Münnich was willing enough to intercede with the Empress Anna on his protégé's behalf. He had not forgotten that many years previously, when he was about the age of the young engineer, he himself had had to ask for time off to settle a family problem[92].

Accordingly, on 11 October 1731 outside the College of War Count von Münnich presented the Empress with a request for the early retirement of Captain Abraham Petrov. The document has enormous value for biographers of Hanibal It is preserved in the archives of the Russian Artillery. Here it is quoted in full:

> *"Abraham Petrov, Captain of the Engineering Corps, here presents a petition to your Imperial Majesty. He has addressed to me a request in which he states that he has been in Your Imperial Majesty's service since 1705. In the reign of your I. M.'s uncle of great and glorious memory, Peter the Great, he took part in all the battles which His Majesty graced with his presence, Dobroe, Lesnaya, Poltava, Hangö, Pruth River, and in numerous other hard-fought campaigns he was always at His Majesty's side.*

> *In 1716, by decree of the Emperor, he was sent to France, where in the pursuit of his military studies and in accordance with the French system he served in the army. In 1718 he received two serious head wounds during the attack on he town of Fontarabie. In 1724 when he returned to Russia, he was made lieutenant of the Company of Bombardiers of the Imperial Guard. In 1727 he was sent to Tobolsk, and from there to Selenginsk on the Chinese frontier to construct the local fort, which he did most conscientiously in accordance with Your Imperial Majesty's decrees.*

> *In 1730, in response to a ukase from the former Supreme Privy Council, he was transferred to the garrison of Tobolsk with the rank of major, and on 25 February, Your Imperial Majesty transferred him by decree to the Department of Engineering, and nominated him captain. He remains in this post until the present.*

He is now in poor health. His eyesight is bad and he has various other problems. He does not feel he is capable of fulfilling the many and difficult engineering tasks that are incumbent on him in his post as captain engineer attached to the Engineering Corps. Consequently I am asking Your Imperial Majesty to favour Captain Petrov with a decree authorising his retirement from the service.

Since he is a foreigner, I would ask your Imperial Majesty of your great generosity to provide for him in his retirement with an allowance of one third of his present salary, that is one hundred roubles per year, depending on a decision by the Senate on the most suitable sum[93]."

Unfortunately the reply was negative. His services were needed. All that happened was that he was summoned to the Chancellery of Artillery and Fortifications in Petersburg and questioned on the state of the fortifications in Siberia "given that he had worked there for some time[94]".

Captain Abraham Petrov was thus obliged to remain in Pernov. Relations with his wife grew rapidly worse and at the end of February 1732, one of the student engineers, Gabriel Kuzminski, informed him that there were plans to poison him...

On 28 February, Abraham sent a written complaint against his wife's lover, Chichkov, to the administration of the Pernov garrison. He accused his wife of adultery, attempted poisoning, and demanded a divorce. An enquiry was opened. Under interrogation Eudoxia Hanibal admitted her guilt. For the month of March she remained in Hanibal's house, but at the end of the month "Eudoxia Andreevna was interned in the offices of the garrison and then moved to the hospital courtyard where the condemned were usually housed[95]".

For the second time in his life in Russia Abraham was confronted with the wickedness and dishonesty of others. Only two years previously he had been in the hell of Siberian exile over six thousand versts from Petersburg. Then he had been liberated through the generosity of Count von Münnich, who had included him in his list of the best qualified engineers. Princess Volkonskaya, though, had been left to die in the monastery of Tihkvin and his other friends were still banned from the Court where the powerful Biren reigned supreme.

His giddy and flirtatious young women friends in Petersburg had no doubt tired of waiting for him, got married and had children. His fate had been to meet his Greek colleague, Dioper, and his beautiful daughter. He thought he could live quietly and anonymously in Pernov, but he had not counted on Eudoxia's refusal to love him, a black man, and her resistance to his attempts to inculcate in her the ways and manners of the Parisian ladies he had known and admired. All in vain, Eudoxia could not love him and would not forgive him for disrupting her life and destroying her secret happiness with Kayserov.

Her disappointment, misery and anger were limitless. He was honest, sincere, and tolerant, and found himself the loser. The first shock was when Eudoxia gave birth to the fair-haired white child, proving her adultery with the naval officer. Next, in spite of the fact that he forgave her and accepted the child as his own, she went on to deceive him with one of his own students. Finally, and even more seriously, she had tried to poison him with the help of her lover. How could he have been so blind?

In the first half of 1732, Abraham once again approached Count von Münnich to help him retire from the service. Von Münnich, always amenable, on 7 June 1732 put the renewed request before the College of War and the Empress. The reply took a year to reach Abraham.

Meanwhile the supreme military authorities who were investigating the affair of the poison plot gave their verdict on 19 February 1732. Captain Petrov received an attestation. The military tribunal declared the mechanic Chichkov guilty "of the intention to poison Captain Petrov, with the connivance of Petrov's wife". Kuzminski, who had denounced Chichkov to the African officer, was accused of complicity for having been in the confidence of the plotters. The document went on: "The mechanics confessed all their crimes and in tears before the tribunal they pleaded for Captain Petrov's Christian pardon. As a result, Captain Petrov, who had been wronged, chose to overlook their evil plot against him and pardoned them everything[96]".

Eudoxia, however, who was accused of fornication and complicity in the poison plot, was held under arrest in the hospital courtyard for the next four years, until 1737.

24. The tsar Peter the Great as a young man in 1697. Engraving by Pieter Stevens van Gunst after Godfrey Kneller original painting.

25. Tsar Peter I with the black child (By Schonebek,1705).

26. Allegorical portrait of Peter the Great, conqueror of the Turks at Azov
and of the Swedes at Poltava, and of his black godson Abraham Petrov
in the costume of the Preobrazhensky Guard (early 18th century).

27. Catherine I (1684-1727) Empress of Russia.

28. Anna Ivanovna (1693-1740),
Empress of Russia, niece of Peter I,
who brought Hanibal back from exile.

29. Elisabeth Petrovna (1709-61),
Empress of Russia, daughter of Peter I
and sister of Hanibal by adoption.

30. Peter I and Hanibal.

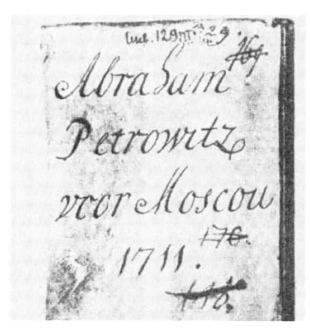

31. Abraham Hanibal's autograph in a geometry book offered to him by Peter the Great in 1711.

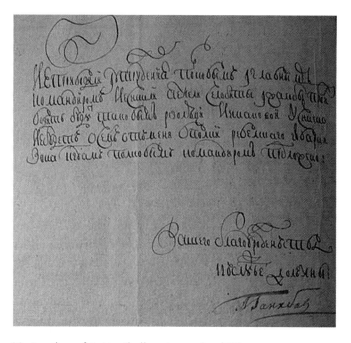

32. Another of A. Hanibal's autographs. (RR)

33. Abraham Hanibal's two volumes written book on geometry and fortifications, 1725-1726.

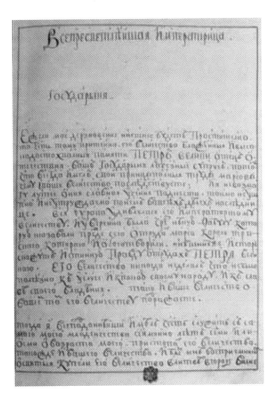

34-38. Extracts from Abraham Hanibal's two volumes written book on geometry and fortifications, 1725-1726: Preface, drawings and trigonometry formulas.

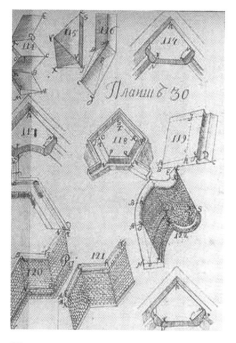

35.

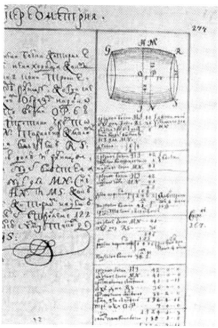

36.

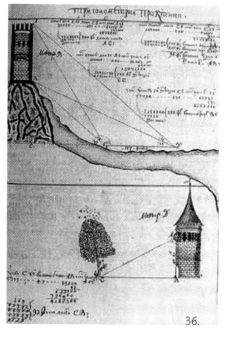

36.

37.

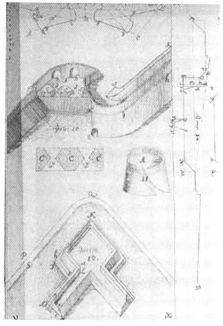

38.

39. Empress Elisabeth's ukase nominating Hanibal as Major-General.

40-41. Hanibal's park and land in his Petrovskoye and Mikhailovskoye estates, near Pskov.

42. View of Reval (Talinn) in the 18th century. Military costumes of the period.

43-44. The commandant's House at Reval (Tallinn) where Hanibal lived as Major-General and military commandant of the Estonian province.

45. Hanibal's house (now museum) at Petrovskoe.

46. Bust of Hanibal at Petrovskoe.

47/48. Hanibal's study.

49/50. The Order of Saint Anne and the Order of Saint Alexander Nevsky.

51. Hanibal's mansion in St.Petersburg.

52. Hanibal's Coat of Arms.

Бюст А.П. Ганнибала
Скульптор В. Шевченко. 1996 г

53. Bust of Hanibal by Chevchenko.

CHAPTER VII

A new life: 1733-1741

In the village of my black ancestor,
Peter's pupil,
beloved by the Tsars and Tsarinas
Their forgotten companion
found refuge here, where
I am waiting for you...

Pushkin. To Yazykov, 20 Sept. 1824

Retirement in the country

Captain Abraham Petrov was finally granted premature retirement on 21 May 1733. He was awarded an annual pension of one hundred roubles.

In 1731, when he first decided to leave the army, Abraham had begun to look for a country property where he could settle down. In 1732 Admiral Golovin, an old acquaintance from Peter I's time, sold him the estate of Kariakula, thirty miles from Reval[97], the provincial capital of Estonia. There he hoped to begin his new life.

The historian Leets, the foremost specialist on the Hanibal's Estonian period, found the deeds of property from that time in the Reval archives. They show that in 1732 the property was already under the name of "Captain Hanibal".

It is only the second time that the name Hanibal appears on an official document – the first being at Irkutsk in Siberia. This time the change was permanent. From then until his death the African captain is referred to in all communications as Hanibal. From 1733 onwards all official Russian documents use the name. In May of that year when his retirement was granted he was awarded a Diploma of Honour by the Empress Anna Ivanovna and Field-Marshal von Münnich. Even on this diploma, the name is Abraham Hanibal.

In retirement, Hanibal became a landed gentleman. He probably made the acquaintance of a Swedish officer in the Reval garrison, Captain Mathias Johann von Sjöberg, at about this time. Von Sjöberg was a member of the Swedish nobility and had been an officer in his country's army, but by force of circumstance was serving in Russia. When in the Swedish army he had been stationed in Riga "in October 1709 he had been commissioned to take 217 Russian prisoners from Riga to Stockholm. He did so, leaving his family and all his property behind." In 1710 Riga was occupied by Peter I's army. Madame von Sjöberg and her children, Christina Regina and Georg-Karl, were taken prisoner and probably "moved to Reval which the Russians occupied on 29 September…"It seems that Captain von Sjöberg left his country later and joined the Russian army in order to find his family[98].

Captain von Sjöberg's wife was a Livonian of ancient stock, born into a noble family of Italian origin, the barons of Albedil . Their first son, Georg-Karl, was born in 1706. After him came three daughters, Christina Regina, Julia-Charlotte and Anna-Gustaviana. The family had been living in Reval for over twenty years. There is no record of how Hanibal first met them. Perhaps he came across von Sjöberg when he was looking for an estate to purchase.

A love affair developed between the black officer and one of the von Sjöberg daughters, Christina Regina, and when the newly de-commissioned captain of Engineers, Hanibal, moved into his property of Kariakula in 1733 he was not alone. Christina Regina von Sjöberg followed him and became his new companion.

True Love

The terrible experiences of his marriage to the faithless Eudoxia Dioper, his first wife, must have made Abraham wary of any new relationship. Yet he had never lived alone during his youth in Moscow and Petersburg, and he would have found it difficult to hide himself away in a lost corner of Estonia without a companion. Everything seems to point to the fact that his new love was the exact opposite of the first.

Christina Regina was in love with him. There was no hypocrisy or ambiguity in the feelings of the young Swedish woman for the black engineer. It was her choice to be his wife and she did all she could to please the man she would later affectionately call "my little black devil". She was young, intelligent, sensitive and well able to manage a household.

Abraham was slow to be convinced but finally decided to share his life with Christina. In the autumn of 1734, she became pregnant. On 5 June 1735, she gave birth to a son. This time there was no doubt about the paternity of the brown-skinned baby the midwife presented to Hanibal. They called him Ivan, the Russian equivalent of Johann, her father's name. The von Sjöberg family had evidently given their blessing to the union even though, so far, it was not officially a marriage.

In the eyes of the law, Abraham Hanibal was still married to Eudoxia Dioper. In his new-found happiness he seems to have forgotten that no divorce had yet been granted. When in the following year he tried to marry Christina he was faced with unforeseen problems. "The priests all refused on different pretexts to marry them – apparently Hanibal had no document authorising him to contract a second marriage. Finally Hanibal came to an arrangement with the priest of the regimental chapel in the Estonian garrison, Peter Ilin. He agreed to marry them on condition they produced "a certificate". Abraham duly acquired this "certificate" from the priest of the church of St. Nicholas in Reval, Ivan Phillipov, and in 1736 Peter Ilin married him to Christina Regina Matveevna von Sjöberg[99]. The happy event took place in St. Nicholas Cathedral in the Estonian capital.

The truth was that in order to obtain the authorisation for his second marriage, given him by the priest Phillipov, Abraham should have appealed to the military tribunal in Pernov. Opatovich explains that this tribunal had judged "the case of the violation of conjugal fidelity by Eudoxia Andreevna" and pronounced the following sentence:

> *"to punish the adulterous woman – she should be whipped round the town with willow rods, then sent to the textile mills to labour for the rest of her life – Hanibal, who is innocent in this matter, to be given an affidavit, signed by all persons present[100]."*

At the time, an unfaithful spouse could be condemned to death; "exiled either in perpetuity or for a given period, men to do forced labour...women to work in manufacturing, etc.[101]."

Eudoxia did not wait for this terrible sentence to be carried out. She moved onto the attack. "She wrote to the General Headquarters of Artillery and Fortifications, demanding that she be brought to Petersburg. Her request was granted. Once there, on 1 March 1737, she addressed a request to the Synod. Eudoxia Andreevna declared that her statement to the administration of the Pernov garrison was false and had been made under threats from her husband, and that the machinist Chichkov, Hanibal's subordinate, had also made a false statement.

She asked the Synod to re-examine the case in the Ecclesiastical Council and to recall her husband and the witnesses for further questioning. She also asked to be set at liberty, 'so as not to die of starvation[102]'."

Six whole years after the birth of the white baby, at the beginning of the scandal, and the subsequent affair of the poison plot, Hanibal's adulterous ex-wife decided to declare she was innocent. She went so far as to accuse him of beating her brutally in order to force her to confess to crimes that she had not committed in front of the Pernov military tribunal. According to Opatovich, the Russian nineteenth century historian who published the first account of Hanibal's divorce, the jealous husband had thrashed and tortured the unfortunate woman almost to death. He "was said to have threatened to kill her if she did not confess to having plotted with Chichkov to poison him and to have committed fornication".

The accusation raises several questions. Vegner, another Russian writer, notes:

"Unfortunately Opatovich does not quote his sources on the story of torture; did it come only from the wife or were there other witnesses? Without this information", Vegner concludes, *"it is impossible to verify its authenticity".*

Another strange omission in Opatovich's article is the 'baby scandal'. He does not even acknowledge it in passing. Certain other Russian writers have thought that the story of the daughter of the adulterous affair was apocryphal and described the new suggestion of torture as typical of the so-called "African temperament"![103]Hanibal's long life-story, however, is that of a man who was consistently generous, tolerant, loyal and of irreproachable morality.

His marriage in 1736 to Christina von Sjöberg brought him great happiness. He respected her right to worship in a different way from himself and he did not ask her as a condition of their marriage to convert from her Lutheran faith to the Greek Orthodox, which had been his from July 1705. Their second child was born in 1737 and was named Elizabeth after Elizabeth Petrovna, Peter I's daughter, whom Hanibal had always regarded as a sister.

In 1739, the Kariakula estate was one of the smallest in Estonia. Leets, who has studied the archives relating to land use at this period, estimates that "the overall area of the estate must have been 120 – 150 hectares[104]".

Hanibal grew rye on about eleven hectares of the arable land. He also had access to a few small peasant farms. A local mayor helped him to administer the area. Each family had to work for the master for eleven daily shifts per week. In summer the rates per shift went up. In addition each family had to make a payment in kind every year: two sheep, four chickens and twenty eggs[105]".

Hanibal's family now consisted of five people: Hanibal, his wife and the children Ivan Abramovich (4 years old), Elisabeth Abramovich (2 years old) and Eudoxia, the child of his first wife's adulterous affair, aged eight.

That year the retired captain requested an increase in his pension from the Russian Government. He did not think that the hundred roubles per year he had been allocated from 1733 onwards was enough for a man with three children to support. The Senate, however, refused to consider his request.

The seasons passed quietly. Christina Hanibal and her husband were in their eighth year at Kariakula. The former mathematics tutor seemed to have settled down to a rural existence. This is the period when "Abraham Petrovich adopted the slow pace of country life – he made no demands, he cherished his memories of Peter and past favours; while he may well have regretted not being able to make full use of his knowledge and education, he was released from the fear of the terrible written orders that could suddenly transport a man from one coast to another[106]".

However, 1740 was the end of an era. Unexpected events at the Petersburg court were to have dramatic repercussions in the life of the Hanibal family.

Reval's Black Lieutenant Colonel

The Empress Anna Ivanovna, the daughter of Peter I's brother, died on 17 October 1740, after reigning for ten years. Her heir was a baby of two months, Ivan VI. The late sovereign's favourite, the all-powerful Biren, Duke of Courland, became Regent. He was not unopposed, however; there were various dignitaries at court who were ready to put an end to "the tyranny" of Biren.

A palace revolution took place on the night of 8 November, only three weeks after Anna Ivanovna's death. Field-Marshal von Münnich arrested the Biren and all the members of his immediate entourage. "The mother of the baby emperor, Anna Leopoldovna, became Regent, and Field-Marshal Count von Münnich, Hanibal's friend and protector, became Prime Minister[107]".

The new twist in the political situation in the Russian Empire would obviously affect the life of the retired captain: less than three months after Count von Münnich became Prime Minister of Russia, Abraham's period of inactivity ended.

He went to Petersburg in January 1741, and the Regent, Anna Leopoldovna, issued a decree appointing him Lieutenant Colonel "for his long and faithful service" to Russia. The appointment was accompanied by a material reward: the village of Ragola, near Reval, a state property, was graciously offered him for life, together with eight serfs. It has been calculated that the new property had an area three times that of the Kariakula estate[108].

When the decree concerning his promotion had been proclaimed Lieutenant Colonel Hanibal presented himself at the College of War where "before the Senate he took the oath of loyalty to Russia[109]".

Hanibal was posted to Reval, the capital of the Province of Estonia. His new rank automatically conferred on him the command of the garrison's artillery. The choice of Reval was not a matter of chance. From the spring of 1740 onwards the threat of another war with Sweden was growing. "The order came that all fortifications, especially those on the Baltic", should be put "in good order as quickly as possible[110].

"Consequently," Leets concludes, "it is not very surprising that in this alarming situation Field-Marshal Count von Münnich should have thought of his former protégé Hanibal, the talented military engineer and artillery expert, who was living in retirement in a village not far from Reval". Hanibal, for his part, would have had no reason to refuse such an offer. At forty-four, he must have felt at the height of his powers. Furthermore, his income would rise substantially and since the offer was to work in Reval he could continue to "oversee the work at Kariakula, only thirty kilometres from his place of work[111]".

Reval – 1741

The Empire's supreme authorities had decided that the command of the artillery in the strategic fort of Reval should go to Abraham Hanibal but their opinion was not shared by the governor of the province, the Danish Baron von Loewendal. He had planned to place his right hand man, a Swede, Major Holmer, in the post. Instead Major Holmer had been posted to Narva.

Baron von Loewendal was furious that the 'Negro', Hanibal, had been appointed in preference to his protégé, and from then on had only one objective: by every means at his disposal to make life so difficult for the new chief of artillery that he would resign of his own accord.

Commander Hanibal was well placed to resist the underhand tactics of the governor and his men. On 22 November, he sent a report with twenty-two points to the Imperial Cabinet, vigorously denouncing the misdeeds of his enemies. The first twelve points condemning the governor relate to the period when Hanibal was acting commander of artillery with the rank of lieutenant colonel. The text below is the first translation from Russian of the text written by Hanibal in 1742. Gastfreynd published the original version in Russia in 1904:

> *"The noble general, Count von Loewendal, Governor of Reval, has shown considerable ill-will towards me. He has made it clear that he does not want me on his staff in Reval and without justification has subjected me to invective and deliberately malicious behaviour. He wishes to give your Majesty a false image of me which will do me wrong...for this reason I humbly submit to Your Imperial Majesty the following report:*
>
> *22 November 1742*
>
> *A. Hanibal*

– 1 –

I was promoted to the rank of lieutenant colonel of the Artillery Regiment of Reval last year by the gracious wish of Your Imperial Majesty.

– 2 –

At that time Count von Loewendal was in Petersburg and I went to visit him as he is my superior. However, when I told him I had been appointed to the Reval Artillery he scolded me as if I were one of his serfs since the incumbent chief of artillery was his protégé, Major Holmer, a Swede who had already received orders to leave for Narva.

– 3 –

Since my arrival at Reval and my assumption of duties as chief of artillery Loewendal has done all he can to cause me to leave. I have been insulted not only by him but also by Debrigny, who was then Commander-in-Chief of Reval – [they wanted] by any means possible to cause my downfall. I was not the only one to find myself in this situation; other senior officers of the garrison were also under attack. They received threats demanding their voluntary resignation, warning that otherwise they would be dismissed with ignominy...

– 4 –

I include as an instance of their reprehensible behaviour towards me [the occasion when] Commander-in-Chief Debrigny sent to ask me to leave my apartment voluntarily; if I did not he would force me to leave against my will and throw my belongings out on the street. I was in the apartment officially assigned to me by the magistrate of Reval, and as my wife was shortly to give birth to a child I sent a senior officer to him requesting him not to take any action in view of my wife's state of health. Debrigny told the officer that he had written to the magistrate to order him to remove me from the apartment. The magistrate did not act upon the letter or respond in any way.

– 5 –

As the aforementioned Debrigny had written to the City Hall claiming that the house had been built by soldiers, I took a copy of the letter and informed Governor Loewendal of this objectionable treatment. I also made a verbal claim but the Governor took no action, which leads me to believe that he had acted jointly with Debrigny to evict me.

– 6 –

Last year following the declaration of war against Sweden Prince von Hesse Homburg[112] sent me orders and sealed instructions commanding me to keep the artillery on the alert and to take precautionary measures against possible enemy attack. Commander-in-chief Debrigny repeatedly gave me verbal orders to remove the cannons from the fort; I replied that at such a time it was not possible to do as he asked.

– 7 –

Since I had not obeyed his verbal instructions, the commandant sent to me a written order to remove the cannons from the town ramparts, which was then done.

– 8 –

The senior officers, the ordinary soldiers and the Russian townsfolk having seen that the majority of the cannons had been removed and that the town consequently faced the enemy without defences began to speak to each other about this and their concern reached Debrigny's ears.

– 9 –

Debrigny realised that he had made an error of judgement and summoned me to his house; there in the presence of several senior officers, which was an affront to my rank, he rebuked me in the most extraordinary manner, claiming that I had removed the cannons on my own responsibility. I answered that I had done so on his orders; he insisted in front of the senior officers that no such order had been given by him to me, at which point I took the order from my pocket and waved it in front of him. Debrigny attempted to seize it but I did not give it to him.

– 10 –

Later Debrigny gave me the order to replace the cannons in their original positions on the town ramparts and I accordingly did so, but many of the soldiers and artillery employees then fell ill as they had to install the cannons in stormy weather.

– 11 –

In the matter of the above malicious attacks against me and attempts at eviction, which I attributed to the Governor and Debrigny the commander in chief at the time, I felt I could no longer endure such a persecution, and wrote an official complaint to Field-Marshal General Grand Master of the Artillery, the Landgrave of Hesse-Homburg, who was so gracious as to reply sympathetically and order the Commander-in-Chief Debrigny to stop troubling and persecuting me.

– 12 –

When Debrigny received the communication from His Excellency he summoned me to his quarters in a tent in the so-called Swedish bastion. I went in the company of an artillery officer and he greeted me in a friendly manner: "I know that you have complained in writing to His Excellency", to which I replied, "I could not endure your insults and your unjustifiable accusations, so I had no choice but to send a complaint"... then he took me by the arm, led me out of earshot of the artillery officer and said in French: "I did not act in this way of my own accord but on the orders of Governor Loewendal. It is the Governor himself who ordered me to find any pretext to send you away from Reval. He had a grudge against you because you were appointed to Reval while Major Holmer was sent to Narva. Then when you had taken command, you sent the Prince von Hesse-Homburg a report on the theft of cloth from the regiment's clothing stores by Major Holmer. You know that I have no personal reason to harass you. You were like a brother to me in the reign of the great and glorious Peter I and we were great friends then." To which I answered: "I thank you for recalling our previous friendship, but I have great difficulty in understanding why you are persecuting me today and try in vain to cause me to suffer."

Hanibal[113]»

In September 1741 Major-General Debrigny, Commander in Chief of Reval, was replaced by the Russian Major General Mikhail Philosophov. Under the command of Philosophov "there were no further disagreements of either a personal or professional nature with A. P. Hanibal".

Christina Hanibal gave birth to another daughter that year. She was named Anna after Peter I's second daughter, Anna Petrovna.

CHAPTER VIII

Major General and statesman 1742-1752

> *"Remember me, Lord,*
> *when you come into your kingdom"*
>
> Luke 23, v. 41

The reign of Elizabeth

Abraham Hanibal settled down peacefully to his work in Reval after the arrival of Major General Philosophov, but in Petersburg another palace revolution was in the making.

> *"Russia was going through a testing period of troubles. People rose to influential positions and fell again just as quickly. – Petersburg made and unmade them all.*

In 1740 one November evening had been long enough to eliminate the universally hated Regent and transfer the administration of the state to an ineffectual princess. In 1741, another night ...was long enough to remove power and liberty from the carefree Princess Regent and replace the baby emperor all had recognised with a new empress on the throne[114] *."*So it happened. In November 1741, there was another change of regime. Eidelman gives a vivid account of that night's events:

> *"During the night of 25 November 1741 the Company of Grenadiers of the Preobrazhensky Regiment overthrew the ruling power in Russia yet again. It was not a large company, only about two hundred men, but the army corps and the main armies had been dispersed to other parts of*

139

the country and the guard had been 'correctly stationed'. It was not the first time the palace had been taken in a surprise attack from its nearest neighbours. The rest of the Empire was to 'receive the official declaration' of the accession of the new sovereign at daybreak.

On this occasion the preparation for the overthrow seems to have been very simple. Ivan Antonovich, in the fourteenth month of his reign and the sixteenth of his life, was not yet able to rule; his mother Anna Leopoldovna had given birth to a daughter, Catherine Antonovna, four months earlier, and as usual was spending weeks in feasting and entertainment. Prince Anton was chiefly concerned with the construction of his new palace and park.

Not much was needed to topple such naïve regents. The main requirement was a claimant from the Tsar's family, and Elisabeth Petrovna, 32 years old, was the daughter of Peter the Great and Catherine I... No-one had taken Elisabeth's claim seriously, which was greatly to her advantage.

The second favourable circumstance was the Russian nobles' jealousy of the 'German faction'. Having got rid of Biren their dream was to remove all the foreigners in charge of ministries, in highly paid posts in the administration and provincial government, move into their places and receive their salaries. There were many young nobles in the Preobrazhensky Regiment of the guard ready to place 'Peter's daughter' on the throne in the twinkling of an eye – all they needed was a signal and some money...

The French Ambassador, the Marquis of Chétardie, was the third 'element' in the plot. A clever master of intrigue, he sent Elisabeth notes through the faithful intermediary of the court doctor and he spared no expense to increase his influence in the Russian court and weaken that of the Germans[115]".

On the morning of 26 November the Russian people were informed that Elizabeth, the daughter of Peter the Great, was the new Empress of All the Russias. When the news reached Reval on the shores of the Baltic Abraham Hanibal was ecstatic. He immediately wrote to the Tsarina. He sent her one of the shortest and most allegorical notes in history. It consisted of nine words Hanibal had taken from the Gospels: "Remember me, Lord, when you come into your kingdom."

Elizabeth Petrovna's response was not long in coming. Hanibal was summoned to the palace in Petersburg. The Empress received him "most charmingly" and overwhelmed him with decorations and gifts of land. Abraham Hanibal was promoted by the Empress's decree to the rank of major general and commander in chief of the garrison of Reval, replacing Major General Philosophov who was transferred to Riga. He was also granted land in the region of Pskov with almost six hundred serfs.

The decree authorising his promotion and the gift of land was signed by the Empress on 12January 1742. The original document still exists in the Russian Central Historical State Archives. It is reproduced below:

> *"It is with the greatest pleasure that we confer on Abraham Petrov Hanibal, Lieutenant Colonel of the Artillery, the rank of Major General in the army and the post of Commander-in-Chief at Reval. The current commander in chief, Major General Philosophov, shall be transferred to Riga to replace the late commander in chief Major General Reding.*
>
> *It is our great pleasure to grant to the aforementioned Abraham Hanibal, in recognition of his long and loyal service, the volost[116] of Mikhailovskoe, in the district of Pskov in the area of Voronovich, which land has been the property of the court since the death of the Tsarevna[117], Catherine Ivanovna, of blessed memory. According to the court records, at the recent census there were five hundred and sixty-nine serfs on the land. We also grant the attached estates in perpetual ownership and instruct Our Senate to put this ukase into effect. The decrees to be sent to all concerned.*
>
>

Saint Petersburg
12 January 1742
Elizabeth
Received this day, 13 January instant by the Senate, number 11[118]

The Empress proved herself generous towards her loyal friends but those who had enjoyed privileges in the previous reign were now stripped of their titles to property. We learn from a request by Hanibal that a decree to this effect was promulgated on 31 December 1741. "Those who received lands from the previous government should return them." Abraham Hanibal had been one of those beneficiaries. A decree of Anna Leopoldovna had granted him the village of Ragola on his promotion to lieutenant colonel in January 1741.

He sent a request to the Empress in January 1742, asking that the village should be taken from him unless he could be given a perpetual interest in it.

His stay in Petersburg brought him back into the secretive world of Russian imperial power. Since the death of his adoptive father in 1725 and that of Catherine I two years later all access to the court had been closed to him.

There had been fifteen long years of exile. Whereas he had survived the rigours of life in deepest Siberia, Menshikov had quickly succumbed. Those of his friends who had survived the effects of exile or banishment from the court were now together again. Cherkasov was brought back from exile in Astrakhan by the new Empress and appointed Secretary to the Imperial Cabinet. He was given the title of Baron, thus becoming one of the great lords of the empire. Veselovsky for his part was appointed to the College of Foreign Affairs and made tutor in Russian language to the Grand Duke Peter Feodorovich[119]. The brothers Bestuzhev-Riumin also returned to high office; Alexis Petrovich became Vice-Chancellor and Mikhail Petrovich Grand-Marshal of the Imperial Court. Sadly, there were those who had not lived to see the great day. Princess Volkonskaya, the sister of the Bestuzhev-Riumin brothers, had died eleven years previously and Major General Pachkov, the former member of the College of War, had died in 1740 while governor of Astrakhan[120].

When he was in the capital in the winter of 1741-42 Hanibal was invited to dine with some old friends, the Suvorovs. The invitation, at first sight quite insignificant, was to have important consequences for the future of one of Russia's greatest men.

Vasili Suvorov, Hanibal's friend, was the public prosecutor of Petersburg. He had a son, Alexander, six years older than Ivan, Hanibal's eldest. Little Alexander's dream was to become a great army leader, but his father refused to send him to military training school because of his delicate health. Suvorov took the opportunity to ask Abraham, the distinguished engineer, for his advice. The African, who had taught in the foremost military school in Petersburg and had been mathematics master to the late Peter II, spent some time talking to the boy about the art of warfare. The Major General was very impressed by the boy's intelligence and told Suvorov he must arrange for his son to attend a military training school. "Let him do as he wishes, old friend. He will do far more than you and me put together[121]."

The prosecutor followed his friend's advice, and to the great good fortune of Russia, a few decades later, Alexander Suvorov, the sickly child, became a general, then a field-marshal, then a Count, then a Prince and famous throughout Europe for his military exploits. He is regarded as one of the most brilliant commanders in Russian military history.

Reval – 1742

1742 was an eventful year for the Hanibal household. First of all their social status was greatly increased as Hanibal was now the chief military officer in the town, second only to the governor of the province. The new land at Mikhailovskoe enabled them to adopt a much wealthier lifestyle. They had more than six hundred families of serfs in their service in their new domain[122]. More generally it should be noted that the rank of major general in the army was at that time the equivalent of second admiral, which in the civilian hierarchy was at the same level as principal councillor of state. Peter I had devised a hierarchical scale of the posts in the imperial system during the 1720s, and major general was the fourth out of fourteen in the notorious "Table of Ranks". In promoting Abraham to the rank of major general the Empress had allowed him, to whom she publicly referred as "my brother", to pass over several stages, for lieutenant colonel is in only seventh place on the military scale. However, Hanibal's service to the state meant that this promotion was richly deserved. If it had not been for the death of Peter I he would have been promoted to the rank of general much earlier, as had most of those of the Emperor's intimates who had not suffered in the repression of the late 1720s.

Abraham Hanibal had become very cautious and wanted all his new privileges to be confirmed by official decrees from the Empress and the Senate. Now that he was a rich landowner with hundreds of serfs he thought it important that a noble title should be officially conferred on him. To this end he wrote as early as January 1742 to the Empress Elizabeth Petrovna. Some extracts from the request follow:

> *"1. I am of African origin, of illustrious noble lineage; I was born in the town of Logone, in the territory of my father who ruled not only this town –but two others besides. In [1704]when I was still a child, I agreed to go to Russia from Constantinople under the auspices of Count Savva Vladislavich. I was taken to Moscow into the household of the Emperor, Peter the Great, of glorious and eternal memory. I was baptised according to the rites of the Greek Orthodox religion in a ceremony which His Majesty graced with his august presence and where he stood as my godfather. From that day onwards I was constantly at His Imperial*

Majesty's side...

3. On the death of their Imperial Majesties, the great Queen and Empress Catherine Alexeevna, and the monarch, Emperor Peter II, I served from 1730 onwards in the Engineering Corps with the rank of captain; in 1741 I was promoted lieutenant colonel in the garrison of Reval and in this year, 1742, by decree from Your almighty and generous Imperial Majesty, I have been promoted to major general and commander in chief of Reval, with an additional grant of lands. However, I do not have and have never had a noble title or coat of arms since such a custom does not exist in Africa.

I am therefore asking Your Imperial Majesty to legalise my noble title by decree and grant me a Diploma of Honour and a coat of arms in remembrance of my ancestry and as a tribute to Your Imperial Majesty's infinite goodness."

While he was waiting for a reply from the Senate Hanibal ordered a seal with the imprint of the emblem he had chosen for the Hanibal family. In the centre there was an elephant, above, an eagle[123] and below the Latin initials FVMMO[124]. The initials are difficult to decipher. Attempts by different Russian researchers continue to this day. Leets has made a suggestion which seems plausible; the initials FVMMO may indicate the Latin phrase : *Fortuna Vitam Meam Mutivit* Oppido (Optime) which would mean: "Fortune has changed my life in marvellous ways".

The Hanibal family left the apartment where they had been living for a year and moved to the "The Commander's House[125]". Shortly afterwards Abraham claimed back his books from the library of the Academy of Sciences in Petersburg where they had been stored since he was exiled to Siberia the late 1720s. His claim gave rise to a correspondence between himself and the Director of the library, Johann-David Schumacher, who was also a member of the Council of the Academy. The originals of these letters were written in French. Below are some addressed to Hanibal from Schumacher. {See translator's appendix for French version with original spelling}

Letter no. 1

Dear Sir,

We have carried out a careful search for the catalogue of your books but so far without success. We will continue the search and are certain to find it eventually, unless Mr. Blumenstrot has kept it. I remember seeing it and I thought it would be among our catalogues or in the Chancellery papers. I wonder, Sir, whether you hold a copy. Even if we do not find it you will lose nothing. In the latter case I will make a collection of books worth two hundred roubles which will be equal to those the Academy has had from you.

I am, Sir, your most respectful....

6th April,1742
(An Herrn General-Major und Ober-Commandanten
von Hannibal à Revall. P.Posto durch Galachnikoff).

Letter no. 2

Dear Sir,

I have asked the Director of Posts, M. d'Asch, to inform me when transport arrives here from Reval, so that I may have the pleasure of sending your books back. Meanwhile I have the honour of sending you a catalogue of the books we have packed up with a note of those which are missing. As for the Gazette, that is a mistake on the part of the man I put in charge. I have repeated the order to send it to you regularly on pain of sanctions. That is the best I can do.

I remain, Sir, yours most respectfully,

At St. Petersburg
This 19 June 1742.
(An Herrn General-Major und Ober-Commandanten
von Hannibal à Revall , P. Posto).

Letter no. 3

Dear Sir,

I am glad to inform you that the postman at the Academy has found further books in his store as noted in the enclosed. The others will come from Holland as I had the honour to inform you in my last communication. If the coachman Stahl, who lives in Reval had not been obliged to take Prof. Tier with him he would have brought your books. He has promised to do so next time he comes. If you should see him, Sir, may I suggest that you speak to him about them yourself.

I am most respectfully...

St. Petersburg, 3 July 1742.
P.S. Discours sur le gouvernement, 8o Vol. 1-3.
Avantures de Neapotolome. 8o
Traité du Nivellement. 8o.
An Herrn General-Major und Ober-Commandanten
von Hannibal à Revall. P. Post

Letter no. 4

Dear Sir,

You will see from the enclosed receipt from Jurgen-Jurgenschen that I have kept my promise in a manner which will be to your satisfaction. I only hope that everything arrives in good condition. If it is possible, Sir, for you to pay the two hundred roubles to the postman at the Academy Bookstore, I should be most grateful. He has been commissioned to buy the same books for the Library. It only remains, Sir, for me to say that if I can be of help here in any way please give the order – you will always find me at your service.

Most respectfully...

At St. Petersburg, this 22 July 1742.
With a Cass. Sig. M.H.
An Herrn General-Major und Ober-Commandanten von Hannibal à Revall).

Letter no.5

Dear Sir

As I have given the order to send the books which were missing,

according to your last note, I hope that you, Sir, will have the goodness to honour the bill of exchange, given in favour of M. D'Asch, Director of Posts, on your account. If you find that I can be of service to you on other occasions, Sir, please let me have your orders.

Yours most respectfully...

11 September 1742
An H. Hannibal à Reval.)

The letters of the Councillor of the Academy, written between April and September,1742, show that everything was done to restore all Hanibal's books to him.

In 1742 Christina Hanibal was expecting another child. She already had one son and two daughters. One may assume she was hoping for a son, and her wish was granted. In July she gave birth to a boy whom they decided to call Peter, in memory of the late Emperor, Peter the Great, Abraham's adoptive father. The new baby did not look like a child of mixed parentage. According to contemporary accounts his skin was as dark as his father's.

A sad occurrence spoiled Christina's happiness. Her father, the retired Swedish Captain, Mathias Johann von Sjöberg, died that year.

The Sjöberg family, however, also gained a new member, as one of the late Captain's daughters, Julia-Charlotte, was married. The bridegroom was a captain in the garrison of Reval called Georg Reynhold Rode.

Hanibal – Defender of Russia's Interests

Only two months after taking up his post as commander in chief, Hanibal was entrusted with deputising for the Governor van Loewendal, who left in March on a military mission to Finland. The Governor was absent from Reval for seven months until October.

On 28 March 1742, Hanibal wrote to one of his closest and most influential friends in the capital, Baron Cherkasov, Secretary to the Cabinet of the Empress Elisabeth. He outlines the state of affairs.

> *"My dear Sir and old patron Ivan Antonovich!*
>
> *Since the departure of the General in Chief and Governor of Reval, Baron von Loewendal, I am the sole person in charge in the town. According to the lists supplied by the regiments of the Reval garrison there are far too few soldiers standing by; in view of the ukases sent out by the Senate and the College of War it was necessary in the present circumstances[126] to recall all those soldiers whose absence was not absolutely essential; I have accordingly ordered the assembly of regimental commanders to recall all soldiers to the barracks..."*

The decision to recall the soldiers was not at all popular. Of the two thousand five hundred and twenty-eight soldiers absent from the garrison a large number had been posted to the "personal service" of various dignitaries in the province, and were not on official military duty. In an attempt to ascertain the real state of affairs the interim military governor "demanded information from the provincial administration on the position of those who were absent" from the regiments. Without success. What is more, those provincial dignitaries who disliked the new military governor's measures decided to be rid of him. The second part of Hanibal's letter clearly shows that he took their threats seriously:

> *"...I have reduced the number of men sent by Governor van Loewendal for service in the province's administration and elsewhere, and you will find attached to this letter a list showing the number of men and where they can be found. I have heard that the provincial administration and others are opposed to their recall; they argue that since it was the Governor who put the soldiers at their disposal, it should be he who recalls them: "We shall send a written complaint to the Governor and to*

the representatives in Moscow"; now, since I am new here... I fear that they will try to discredit me. I am therefore writing to you, my dear sir and former benefactor, to ask you to examine the staffing of the garrison now and in previous years... and to defend me because the Governor has been my enemy for many years... Perhaps the complaints about me will come from the said Governor; perhaps from the deputies of Reval, in which case it would be best to speak to those concerned and report on the exact circumstances in which the complaint has been made...I have the greatest confidence in you.

Reval, Your devoted servant
28 March, 1742. A. Hanibal

Hanibal had quickly realised that the practices of his predecessors in the administration of the affairs of the province were incompatible with his own concept of duty to the state. One of his descendants, Anna S. Hannibal, writing at the beginning of the twentieth century, describes this period in her ancestor's life as follows:

"Abraham Petrovich was by nature so energetic that he was constantly occupied; he exercised his duties with enthusiasm; he never failed to report to the authorities the abuses committed in Reval and struggled against them unremittingly; he advised of urgent requirements, the decline of discipline – in short, the poor state of the military system. All this annoyed certain people. His colleagues and his subordinates disliked his demanding nature and his unfailing determination to restore legality in an area which had sunk into indiscipline and arbitrary decision-making. They tried in every possible way to impede him."

One of the occasions on which his enemies tried to discredit him was the coronation of the Empress Elisabeth. They released to the press an account of the commemoration at Reval as if it had been organised by the Governor's councillor and not the commander in chief. Elisabeth was crowned Empress of All the Russias at St. Petersburg on 25 April 1742, and the event was celebrated in every town in the Empire. In Reval, the man deputising for the absent Governor was one of the most loyal of the Tsarina's supporters, Abraham Hanibal, the black godson of the new sovereign's father.

Hanibal had organised a grandiose celebration to which he had invited "the Corps of Army Generals, the Admirals of the Fleet, the

Senior Officers of the Artillery staff, the Engineering Corps and the town's garrison, the Landgraves of the duchy of Estliandia and many other illustrious people."

Imagine Hanibal's surprise when he read in No. 37 of the *St. Petersburg Bulletin* that the festivities in Reval in honour of the Empress had been organised by the provincial councillor, De Brevern. He immediately demanded justice through his right of reply.

The St. Petersburg Bulletin was edited at the time under the auspices of the Academy of Sciences. Abraham accordingly wrote to J. D. Schumacher to expose the false report and ask for the publication of a text he had prepared himself, describing what had in fact happened on 25 April in Reval.

M. Schumacher ordered that Hanibal's text should be published in No.42 of the *St. Petersburg Bulletin*. He replied personally to the Commander, whom he held in great esteem, to explain that the report had been published in good faith:

> *"Your Excellency Major-General and Commander in Chief,*
>
> *Sir,*
>
> *In response to Your Excellency's request I have arranged to publish the account you sent me for the St. Petersburg Bulletin, concerning the festivities organised in Reval on the occasion of Her Majesty's coronation. It appeared in full in No. 42 of the paper. As far as the previous article was concerned, which as you indicated in your letter had been sent in bad faith, I must assure Your Excellency that it was sent to us by someone in whom we have confidence and who has always sent us reliable reports on Reval...[127]"*

Abraham Hanibal was satisfied at receiving his right to reply in the journal and considered the matter closed.

In early summer 1742 military operations between Russia and Sweden intensified. The Russian military authorities feared that the principal Baltic towns, Riga and Reval, would be attacked from the sea. The military commanders of the two towns, Major General Philosophov and Major General Hanibal, accordingly received a series of ukases from the Senate and the Empress regarding the measures to be taken for the security and defence of the area.

At Reval the commander in chief, acting in his capacity as provisional military governor, requisitioned labour from the city's inhabitants to work on the improvement of the fortifications. His enemies immediately spread the rumour that the major general was "forcing the inhabitants" to work "without having received a decree from the Senate ordering the repair of the city's fortifications". The rumours were without foundation as Hanibal had received no less than six decrees on the subject, dated 22 January, 23 February, 18 and 19 June, 6 and 27 July 1742[128].

In the absence of Baron von Loewendal, Hanibal proved to be an ardent defender of the Russian Empire and its Empress. He was vigilant in matters of security and counter-espionage. The archives of the Russian Senate for this period contain numerous confidential reports to the authorities from Hanibal. He knew that the opposition of certain dignitaries in the province was linked to their rejection of Russian rule. The region was traditionally pro-Swedish and there was little enthusiasm for consolidating Russian military power. In a letter of July 1742 to the principal Councillor of State, Ivan Cherkasov, Hanibal complains about the refusal of the local townsfolk to finance the work on the fortifications: "When they were under Swedish rule they were responsible not only for the repair and maintenance of the fortifications but for the artillery as well. Since Reval came under the rule of His Imperial Majesty, our sovereign of great and enduring memory, the Emperor Peter the Great, thirty-two years ago[129], they have never stopped asking for postponements. These have several times been granted...and now they want to profit from the funds that have been collected by using them as they please; when they are asked to pay a levy they claim to have been ruined in the last war and to be in no position (to pay). There has been no disaster for thirty-two years and the money they have accumulated through their privileges would suffice to finance all the work in the town, the artillery and the fort[130]."

Nothing could deter Hanibal from acting on the orders of the Empress. He succeeded in spite of the initial hostility. The town's fortifications were reconstructed and control towers built from which to survey the movements of "the enemy fleet". Thanks to the regular reports he sent to the capital the College of War was aware of "every event in the Baltic area[131]". He maintained the liaison between the College of the Admiralty in Petersburg and the Vice-Admiral Michukov, the commander of the Russian fleet in the Baltic.

At the time fortune was smiling on the Russian troops and they won some decisive victories over the Swedes. Abo (Turku today), which was then the capital of Finland, and the town of Helsingfors (Helsinki) were occupied by the Russian army under Field-Marshal Lassy. The situation forced the Swedes into peace negotiations with the Russians. The negotiations lasted almost a year and ended on 16 July 1743 with the signing of the Treaty of Abo, in Russia's favour.

In October 1742 the Governor of Estonia, Baron von Loewendal, returned from Finland. He learned of the decisions taken in his absence by the black commander and raised objections. Once again he looked for ways to be rid of him and renewed friction arose between the two men who had disliked each other from their very first meeting.

For Hanibal the situation became untenable. He denounced the Governor's manoeuvres in a letter to the Imperial Cabinet. He accused him of abusing his rights over the soldiers in the garrison by making them work for him on his lands like slaves. He defended the "poor soldiers" who were, additionally, deprived of firewood in the winter, which explained the frequent illnesses that afflicted them. He was infuriated by the Governor's ill will towards him and asked for a transfer to Narva. The authorities in Petersburg, however, were evidently satisfied with the dedication of their commander and kept him there for ten years! As for the Governor, the Danish Waldemar von Loewendal, he left Russia in 1743 to serve under Louis XV in France. He died in Paris in 1755 with the rank of Marshal of France.

The von Tiren Affair

An amazing lawsuit rocked Estonia in 1743. The High Court of Reval, the organ of justice for the local nobility, was asked to try a case which had no precedent in local legal records, nor even in the annals of eighteenth century Russian serfdom. The case was brought by two noble and extremely rich provincial landowners. They were suing each other in an affair which principally affected the peasants of Estonia, "the people without a voice" in a period when serfs were treated like animals.

The two protagonists were highly cultivated men. One, Joachim von Tiren, was a professor, the other, Abraham Hanibal, also a professor, was the military commander in chief of the province. Their distinguishing characteristics were the unscrupulous cruelty of the former and the profound humanitarianism of the latter.

In March 1743, a few months before the two men brought the case to court, Hanibal had arranged to lease two thirds of his property at Ragola to Professor von Tiren. As Reval's commander-in-chief Hanibal was preoccupied by the unstable relations between Russia and Sweden[132] and was unable to supervise in person the running of his estate. Accordingly he made the decision to "lease two thirds of the village, including the peasants and the agricultural equipment to Professor von Tiren for an annual sum of 60 roubles[133]. The remaining land was leased to a different wealthy landowner. A written contract made the agreement binding between Hanibal and the two men.

The contract was in itself an unusual document for the period. Hanibal had included a special clause forbidding the new landlords to administer corporal punishment to the serfs. Masters at the time had the power of life and death over them. Whipping was a normal procedure and a legal right of the landowners. The African proprietor, however, was opposed to the barbaric practices of his contemporaries. While punctilious in his respect for the law he was also humane and kind-hearted. It was he who had been shocked to discover that the high command in the province had had no compunction in using hundreds of soldiers as a matter of course as labour on their privately owned land, and that the same soldiers had been deprived of firewood in winter because it had been requisitioned by the authorities. He had vigorously denounced many abuses of power and he was not the one to tolerate the gratuitous cruelty of master to slave without speaking out. Naturally he could not intervene when serfs were whipped on the neighbouring estates but at Ragola and Kariakula, where he was master, such punishment was never used.

Hanibal had made the rules regarding the treatment of his peasants perfectly clear to von Tiren; but he had also taken the precaution, knowing local custom, of including in the contract article no. 4 which stipulated: "The leaseholder is not authorised to increase the dues of the peasants; he shall retain the present level of obligatory labour; he shall not penalise peasants for previous litigation or wrongdoing. *This present contract is nul and void if traditional levels of obligatory labour are imposed or if the peasants are whipped or subjected to any form of physical oppression.[134]"*.

Professor von Tiren "had no thought for anything but his own personal profit" and paid no attention to the clause, running the Ragola estate in his own way. "When there was a great deal of work to be done and the local landowners needed supplementary labour von Tiren had no hesitation in 'lending' them Hanibal's peasants in return for payment to himself." That was not the only infringement of the clause. He also habitually had the poor men violently whipped.

In desperation over von Tiren's rough treatment the peasants held a secret meeting and resolved to inform their black master of the situation. They chose two messengers, Esko Yann and Nutto Hendrik "who were to go to Reval and tell the commander in chief of the violence meted out to his peasants by the lessee." The two men duly met their master and reported von Tiren's abuses in detail.

On their return von Tiren discovered what had happened. Yann Esko was held responsible for "daring to disturb" his lordship the commander in chief and was so savagely beaten that he could not stand for four weeks".

Hanibal's reaction was swift. He demanded an explanation from von Tiren who attempted to justify himself on the grounds that local law authorised physical punishment. Such savage cruelty, however, was not in any way justifiable in the eyes of the major general. He pointed out the terms of the contract and terminated it then and there. The matter was referred to the High Court. A magistrate, Pilar von Pilhau, was sent to Ragola to investigate the peasants' complaints and von Tiren's abuse of the lease. The nobles who assembled to hear the case were incredulous. Here was one of their number accused of a crime which was no crime. "At the trial," writes Leets, "von Tiren claimed that he had received 'verbal authorisation' from the major general and commander in chief to punish the peasants as he wished. Hanibal denied any such authorisation and pointed to Article no.4 of the contract which imposed on the signatories strict fulfilment of its conditions. The High Court ruled that von Tiren had broken the terms of the contract and declared it void.

Abraham Hanibal had won his case. The real beneficiaries were the Estonian peasants. For the first time a master had been taken to court for an offence which concerned, not another landowner but the peasants themselves, who had been unjustly whipped and forced to do extra obligatory labour. The life of peasants at the time was no more than that – whippings and forced labour. Leets writes: "Hanibal's defence of the peasants' interests was an extraordinary phenomenon. The trial, which must have been unique of its kind, challenged in the public court of the nobles the arbitrary powers of the landowners at a time when serfdom was increasing. Hanibal must have enjoyed a certain popularity among the local Estonian population and have been respected, if for nothing else, as a generous master[135]."

After the lawsuit, Hanibal entrusted the running of his estate to his brother-in-law, Georg-Karl Sjöberg, probably at his wife's suggestion. Her brother was at the time an officer in the Reval garrison, 37 years old and unmarried.

Holmer the Rebel

On 1 November 1743, a new governor was installed in Reval in place of von Loewendal who had left for France. The new governor, a lieutenant general in the Russian Army, was Prince von Holstein-Bek, the son of a Prussian general with powerful support in the Court of St. Petersburg. Since her accession, Elizabeth had welcomed the Holstein princes at court. Henri Troyat writes: "There were ties of blood between the house of Holstein...and the Russian Imperial family. Peter the Great's eldest daughter, Anna Petrovna, had married Karl-Friedrich von Holstein-Gottorp and had a son,...Peter-Ulrich...the second daughter, Empress Elizabeth Petrovna, had been betrothed to the young and charming Karl-August, one of the brothers of Johanna (von Anhalt-Zerbst, born Holstein-Gottorp and the mother of the future Catherine II). He died of smallpox shortly after the betrothal and Elisabeth was said never to have reconciled herself to his early death[136]." In the very first month of her reign she named her young nephew, Peter Feodorovich, as the heir to the Russian throne.

In Reval Abraham Hanibal, as commander in chief of the garrison, was having trouble with one of his subordinates, Major Holmer. He was the same man that the former governor, van Loewendal, had wanted to command the artillery in 1740. At the time, the military authorities had appointed the black officer to the position Holmer coveted and he himself had been transferred to Narva. On taking up his new post, Hanibal had discovered that the clothing stores had been mismanaged by Holmer and had reported the matter to the authorities.

In January 1742, Governor von Loewendal finally succeeded in obtaining the post of commander of the artillery at Reval for his friend Holmer. The position had become vacant on Hanibal's promotion as commander in chief of the garrison. From the beginning, Holmer, nursing his resentment against his new superior, was persistently insubordinate.

By the beginning of 1744, relations between the two men had become so bad that Hanibal wrote a formal letter of complaint about

Major Holmer's flagrant breaches of discipline to the Grand Master of the Artillery, Field-Marshal von Hesse-Homburg. The Prince's reply demanded that Major Holmer should behave correctly.Only a few months passed before there was another dispute. Major Holmer behaved with deliberate disrespect towards the commander in chief. He "made grimaces" at him, was insolent, passed insulting remarks and boasted of his powerful friends at court.As commander of the artillery, he did not think he should be answerable to the commander in chief of the garrison. None of Major General Hanibal's reprimands had any effect; he remained incorrigible. He threatened Hanibal in the presence of other officers, and, as Hanibal was to learn later from his friends in the capital, who had followed the whole affair closely, he had solemnly vowed to set the commander in chief and the new governor against each other. In this, he succeeded, for in December 1744 relations between the commander in chief and the governor broke down completely. From that time on Major Holmer was not the only one to send complaints about Major General Hanibal to Prince von Hesse-Homburg.

The governor accused the commander in chief of failing to inform him of decisions concerning the fortress and the garrison. The regulations were in fact very unclear on the matter of prerogatives between the governors of the provinces and the commanders of the garrisons. Hanibal proposed that a way out of their difficulties would be to return to the rules laid down by Peter I, which had remained in force until 1736. Citing the area of Reval, he proved that there had been no conflict of authority between 1710 and 1736 as the functions of the commander in chief and the governor had been clearly defined. He wrote: "The governor was responsible for the affairs of the province and the commander in chief for the garrison ...neither had authority over the other." The General Directorate of Artillery and Fortifications did not respond with any immediate solution, the conflict was not resolved, and Hanibal in turn accused the Governor of abusing his authority.

Once more, Hanibal found his situation untenable. He decided he must leave Reval. He sent a 'memorandum' to the Empress's Cabinet, requesting a posting elsewhere. The document throws an interesting light on the way the Russian military administration functioned at the time. Hanibal requested a new posting:

1. To St. Petersburg as commander in chief to replace M. Ignatiev, who had applied for retirement on grounds of poor health and old age.

2. Or to Vyborg to replace the late major general and former governor, Prince Repnin.

3. Or to Moscow, as commander in chief in place of Von Taneev who intended to retire on grounds of age.

4. Wisely enough, however, Hanibal suggested a fourth alternative:

If Her Imperial Majesty should decide to let him remain in his post as commander in chief at Reval, he hoped he would be allowed to exercise his functions according to the system in force at the time of his Imperial Majesty, Peter I.

He explained further that in those days the garrison, the artillery and the engineering corps were under the sole command of the commander in chief with the result that there was no disruption when His Imperial Majesty's interests were over-riding. The commander in chief of Reval was thus answerable directly to the College of War and not to the governor of the province. His responsibilities included restoration work on the palace, in accordance with a ukase from the Senate, and oversight of the military port of Reval, on the instructions of the College of War.

Finally, Hanibal claimed payment of the salary appropriate to his rank as major general in the army. Since 1742, he had received the allowance as commander in chief but the difference in salary since his latest promotion had not been paid.

Apparently, the failure to pay him his full salary was not just a case of forgetfulness in the service concerned. Hanibal thought it was a deliberate action motivated by 'hatred'. In a letter to his old friend, Cherkasov, dated 8 August 1745, he makes it point no.2[137].

The letter is a veritable cry of despair from Hanibal to the Baron. He is sickened by the treacherous and vicious behaviour of the people in Reval whose unlawful activities have been exposed thanks to his own integrity and devotion to duty. He is sad and disheartened at being the object of so much hatred, the more so as his enemies have not hesitated to use his race against him. In the depths of his current misery and despair he has concluded that there are three major traits in his character – he is totally honest, totally dedicated to his work – and he is black. Of these three traits he would only wish the first two on anyone Russian. He is hated, not just because of his integrity and dedication, but because he is black.

Never before had Hanibal ever referred to racial hatred as one of the sources of his misery. His conflicts have been with the various dignitaries who resented his uncompromising honesty in exposing their unlawful exploitation of the garrison's soldiers, and with colleagues such as Major Holmer and the previous and present governors who reduced him to a state of despair.

> "I could wish," he writes in the letter of 8 April 1745, "that everyone was like me in my sincerity and dedication (but not in my black skin). My dear friend, do not be angry with me for writing like this —my heart is full of pain and sorrow; you may spurn me as you would a foul monster and consign me to oblivion, or retain your love for me as God does, saving me from the wicked designs of men."

Only a small number of individuals in Reval were hostile to the black commander in chief. In spite of a certain amount of opposition, he had an excellent record of activity. Proof of this is in a letter of congratulation sent him a year previously (1744) by the Municipal Council of the Estonian capital. In it the municipal authorities assure him of their complete confidence in him and "thank him for the support he has given the town".

The Municipal Council of Reval had concluded that "the over-riding demands of the commander in chief and his rigorous leadership of the garrison had been in the interests of the townspeople."

In Petersburg, similarly, the authorities (the Senate, the College of War, the General Administration of Artillery and Fortifications), were totally satisfied with the work Hanibal had done in restoring the entire defence system of the town.

The Russian population of Reval saw the black military chief as a redresser of wrongs and the true representative of Russian power in the Province.

Mission to Finland

Russia and Sweden signed the Treaty of Abo on 16 June 1743. Once military operations had ceased there remained the thorny question of the future boundaries between the two great northern powers. There was no hope of a permanent peace until it was settled. Fully aware of the importance of the issue the former enemies appointed a government commission, representative of all parties, to agree on the frontiers. The commission met in Stockfors in Finland with the formidable task of reconciling the two parties' conflicting interests. Malevanov writes, "On declaring war the Swedish lords had wanted to restore the Russian frontier to the line of 1617, that is, they had wanted to win back not only the Baltic territories and Ingria but the Lake Ladoga region as well. They realised that they had failed in this ambition, but they stood by their demand for a return to the frontiers of 1700."

Each country naturally selected its best diplomats and the most reliable and patriotic of its top civil servants to act as delegates. On the Russian side, the Empress Elisabeth issued a decree on 15 June naming Major General Abraham Hanibal as head of the delegation. The nomination of Hanibal was yet another indication of the confidence the rulers placed in him. He stayed on the commission for one and a half years, from June 1745 to October 1746. Malevanov points out that for Hanibal the appointment was a great honour as well as a considerable responsibility: the previous head of the delegation having been Prince Repnin, Adjutant General and Chief of Staff of the Russian Imperial Army. Hanibal's instructions were "in his capacity as military engineer, first to settle the Russian frontier along lines that would be the most advantageous militarily, and second to indicate the position of future fortifications which would be indispensable for its defence[138]."

Hanibal was away from Reval during the whole period. Then at the end of the summer of 1746, he took advantage of a regulation of 1727 "which authorised a certain number of officers and soldiers of noble origin to take leave to manage their estates." Hanibal took prolonged leave but declared himself ready to return to the commission if his services were needed[139].

The Black Russian Nobleman

On his return from Finland in the autumn of 1746, Hanibal decided to devote his time to his family and the management of his estates. He had sold his village of Kariakula in 1744 with the intention of investing the proceeds in the development of his lands at Ragola. From 1743, the year of his famous law-suit against Professor von Tiren, the estate had been managed by his brother-in-law, Georg-Karl von Sjöberg, who was an officer in the Reval garrison and promoted to lieutenant in 1744.

In February 1746, the Senate published a decree awarding a Diploma of Honour to Hanibal. The Senate granted him the 'volost' of Mikhailovskoe in perpetuity, which meant that he no longer needed to fear that he might lose possession of this vast domain "if times changed". He decided to develop to the full this rural district, which had 41 little villages and almost 600 peasant families, and he naturally made it his centre of operations. He chose one of the villages, named it Petrovskoe (Peter's Village) in memory of Peter the Great and built his main residence there[140].

During his absence from Reval his vice-commander, Feodor Contsevich, had filled his place. Hanibal made only brief appearances in the town between 1746 and 1752, when he checked the progress on several major projects. In 1747, the port and the coastal battery were reconstructed in stone to replace the original timber[141]; in 1748, the high land of Taygues was leveled; in 1749, a small fort was built on the island of Maly Karlouss; in 1750, the restoration of the port of Reval was approved and in 1751 reconstruction work on it began[142].

In 1748, Hanibal received secret orders to return to the negotiations with the Swedes. He was to make sure "that places and lines of communication between Russian territories were not lost (to the Russians) or alienated[143]. He spent several months in Finland that year with one of his friends, Ivan von Bauman, as his secretary.

An ardent defender of the interests of his second homeland, Hanibal, as the representative of Imperial Russia, insisted on claiming from the opposite party "a certain small island which had not previously been included"[144]. The representative of the Swedish king naturally refused to cede it and a confrontation developed between the two delegations. On 21 August 1748 negotiations were postponed to a later date but were successfully completed by the end of the year. Hanibal was received with great ceremony at the Court of St. Petersburg. His "sister", the Empress Elisabeth, decorated him, putting the Order of Chivalry of the Russian Empire round his neck. He thus became Chevalier A. Hanibal[145]. This visit to the capital was also the occasion to renew his old friendships, notably with Alexis Bestuzhev-Riumin, who had become Grand Chancellor in 1744.

There had been other additions to Hanibal's family since the birth of their son Peter in 1742. While they were still in Reval, on 20 January 1744, Christina Regina had given birth to Osip, their third son and in 1747 another son was born. He was named Isaac after Count Savva (the Russian diminutive of Isaac) Raguzinsky, the rich merchant who had been instrumental in bringing the young Abraham from Constantinople to the court of Peter I in 1704. Their last son, Jacob, was born in 1748. Hanibal and Christina now had five sons and two daughters. The family of ten included Eudoxia (aged 17), the daughter of Hanibal's first wife.

Ivan, their eldest son, went into the army in 1744 at the age of 13, when his sister Elisabeth was 11 and Anna 7. His brothers Peter and Osip were then 6 and 4 respectively.

Christina Regina's brother and two sisters had also had eventful lives since the marriage of Julia-Charlotte in 1742. In 1743 Julia-Charlotte had a daughter, and called her Christina Regina after her sister. Anna-Gustaviana was married in 1746 to a clerk of works in the Engineering Department called Georg-Simon von Sokolovski and in the same year Georg-Karl von Sjöberg was promoted to the rank of captain at Reval.

The Shadow of Eudoxia

Up until 1749, the happy family life of the Hanibal was liable to be broken up at any moment. Hanibal's divorce from Eudoxia had never been formalised. Captain Dioper's daughter had lodged a complaint against her husband with the Synod in March 1737, still using the name of the black man she hated. She remained in prison until the Synod held its enquiry into the affair, which was not until 1743, six years later. The Archbishop released her on bail in expectation of a decision being taken. Three years passed. In 1746, Eudoxia became pregnant, which should have been unthinkable for a woman in her position, making her predicament much worse. On the advice of her priest, André Nikiforov, she wrote to the Consistory, admitting her faults and asking that her marriage to Abraham Hanibal be annulled as he had remarried and had several children. The Consistory began a new enquiry and sent Hanibal the following list of questions:-

1. Was he really married?

2. Who celebrated the marriage in which church?

3. Who had authorised the marriage?

4. What type of marriage was it?

Hanibal replied only in part as he had already given a full explanation to the Empress. The affair was referred back to the Synod and once again, there was a three-year wait. Eudoxia gave birth to a daughter, named Agrippina, who only lived a short time.

By September 1749, Hanibal had decided that the delay in making a decision had been too great. "[I] ask the Consistory, in view of my long and unimpeachable service, to have the goodness to protect me by keeping my former wife Eudoxia in custody in the Consistory. Because of her adulterous behaviour I wish that any association with me should be completely removed and that she should no longer be regarded as my wife. If she is allowed her liberty, I fear she will dishonour my name with her reprehensible actions"[146].

With his request, Hanibal enclosed the affidavit he had been given in February 1733 by the military tribunal, which had pronounced Eudoxia and her lover Chikov guilty of an attempt at poisoning.

He had serious reasons for asking the ecclesiastical authorities to make a firm decision in his favour against his adulterous wife. The future of his seven children was in doubt as long as the Church failed to recognise his second marriage:

> "Hanibal's first marriage had never been annulled, and the second could not be recognised as legitimate. Consequently the children of the second marriage would be regarded as illegitimate and denied access to any establishment or class except that of the peasantry"[147].

The Archbishop of St. Petersburg was at last moved to take action. He adopted three resolutions.

1. To separate Eudoxia Andreevna from Hanibal.

2. By virtue of the sentence passed on her on 8 April 1744 to send Eudoxia Andreevna to Orenburg; or in deference to the opinion of the Synod to a distant convent for monastic duties in perpetuity since "a person of such depravity cannot remain in the city."

3. Major General A. Hanibal remarried in good faith, as might any individual in ignorance of canonical law, believing that his divorce was genuine as a result of the ruling of the military tribunal, which condemned his wife to corporal punishment and hard labour for life in the spinning mills. He has lived in a state of matrimony with his second wife for thirteen years and has six children. Rather than separate them we should impose a fine on him, ask him to do penance and validate the second marriage."[148]

Archbishop Theodose's decision, however still had to be voted upon by the Synod. Eudoxia was entrusted to the care of her guarantors. Unfortunately, for her, on 5 December 1749 her protectors refused to continue taking responsibility for her moral conduct. Hanibal then requested that she be detained at the Consistory and promised to pay for her upkeep until such time as the Synod reached a decision.

Eudoxia was sent back to the Consistory as a result of the Archbishop's decision and again nothing further happened. By 1750 the city of St. Petersburg had a new Archbishop, Sylvester Kuliabka.

The Holy Synod sent the case back to him on 17 November 1750. He seemed to think the dossier was incomplete and ordered a new enquiry into the religion of Hanibal's second wife and the basis on which the marriage had been celebrated. Since Christina Regina was Lutheran and Hanibal Orthodox a special dispensation would have been required for such a marriage. In 1736, Hanibal had not given the matter any thought. There was only one thing to do – find the priest, Peter Ilin, who had celebrated the marriage in Reval fourteen years previously. Predictably, the search lasted for months. Finally, the Archbishop learned that he priest had been dead for some years.

It was in 1750 that Hanibal and Christina visited the capital and met her confessor, Pastor Helarius Henning. They were looking for a French language tutor for their children. Their stipulations were that he must be conscientious, of university standard and fully qualified in the French language.[149]. Pastor Henning was a close friend of the family and quite willing to look abroad for a teacher who would meet their requirements. He wrote the following letter on 21 February 1750 to Jacob Baumgarten, Professor of Theology in the University of Halle in Saxony.

"I have the honour to inform you that there is a vacancy for a student [who would be] conscientious and have a particular knowledge of French...in the household of an eminent gentleman in this country, Major General Hanibal. His wife is a member of my congregation and goes to confession and takes communion in my church. He is an African Negro by birth, a highly talented man in the scientific sphere in which he operates. He himself is a practising member of the Greek church and according to the laws of this country all the children, without exception, belong to the Russian church...it so happens that they have asked me to find them a student with a proven record of proficiency in French...naturally the man and his wife would be happy if you could find them a theology student who would like to take up this invitation. Such a person may be hard to find, in which case the General would be prepared to employ a Frenchman with a good personal record...a theologian, a lawyer or a doctor – it would not matter...sometimes students of languages or other disciplines are anxious to travel abroad – the General has lived in France, loves the French language and has a well-stocked library. He has an excellent command of French and anyone who wished to improve his own knowledge of the language would have the opportunity to converse with him on frequent occasions...the General's Lady is a woman of refinement and good character in the prime of life..."[150]

No one at the University of Halle would have been surprised to learn that there was a black general in the Russian Imperial Army. One of its most brilliant students had been an African, William Anthony Amo, who came from the Gold Coast (present day Ghana) and studied there from 1727 to 1734, obtaining a doctorate in philosophy at the University of Wittenberg in 1734. He became a professor and the author of two books on philosophy and eventually a Councilor of State in Berlin.

Pastor Henning's letter to the professor at the University of Halle is of interest for the precious information it gives us about Christina Regina Hanibal. He refers to her as the General's Lady and it is clear that Hanibal's Swedish wife was a woman of some standing. It is understandable that Hanibal was increasingly irritated by the extreme reluctance of the religious authorities to pronounce his divorce from his first wife. 'The regrettable business' had begun in 1731 when the young Greek woman had given birth to a white baby and until it was settled the shadow of the faithless wife would hover menacingly over the conjugal bliss Abraham and Christine had enjoyed since 1733.

CHAPTER IX

Chief engineer 1752-1762

"In the history of the Engineering Department Abraham Petrovich (Hanibal) is one of the outstanding personalities of his time."

Vegner, "Pushkin's Ancestors", (1937) p. 115.

"Hanibal was a great humanist and an exemplary figure in his time for the society of Russia (his second homeland)."

Malevanov.

Hanibal, technical director of the Russian Imperial Army

Major General Abraham Hanibal was transferred to the Department of Fortifications in St. Petersburg on 25 April 1752. He had been appointed Head of Technical Management in the Russian Imperial Army.

At the time the Department of Fortifications was part of the Chancellery of Artillery and Fortifications under the authority of the Senate.[151]A general staff of three generals, of whom Hanibal was one,was in charge of the department, made up of three major services, administration, engineering and inspection. The ukase from the College of War appointed him to be in charge of the Engineering Corps. He had two engineers as assistants in his new office, colonels Liudvig and Bibikov. He was directly responsible for his new work to the College of War.

Immediately on taking up his duties he sent orders all over the Russian Empire asking for weekly and monthly reports on all the fortification projects in progress, with information on the workforce employed at each site and the technical equipment needed to complete each project. He also asked for relief plans of all the fortresses. The largest sites were the fortresses of St. Petersburg and Schlüsselburg. Another responsibility was the training programme in the Schools of Engineering in Russia's two great cities, Moscow and St. Petersburg. Here too he asked for "weekly and monthly reports on the condition of the students" and kept himself fully informed of the curriculum. According to several Russian writers it was almost certainly the African who originated the project of merging the two Schools of Engineering and Artillery, a merger which was effected in the same year as he took office. As a former student at the School of Artillery of La Fère, Hanibal himself was the model for military engineers who had studied both artillery and engineering. In his opinion, artillery and engineering officers should be trained in the same institution.

The Senate had issued a decree in February 1752 for work to begin on a line of fortifications in Western Siberia. The new Technical Director had the task of overseeing the military works in the region of Tobol-Ichimsk, which took two years to complete.

There was no lack of opportunity for Hanibal to prove his talent in designing fortifications. With his usual enthusiasm, he supervised all the work on fortification throughout the vast Russian Empire. He carried out the renovation of the entire defence system of the western and north-western frontiers. In 1753 the Senate ordered that all the work on fortification in Kronstadt, Riga, Vyborg, Pernov and the fortress of Peter and Paul (in St. Petersburg) should be carried out "in accordance with the good judgment" of Hanibal[152].

He was asked to direct in person the work on the renovation of the Peter and Paul fortress in the capital and to supervise the recruitment of workers. There was work in progress on fortifications at Novoserbsk and Slavianoserbsk in the south of Russia, and Hanibal was also in charge of all the reports sent in by the directors on these sites...

The autumn of that year brought news of great importance for Hanibal's private life. He finally received the Synod's verdict on the long dispute between himself and his former wife. Eudoxia was declared guilty of having had sexual relations with the naval lieutenant Kayserov before her marriage. The judgement confirmed that the said Kayserov was the father of the white child, Eudoxia, whose birth many years earlier in 1731 had caused such consternation – and not only to the black husband of the errant wife – in the town of Pernov (Estonia).

Eudoxia Hanibal was also declared guilty on the second count of adultery with the 'Don Juan 'of Pernov, Lieutenant Chichkov and on a third count of the adulterous liaison with Abumov, a clerk at the library of the Academy of Sciences in St. Petersburg, which had led to the birth of a daughter, Agrippina.

The Synod consequently was able to grant the divorce of the couple and Eudoxia was condemned to exile in the convent of Staroladhozhky. The Synod also decided to recognise Hanibal's second marriage to Christina von Sjöberg subject to his paying a fine and performing a penance. Eudoxia was required to swear that she would not use the name of her former husband "and that she would not commit further acts of fornication on pain of the severest punishment; she should make a full confession of her previous crimes to her spiritual confessor and perform in every detail the penance he should impose."[153]

She was escorted to the convent of Staroladhozhky a few months later on 24 January 1754, and remained there for the rest of her life.

Abraham Hanibal had waited 21 years, from his first complaint against his wife in February 1732 to September 1753, when the clergy granted an official divorce. He had already been married for 20 years to his second wife, Christina Regina. Their eldest son, Ivan, a tall young man of 18, was an officer in the navy. Peter and Osip, aged 13 and 11 respectively, were sergeants in the artillery, while the two other boys, Isaac (6) and Jacob (4) were still too young for military training.

In the Russian army of the time, the artillery corps was the most prestigious and it is not surprising that Hanibal encouraged his sons to enter it. The whole family was now living in a house Hanibal had bought on Vasilevskiy Island.

At the end of 1753, Hanibal was sent back to Stockfors (Finland) by the College of Foreign Affairs. He took part in further negotiations on the delimitation of the frontiers between Russia and Sweden. On his return in January 1754, he was commissioned to study a project for the reconstruction of a fortress at Kiev (Ukraine) and submit the necessary technical documentation to the Chancellery of Artillery and Fortifications. This he did and submitted his conclusions and a plan he himself had drawn up[154].

In 1754, in the course of work on the fortress in the capital Hanibal was responsible for an innovation. When it came to cladding the walls with brick, he suggested that stone would be preferable as 'stone would be more durable'. An initial section with stone cladding was tried at his suggestion. When the military authorities and leading civilian architects heard of his innovation they made a special journey to the Peter and Paul fortress to witness the second phase. On 9 August 1754 to show that the ruined walls could take stone cladding the whole corps of officers and generals and St. Petersburg's most eminent architects, S. Shevakinsky, O. Trezzini and M. Bachmakov came to join Hanibal. The demonstration was so convincing that "in the report of the inspection presented by these experts it was recommended that 'this should be applied' to all the walls of the Fort.[155]"

Another innovation in 1754 was Hanibal's introduction of the study of civil architecture into the curriculum of the Schools of Engineering. Such was his personal contribution to the history of military technical training in Russia.

His presence was required at all corners of the Empire. As he was in such demand, he was frequently out of the capital. One of the journeys he made that year was to supervise the fortification of Elisabethgrad, and it was under his direction that the first stone of Fort Elisabeth was laid. In the following February the Chancellery of Artillery and Fortifications approved a report submitted by Hanibal one year previously with his plans for the reconstruction of the fort at Kiev-Petchersk.

Director of Works on the Kronstadt Canal and Head of the Engineering Corps 1755-1759

Since his promotion to the Department of Fortification in 1752, Major General Hanibal had worked untiringly to improve the Russian Empire's defence system, constructing new fortifications and renovating old ones. He had an excellent command of the science of fortification and was also an expert on hydraulics. The latter qualification did not escape the attention of the Senate. On 30 March 1755, a decree was issued by the Senate nominating him commander in chief "of the work on construction and maintenance of the canal and docks" at Kronstadt. He was also made a member of the "Commission on the port of Rogervik, the future port on the Baltic, and the canals of Kronstadt and Ladoga." As the chief officer in charge of the Kronstadt Canal Hanibal was responsible for "one of the most impressive hydraulic engineering achievements of eighteenth century Russia, begun under Peter I. (There was no comparable project in Western Europe at the time)". The choice of Hanibal to fill this important post was the obvious one for the Russian Senate. The decree stated that he "was well known to the Senatorial Conference and fully competent in this matter".

Hanibal was 59 years old in 1755. In spite of his age, he had not changed. One of his Russian biographers, Malevanov, writes that he was still "a demanding leader and as conscientious as he had been in his youth." His concern for work well done and his profound humanitarian feeling had never left him. On the contrary, it would seem that the higher he rose in the military and social hierarchy the greater his desire to improve the lot of the poor. Perhaps it was a legacy from his childhood in Logone, it being a key principle in traditional African society that power and wealth must be used for the benefit of the poor.

It is a fact that the russified African was "a great humanitarian and an exemplary figure for the Russian society of his time. As far as possible," notes Malevanov, "he tried to alleviate the harsh conditions in which the workforce, consisting of hundreds of skilled men and labourers, lived while they worked on the construction of the canal and the wharves at the ports.

Soon after becoming principal director of the Kronstadt Canal Hanibal proposed to the Office of Works in the town that a hospital should be provided.There were no special funds available for the treatment of the sick but he went on to found the first hospital for working men."

The way the project was carried out was remarkable for the period. Hanibal himself spoke to the workmen. He asked them to put aside one kopek for every rouble they earned and in that way to create a fund to set up the hospital. The workforce accepted the idea with enthusiasm and all began to subscribe. However, it soon became clear to Hanibal that their contributions would never meet the target. He then had recourse to other means: he approached the tradesmen and officers of Kronstadt. He went to the Office of Works in the town and "suggested that a small sum should be deducted when allowances were paid to officers and when traders paid for goods on delivery." He appealed to the Christian charity of such people. A certain number of traders had already taken a charitable interest and he naturally hoped that "everyone would give according to his means" in order to set up the hospital. His faith was rewarded and to the general amazement a sufficient sum of money was raised. The hospital was opened without delay and from then on workmen who fell sick in Kronstadt were cared for and given food[156].

1755 was also the year that the first Russian university was founded in Moscow on the initiative of the Empress Elisabeth with the help of the great scholar Lomonosov.

On Christmas Day Hanibal learnt that he had been promoted to the rank of Lieutenant General. The promotion elevated him to the third rank of the civil and military hierarchy and he thus became one of the Empire's elite. A lieutenant general was equivalent to a vice-admiral in the navy or a privy councillor in the higher administration of the Empire. The decree of 25 December had another clause. Hanibal, was nominated governor of the province of Vyborg on the Finnish frontier. It was a high office and carried considerable prestige, but the Ministry of War quickly realised that Hanibal's appointment to a political and administrative post would deprive it of the service of their most gifted engineer.

For several months, Hanibal had been head of the Engineering Corps of the Imperial Army in addition to his responsibilities as

Director of Operations at Kronstadt; as a member of the Commission on Ports and Canals and in the Department of Fortifications...he was considered to be "irreplaceable in the specialist areas" where he was active.

We shall never know whether Hanibal would have been willing to abandon his responsibilities in the military and technical sphere in order to become Governor of Vyborg. He would certainly have been overjoyed to accept such a position twelve or thirteen years previously. On the other hand, even in 1726 when he presented Empress Catherine I with the two volumes of his huge book "*Geometry and Fortifications*", it had always been his dream to make a career in military engineering. In the 1750s, his passion for mathematics, engineering and hydraulics was stronger than ever and it is possible that it was his wish to stay on in the army and make his mark with the major works that demanded so much of his intelligence, inventiveness and technical skill.

Whatever his thoughts may have been at the end of 1755, the College of War, the Empire's highest military authority, made the decision that he should stay in St. Petersburg at the head of the Engineering Corps, which was where he was most needed. The decision was communicated to him on 3 January 1756, barely ten days after his appointment as governor of Vyborg. The proceedings of the College of War as recorded on 3 January 1756 were unequivocal:

> Her Imperial Majesty has most graciously willed that Lieutenant General Lord Hanibal should remain as previously in the Engineering Corps... since the Lieutenant General Lord Hanibal is at present in command of the whole Department of Engineers and is responsible for all matters concerning the Corps and the personnel of the Department...[157]

Hanibal therefore remained in St. Petersburg. He installed a training range there for the use of students of artillery and engineering. Students of artillery were able to practise shots while students of engineering learnt how to take forts by assault[158]. As a former student at the Military School of La Fère Hanibal was fully aware of the importance of practical training. Thirty-four years previously he had pleaded desperately to be allowed to stay a further year in France in order to be initiated into the construction of trenches and the laying of mines...

In the mid-1750s Count Peter Shuvalov, a brother of the Empress's favourite, Ivan Shuvalov[159], became Grand Master of the Artillery and President of the College of War. Count Shuvalov "considered the Artillery to be the principal army corps" and immediately took steps to make this branch of the armed forces much stronger. In 1756, he amalgamated the Artillery and the Engineers, something that Hanibal had suggested several years previously. Interestingly enough at the same time in France, where Hanibal had received such a solid military training, the same kind of reform was taking place. On 8 December 1755, there was an "Order from the King (Louis XV) to unite the Artillery with the Engineers under the immediate authority of His Majesty". The King's reasons for the move were made clear in Article 1 of the decree, stipulating: "His Majesty judges it conducive to the good of his forces... to unite the Artillery and the Engineers into one corps confident that the satisfaction he has felt with the two corps' considerable services as separate units can only be augmented by their amalgamation. The members of both corps shall use their capacity jointly under his immediate authority for the successful outcome of the tasks enjoined upon them...His Majesty wishes the battalions of the Royal Artillery Regiment, the companies of mining engineers and the workmen who serve them, the officers of the Artillery and those of the Engineering Corps to form one sole corps to be known from now on as the Royal Corps of Artillery and Engineering[160]".

The French military authorities, however, were not in favour of the amalgamation. Anne Blanchard, a French military historian, gives the following explanation:

> *"The measure was inspired by a senior official in the Ministry of War, M. Dubois, who was anxious to cut costs and increase efficiency. He assumed he could bring together two corps who were equally skilled in warfare and sieges, but ignored the fact that they were traditional rivals with similar technical strengths.The Comte d'Argenson[161]saw a further advantage. He suppressed the office of Grand Master of the Artillery of France and took over the artillery himself. Artillery men benefited to some extent from the reinforcement but the move was not welcomed by the great chiefs on either side nor by their subordinates..."*

If in France some people opposed the merger, in Russia it seems to have gone smoothly.

On 4 July, Abraham Hanibal was made Engineer-in Chief. He was now the principal military engineer of the entire Russian Empire. Nine days later, he celebrated his sixtieth birthday. He had spent fifty-two of his sixty years in Russia and more than half a century had passed since that memorable day in Vilna when, before God, Peter I had chosen to be his godfather. Then the little prince from black Africa had had little idea that his fate would be in an unknown land. In the cold climate of Russia, he had been warmly welcomed and in that completely alien environment so far from his native Logone, he had nevertheless been able to put down roots. His large family of five sons and two daughters was proof enough. His son Isaac, aged nine, had just left to join his older brothers in the School of Artillery. It seems that the youngest, Jacob, died that year at the early age of eight.

In his role as Engineer-in-Chief Abraham Hanibal was required to sit on a committee to examine all the administrative procedures in connection with the activities of the Chancellery of Artillery and Engineering. As a purely bureaucratic task, it was not at all to Hanibal's taste as a technician and man of action. He was unsurprisingly absent from every meeting of the committee from July 1756 to November 1757, almost one and a half years, and his signature is missing on 2755 sets of minutes and 189 registers! Peter Shuvalov, the chair of the committee, issued various injunctions, but the representative of the Engineering Corps did not want to waste his time on paper work and did not respond. Finally Shuvalov found a replacement for him on the Committee.

On 21 May 1757, a "Commission to study the state of repair of Russia's fortifications" was set up. There were eight members. The chair was Chief of Staff General Fermor, a brilliant administrator and second lieutenant to Field Marshal Apraxin, the Supreme Commander of the Russian armed forces. Hanibal was made vice-president of the Commission. Its brief was to make a study of the entire system of the country's fortifications, particularly those along the frontiers, and to see which were still of strategic importance and which had no further use in the defence system so that funds could be allocated for renovation and reconstruction.

Since 1756, Russia had been engaged in the Seven Years War, which involved many European nations[162]. Field Marshal Apraxin, the leader of the Russian forces, won some major battles against the Prussians in July 1757. Strangely, he did not attempt to make use of his military advantage but ordered a retreat. The Empress Elisabeth was furious and replaced him with the German, General Fermor, who on becoming Supreme Commander of the Russian forces resigned from the presidency of the Commission on Fortifications. Abraham Hanibal automatically took his place and as Head of the Commission was given access to highly confidential documents by the Central Bureau of Fortifications and Artillery. These included the book: *"The Power of the Russian Empire"* and "plans and maps of all Imperial Russia's frontiers, the forts and lines of defence linked to them... as well as general plans of the interior of the country."[163]

Hanibal was indefatigable and his new responsibilities did not prevent him from continuing to direct the great hydraulic works in progress. He regularly visited Kronstadt, Ladoga, the largest lake in Europe, and Rogervik. He supervised the dredging and deepening of the Ladoga canal in 1757.

He was a regular visitor in Kronstadt and was appalled by the extreme poverty of the families of the men working on the canal. The streets of the town were full of children running around with nothing to do. They were the canal children. For many years the gigantic project had employed hundreds of labourers as well as overseers and engineers. Labourers and craftsmen were paid very little but had large families to support. The gulf between the lower classes of society and the landed nobility was immense. Earlier, as Chief Director of Works on the canal, Hanibal had taken steps to improve health care for the workers; now he set about helping their children.

He made the immediate decision to found a school for all the children of workmen at all levels, skilled and unskilled. Land belonging to the canal was used and children who enrolled there were taught to read and write, but that was not all. They were also given technical training as carpenters, locksmiths, iron-workers, fitters, mechanics and even health assistants. The Chief Director of Works was not too proud to go out into the streets of Kronstadt to look for poverty-stricken children and bring them in. Malevanov pays Hanibal an eloquent tribute for his dynamic action and social concern: "Abraham Petrovich took a truly paternal interest in the children of both the craftsmen and the labourers. On his visits to Kronstadt he would advise adolescents between ten and sixteen years old on the best course for their studies: he directed some into work as office clerks or nurses, others into the trades of carpentry, lock-making or iron-working. Success in their studies led to higher awards for the best students "for their dedicated application to the sciences" and "in order to encourage others to do their best." At the end of August 1756, he noticed two particularly keen young apprentice turners, Semion Eremeev and Maxim Timofeev, and promptly went to the Office of Works in Kronstadt to arrange an increase of ten kopeks in their allowance in recognition of their scholastic achievements. He arranged for the same thing for any pupil who had proved his ability in any other trade...[164].

Hanibal, the protector of Kronstadt's children, fought unremittingly for several years to give them a chance in life. Two of the best pupils, Roman Dimitriev and Theodore Borzov would distinguish themselves years later by building the Russian Navy's first steam engines.

Imperial Russia's first black General in Chief

Count Peter Shuvalov had observed that some things were lacking in the training of officers in the Artillery and Engineering Corps, and wanted to tackle the problem. In January 1758, he asked the representatives of the two corps he headed to instigate "the teaching of fortification in the Schools of Artillery and of artillery in the Schools of Engineering". The Head of the Artillery was Lieutenant General Glebov and the Head of Engineering was Hanibal. Together they founded the United School of Artillery and Engineering in 1758 in St. Petersburg.

In France at that time, the amalgamation of the two corps was an acknowledged failure and Louis was forced to separate them again on 5 May 1758. A new Royal Ordinance was issued in March 1759, which "conferred on the Engineering Corps the administration and disposition of mine-laying personnel under the orders of Belidor, the inspector of these companies." Belidor, the man appointed as head of the French army's engineering companies was none other than Hanibal's former mathematics tutor. The distinguished mathematician and military engineer was still very active and had written several books on "the science of the engineer". He was also an associate member of the French Academy of Sciences.[165]

We do not know whether the two men were acquainted with the progress of each others' careers but Belidor would certainly have been as proud as any teacher would to learn that his former pupil at La Fère had reached such a high rank in Russia.

In St. Petersburg Hanibal was not afraid to speak out against the Senate's ukases, put forward by the Grand-Master of the Artillery, when in his judgement they were not in the interests of the projects for which he was responsible. He opposed the execution of a decree of May 1759 relating to the organisation of works on the Kronstadt Canal. He addressed a counter-proposal to the Senate on a better use of qualified personnel. Count Shuvalov was a member of the Senate and much too powerful to be outvoted by his peers. The Senate rejected the Chief Engineer's advice while recognising that "his suggestions were reasonable and well founded"[166].

In spite of the difference of opinion Hanibal's career suffered no further setbacks. On 23 October 1759, he was made General in Chief of the army and Director-General of the works at Lake Ladoga and of the Commission on the works at Kronstadt and Rogervik. He was thus in charge of the greatest undertakings of the greatest empire in Europe. A year later the Empress Elizabeth awarded him the *Cordon Rouge* of St. Alexander Nevsky – he was now a knight of two orders, St.Alexander Nevsky and St. Anne.

As well as all his official activities in this period General in Chief Hanibal was continually involved in defending the rights of his subordinates. Where their interests were concerned he lost no time in presenting their case to the Senate. Whenever he travelled to Kronstadt or other cities, he was accompanied by his mobile military chancery where his orders were taken down and transmitted to the relevant bodies.

On Christmas Eve 1761, the Empress became seriously ill to the point of "receiving the extreme unction."[167] On 25 December Prince Nikita Trubetskoy came out to the dignitaries assembled in the Imperial Palace and announced that the Empress had given the order to "live long". "That," writes the Academician Henri Troyat, "was the time-honoured formula in Russia for announcing the death of a person, be it king or peasant. Then as weeping broke out at the sad news Prince Trubetskoy proclaimed the accession of Peter III."[168]

In 1727 the death of Catherine I had marked the end of an era in the life of the black general. In the winter of 1762 would the death of her daughter have the same devastating effect? Hanibal mourned the passing of his patron's daughter and benefactress, the Empress Elizabeth, and then swore allegiance to her chosen successor, Peter III. He also had to attend the funeral of his superior, Count Peter Shuvalov, who died in January 1762. The interim, while a new Grand Master of the Artillery was being sought, was filled by Lieutenant General Glebov[169].

From January to March 1762 work on the canals stopped as it did every winter when the lakes were frozen. Hanibal remained in the capital with all the members of his chancery. Announcements appeared in the various Petersburg newspapers inviting "all those who wish to supply the workforce on the Kronstadt and Oranienbaum canals to present themselves at the offices in the capital[170].

At the Imperial Court various people were emerging from the shadows. Well-known exiles, including Biren, von Münnich and Lestocq were recalled from Siberia[171]. Prince George of Holstein was appointed Chief of the Armed Forces. Another Holstein prince, the governor of Estonia and Hanibal's enemy from the 1740s, was made Field Marshal on 9 January. By 18 May Peter von Holstein-Bek had become a member of the Special Assembly nearest to the Imperial Court. As the Emperor's right hand man,[172] he could finally take his revenge on the "insolent" ex-commander of Reval and black defender of "Russian interests over those of the Germans"[173].

Three weeks later, on 9 June 1762, Imperial Russia's leading engineer, General in Chief Hanibal was retired from the army – on grounds of age! He was 66 years old and at the height of his powers. The new emperor, Peter III, the 'German' descendant of Peter I, signed the decree and there was no appeal. The retirement order was not even accompanied by promotion as was traditional in the Russian army. Hanibal would have expected to be made Field Marshal and receive royal grants on retiring with the grade of General in Chief but he received nothing. Was he really too old? That cannot have been the real reason. The man Peter III appointed in his place was the 79-year-old Count von Münnich. The former Field Marshal had returned from his twenty years of exile to become Head of the Engineering Corps.It would have been difficult to find anyone else whose abilities could compare with the African's!

On the evening of 9 June, Peter III "gave a dinner party for 400 people to celebrate the ratification of the peace treaty with Prussia. For the event he dressed in Prussian uniform..." No doubt the former governor of Reval was one of the distinguished guests on this occasion, savouring his revenge on his black opponent.

Peter III was deposed less than three weeks later in another coup d'état. His wife, Sophie von Anhalt-Zerbst, ascended the throne of Imperial Russia. She had changed her name to Ekaterina Alexeevna in June 1744[174], in accordance with the wishes of Empress Elizabeth and now took the title of Catherine II.

Hanibal, who had followed events closely, wrote to the new Empress after her enthronement in July 1762. He reminded Catherine that he had been the faithful servant of the Imperial family for 57 years. With no fault on his side, he had been removed from his post on June 9 without reason and without any of the customary grants. He asked the Empress to grant him land in Ingria in view of his loyal service[175].

July, however, was the month when the new Tsarina found herself in serious personal difficulties. A week after her accession her husband, whom she had confined to his residence, had been killed. The murderers were her close advisors. She announced that he had died of an attack of "haemorrhoidal colic" but she had to defend herself against accusations of 'regicide' at the same time as she was trying to consolidate her position. To reassure people she promised she would remedy all injustices and as a result received innumerable petitions from victims of former regimes. She was soon overwhelmed by "the flood of letters and three-quarters of them were left unanswered."[176]

Abraham's letter to Catherine II met the same fate. On the original, an unidentified member of the Court wrote: "No decision was taken."[177]

When Hanibal finally retired from the army in 1762 yet another period of unrest was beginning in his adopted homeland. At the age of sixty-six he had known every Tsar and Tsarina who had ruled since the beginning of the century. A child of Africa, born in the seventeenth century, he became part of the history of another continent, Europe, and another century, the eighteenth.

CHAPTER X

The black lord

My negro grandfather
Unmindful of Elizabeth and the others
Of the court and the sumptuous banquets
Sat in the shade of the lime tree avenue
Thinking of his distant Africa
In the cold European summers

Pushkin, To Yazykov
20 September 1824

Retirement in Suyda

Late in the 1750s, Hanibal had increased his property holdings by buying extensive estates and dozens of villages in the St. Petersburg region. By the summer of 1762 when he retired from the Directorship of the Engineering Corps and the supervision of the major engineering work he owned two large domains – Mikhailovskoe, on the Estonian border, with its many villages in the Pskov region, and Suyda, about thirty kilometres from the capital, in the St. Petersburg region. Suyda was made up of the farms of Runovo, Yelitsy, Taytsy and their villages. In the capital itself he possessed a large residence on Vasilievsky Island which he later sold in order to build a new house.

He had acquired a taste for rural existence in the 1730s and now chose to pass his final years in the countryside, devoting his time to the management of his estates and the education of his youngest daughter,

Sophie, who was only three years old at the time of his retirement. His two elder daughters, Elizabeth and Anna, whom he had named after Peter I's daughters, had been married for some time.

Elisabeth Abramovna (meaning Abraham's daughter) no longer used the family name of Hanibal. She had married Lieutenant Colonel André Pushkin, a military engineer in her father's corps. The Pushkins were a very old noble family who had always been close to the Tsars. Hanibal, 'a veteran of the age of Peter the Great' must have looked very favourably on that match. His second daughter, Anna Abramovna, had married Major General Semion S. Neelov.

His son, Peter Abramovich Hanibal, was promoted to captain in the artillery on 1 July 1763.

The General's peaceful existence was disturbed briefly in September 1765 by a messenger from the Imperial Palace bringing a letter from Catherine II [178]

Letter from Catherine the Great.

"Abraham Petrovich!

I am aware of the fact that at the time of our Sovereign of great and glorious memory, Peter the Great, you had charge of the papers relating to his numerous projects, since he had a high opinion of you and employed you for various duties.For this reason, I believe some documents you found to be of interest may have been retained in your possession in memory of our great Sovereign and your years in his service. I have been informed that he planned the construction of a canal between Moscow and St. Petersburg and that the plans had already been drafted. Even if there is only a rough sketch, assuming that you have any such papers in your possession, I should be greatly pleased to have it together with any further notes relating to the project.

If nothing of this kind is in your possession can you at least let me know where I might find such information, as I am most anxious to have it. On the same matter, if you ever heard His Majesty make any comment on the subject I would ask you to write to me with what you remember. I remain benevolently yours.

Tsarskoe Selo, 2 September 1765
Catherine"

General Hanibal replied immediately to the Tsarina.

Letter from Abraham Hanibal to Catherine the Great

"Madam!

In reply to Your Imperial Majesty's gracious communication, I humbly wish to report as follows:

During the reign of our Sovereign of blessed and eternal memory, Peter the Great, I had the honour of being in charge of His Majesty's Privy Cabinet, which contained all the plans and projects and also the library; however, after so many years I do not now recall having ever heard any discussion of a canal between Moscow and St. Petersburg. There was a prospective shortened route to Moscow, which His Majesty was often pleased to say [he hoped] to construct one day. Since the death of our Great Sovereign... I have seen books and other relics from the Privy Cabinet at the Academy of Sciences. All the projects and plans were stored together so they should all be either there or in the Archives of the Privy Cabinet.

Your Imperial Majesty's... most humble servant
A. Hanibal[179]."

Ivan A. Hanibal, Abraham's eldest son handed the letter to Senator Gregory Teplov, who passed it to Catherine II on 7 September 1765. The Empress read the reply and made the following note in the margin:

"If the plans are in the Academy it is almost certain they will be of no use as they will already have been stolen."

Reasons to be proud

Hanibal spent the quiet years of his retirement at the side of his admirable wife, known affectionately as 'Krestina'. When they relaxed on the big stone bench outside in the garden, Abraham, who had an amazing memory, would tell her stories of his "distant Africa" His descendants remember how he wept whenever he spoke of his kidnapping in Logone. Not only had he been parted forever from his family – the tragedy had been made even more dreadful by a related incident. His only sister, Lagane, had thrown herself into the water in a desperate attempt to save her young brother from the clutches of the traders who were abducting him. As the boat moved away, he saw her drown in the waters of the great river...[180]

The Hanibals followed the progress of their four sons with pride. Their respective military careers had begun some years earlier. In 1768, Turkey had declared war on Catherine II's Russia. Ivan Hanibal, a lieutenant colonel in the navy, was promoted on 10 February 1769 to the rank of commander of naval artillery. When Admiral Spiritov's squadron sailed from the Baltic to the Mediterranean, Ivan Hanibal was with him and headed a landing force of 2,500 men[181]. He played a heroic role in the military campaign in the Greek archipelago. The admiral was searching for a safe landing place for the Russian troops on the Morea peninsula. He decided to take the port of Navarino, and ordered "Major Prince Dolgorukov to invade." The Prince refused saying it would be "impossible to take the fort by storm as it was well armed and had a large garrison to defend it." The Admiral was determined to gain control of the fort because of its strategic importance for future operations and ordered Ivan Hanibal to take it. "When he reached Navarino with one frigate and two warships, Hanibal first exchanged fire with the fort. He then landed three hundred Russians and some Greek volunteers, placed several big guns on the shore and installed batteries to the east and west. The siege lasted fifteen days and the fort finally fell on 10 April 1770. Ivan Hanibal then became its commander and was given the task of its restoration.[182]. He was knighted and awarded the Order of St. George for his courage. He was just thirty-five years old.

Abraham and Christina had scarcely had the time to congratulate each other on their son's heroism before they learned that ten weeks later (on 24-26 June) he had further distinguished himself in the great naval battle against the Turks at Chesme in the Aegean Sea. The official war dispatches record that the military genius of the commander of the unified artillery squadron, Ivan Hanibal, "contributed to the destruction of the Turkish fleet."[183]

Two of Hanibal's other sons, Peter Abramovich and Osip Abramovich were promoted to the rank of army major on 13 and 29 December 1770. The youngest son, Isaac Abramovich, was serving in Poland where the Russian army was also fighting. He was already a captain in the artillery and in command of a detachment of artillery men in the infantry regiment at Naschenburg[184]. He distinguished himself in September 1771 for "daring and courage" and was mentioned on 12 September by Alexander Suvorov, commander of the forces fighting the hetman Oguinsky[185], in his dispatches to General Veyman, the Supreme Chief of the Russian army in Poland.

Ivan Hanibal was promoted to the rank of Major General of the Imperial Russian army on 7 December 1772.

Osip Abramovich married a few months later in 1773. His bride was Maria Alekseevna, another member of the Pushkin family. Osip was an elegant young man, well educated but with very little understanding of marriage. He was the most unruly of the four sons and his father was profoundly irritated by his frivolous and spendthrift way of life, so unlike his own. He was very angry with Osip and accused him of dissolute behaviour, ruining his army career and marrying without his permission[186]. He refused to see him and cut off his allowance. The young wife, Maria, "did her utmost to reconcile her husband to his father" and ultimately succeeded: Hanibal did in fact "pardon him and allow him to visit." "The young couple then moved to the parents' home in Suyda and settled down[187]. Their only daughter was born there on 21 June 1775. She was named after Maria Hanibal's elder sister, Nadine or 'Nadezhda' and was "the future mother of the poet (Pushkin)."

Meanwhile, Ivan Hanibal was in St. Petersburg to receive the Order of Saint Anne from Catherine II and Peter Hanibal was promoted to the rank of lieutenant colonel of the infantry on 10 July. A year later, to Hanibal's great joy, Ivan became head of artillery of the whole Russian Navy with the rank of commander general. Six days before his eightieth birthday the veteran of the days of Peter the Great could not have hoped for more welcome news.

On 17 July 1776 at Hanibal's great house in Suyda there were crowds of people celebrating the eightieth birthday of Russia's most eminent military engineer. The guests included Ivan N. von Baumann, formerly his secretary in Finland, and now State Councillor[188], Baron Alexander P. von Voberzer, a councillor at court and Hanibal's former colleague, who had retired four years previously[189]; the assistant judge, Kaspar von Tirol, the Orthodox priest, Sergei Romanov, Hanibal's confessor and the incumbent of the Suyda church, and Savva Chelpanov, a clerk in the Office of Livonian, Estonian and Finnish Affairs. These were all old friends of the Hanibal family and he had summoned them to witness his last will and testament.

Chelpanov was asked to draw up the document. The old engineer felt that on account of his great age it was time to distribute fairly between his beloved wife and his children the considerable wealth he would leave at his death.

Hanibal's Will

"*In the name of the Holy Trinity, Father, Son and Holy Ghost, Amen.*

I, the undersigned Abraham Petrov Hanibal, General-in-Chief and Lord of the Orders of Saint Alexander Nevsky and Saint Anne, having, as was my duty, supported my sons, educated them all alike, holding them still in my affection, it is my wish that after my death they should remain together in brotherly love for ever.

With this intention, in order to avoid any disagreements between them, I, being of sound mind and body, do confirm that this is my present will in the presence of the witnesses whose signatures appear below. The aim of my will is to enable my sons Ivan, Peter, Joseph[190] and Isaac Hanibal to share the inheritance between them without dissension. I herewith define the share of my property, moveable and immoveable, that shall go to each one.

To Ivan I bequeath the lands in the province of Pskov granted me by Her Imperial Majesty in perpetuity and for due inheritance, comprising the volost of Mikhailovskoe with its houses, dependants and villages, together with the estate of Suyda which I bought in the district of Koporsky in Ingria, with all the villages belonging to the estate and all the serfs of either sex.

To Peter – the estate of Elitsy on the land which I acquired in the Koporsky district of Ingria, with all the villages attached to it.

To Joseph – the estate of Runovo in the Koporsky district of Ingria with its villages and all the serfs of either sex.

To Isaac – the estate of Taytsy also in the Koporsky district of Ingria with its attached villages and all the serfs, men and women, living there.

Additionally to Peter, Joseph and Isaac the sum of 5,000 roubles each.

To my young daughter, Sophie[191] I give 5,000 roubles; she has no claim on my immoveable property. My daughters, Elizabeth Pushkin, widow, and Anna Neelova have no claim on any property, moveable or immoveable, since they received substantial sums of money from me on their marriage.

In addition, I direct:

Firstly: on my death any further purchases of land that I may make in this neighbourhood during my lifetime shall become the property of my eldest son, Ivan. In no circumstances shall this land be broken up.

Secondly: on my death all my property, moveable and immoveable, and all my revenues shall go to my wife, Christina Matveevna, for her to use at her pleasure until her death... and while she lives, my children may not inherit the above; when by the will of the Almighty she leaves this world my children may claim their inheritance as detailed above; they should also share our servants between them by amicable agreement.

The above arrangements should be permanent. It will be incumbent on them, if they have sons, to bequeath all their immoveable property to the eldest; if they have no sons, and at least one brother still living, the eldest brother should inherit. The aforementioned properties will thus remain in the possession of the Hanibal family and will not be divided up between brothers and sisters or daughters. Land should not be given as dowry to the females of the family; by this system the aforementioned properties should fall in perpetuity to the eldest in the family; none of the heirs shall have the right to sell or mortgage or even to use them as surety for purchases or promissory notes...

That no one shall violate the terms of my will, I here confirm that it is my will and sign it in the presence of my confessor, Sergei Romanov, priest at the Orthodox Church of Christ's Resurrection in the district of Koporsky on my estate at Suyda.

Made on the above estate of Suyda on thirteenth July 1776. The above will and testament was written by the Clerk to the Office of Livonian, Estonian and Finnish Affairs, Savva Chelpanov.

Signed as follows:

General-in-Chief Lord Abraham Petrov Hanibal

His spiritual father Sergey Romanov

State Councillor Ivan Nicolas von Baumann (witness)

Baron Alexander Petrov von Voberzer, Court Councillor (witness)

and the Assistant Judge Kaspar Yuriev Tirol (witness)

This will was placed in the Offices of the Judiciary on 15 July 1776[192].

A remarkable feature of the will was the passage concerning the black patriarch's Swedish wife. In general, Hanibal had remained faithful to the old code of inheritance which Peter I had instituted in 1714 (subsequently revoked in 1731). Peter had intended "to prevent the large estates breaking up" but gave no rights to women. Hanibal firmly intended to break with established practice when it came to his wife. He bequeathed all his property, including his lands, to the woman he loved so deeply and trusted absolutely. "Surprisingly tender feelings show through his words about Christina Matveevna", writes Nathalia Teletova[193]. Although he forbids the women of the family to inherit land he makes an exception for Christina. They had spent forty-three years together and their eldest son, Ivan, their pride and joy, had celebrated his forty-first birthday a month previously. 1776 was also the Hanibal couple's jubilee. Forty years earlier in the cathedral of St. Nicholas in Reval (Tallinn) their destinies had been united in the sight of God.

In 1777, Catherine II made Ivan Hanibal a member of the College of the Admiralty. A year later, his brother Osip (Joseph) became a member of the Town Council of Pskov and Ivan received a new commission. He was put in charge of the new town and harbour of Kherson in the Crimea, where he also had to construct a fort. An Imperial order in Catherine II's own hand came from Tsarskoe Selo on 25 July 1778[194]. It instructed him to go to the Dnieper to "build a town near the village of Alexandrovskoe, fully fortified, with a naval yard and admiralty headquarters."[195]

Ivan Hanibal was the son of an expert on fortification and his talents as an administrator and builder had evidently made a great impression on the Empress. "The speed with which the town of Kherson was built was unbelievable, despite the difficulties of the damp and marshy site (badly chosen by Potemkin) and the great distance from sources of supply and construction materials."

In recognition of his achievements in the summer of 1778 as Director of Works at Kherson Ivan Hanibal was promoted to the rank of Lieutenant General on 1 January 1779 "retaining his position as commander of the naval artillery." Six weeks earlier, on 20 November 1778, the Empress had sent him a tobacco box with her portrait as a token of her gratitude"[196].

The death of the Patriarch

Abraham and Christina's last years were spent at Suyda. His family remembered him as a wise and philosophical old man. In 1779, when he was eighty-three, he was still very active and personally supervised the building of his new house in St. Petersburg. Friends often made the journey to Suyda to visit him. The Suvorovs, father and son, were friends of long-standing and frequent visitors to the black 'barine' (lord) as he was known to the thousands of serfs in the numerous villages in his domains.

At Pskov, the incorrigible Osip Abramovich had deceived the local priest into believing that he was a widower and on 9 January 1779, he married a certain Ustina Tolstoya, a 'femme fatale', rumoured to be somewhat 'disreputable'. Osip's first marriage to Maria Alekseevna had been a disaster. She was extremely jealous and he was a thoughtless and irresponsible father. There were long and bitter negotiations between them before Maria could be allowed to keep their attractive little daughter, Nadezhda.

Osip Hanibal was transferred to St. Petersburg in April 1780, where he became a member of the Council of Government[197]. His distinguished brother, Ivan, was rewarded for his high achievements at about the same time by the Empress Catherine II, receiving 10,000 deciatines (27,000 acres) of land. He was decorated with the Order of Saint Alexander Nevsky the following year.

Ivan was in Kherson when he received the news of his mother's death. Hanibal's highly respected faithful Swedish wife died on February 1781[198]. Ivan went to Suyda on the sad occasion and wrote to Osip on 25 March: "We have buried our mother; Father is seriously ill and grows weaker by the hour; he will not live much longer. There is little hope for him. All our servants are here[199]." Hanibal did not long outlive his wife. He died on 20 April 1781, aged eighty-five.

Hanibal had been born in 1696 in Logone in far away Africa, adopted by the famous ruler, Peter the Great and had proved himself a genius, one of Imperial Russia's most distinguished sons. He was an ardent defender of the interests of Russia, his second homeland, and at the same time the most outstanding representative of Africa in the land of the Tsars. In the nineteenth century, in the cause of perpetuating black slavery, "scholarly anthropologists" in Europe invented the racist myth and decreed that the black races were inferior. In Russia there were people in a position to denounce the myth as an aberration by reference to Abraham Hanibal. In 1867 Prince Dolgorukov, a descendant of one of Tsarist Russia's most noble families, paid Hanibal a ringing tribute in his *Memoirs*. "Abraham Ganniball proves most vividly the injustice of the dreadful prejudice against the black race which lays upon it the reputation of intellectual and moral inferiority. He was an immensely talented man with a tremendous ability for study, a rare understanding of mathematics and the many branches of human knowledge to which mathematics is the key. In character he was noble and upright and incorruptibly honest in all his dealings."[200]

In commemoration of the black eaglet "from Peter the Great's nest" the Russians have converted one of his former properties, the volost of Mikhailovskoe, into a museum. On his grave in Suyda (near Gatchina in the St. Petersburg region), they have erected an obelisk[201] with the following epitaph:

Here lies
The great-grandfather of A. S. Pushkin
Abraham Petrovich
HANNIBAL
The eminent Russian mathematician
and expert in fortification and hydraulics

1697-1781

54. Alexander Pushkin by Kipriensky.

55-56. Lauritz Galtung (c. 1615-1661), a Norwegian nobleman of the Galtung-family, admiral of the Dano-Norwegian joint fleet and his wife Barbara Grabo. They are the great great parebts of Abraham Hanibal's wife, Chrstina Regina Schoberg.

57. Lauritz Galtung and Barbara Grabo's children. Their eldest daughter, Klara Maria is Christina Regina's grand-mother.

58. General and admiral Ivan Hanibal, Abraham Hanibal's eldest son. Russian war hero, builder of Crimea city and port of Khirson.

59. Peter the Great waiting for his godson returning from France. By Shteyne, 1999.

60. General and admiral Ivan Hanibal, Abraham Hanibal's eldest son. Russian war hero, builder of Crimea city and port of Khirson.

61. Baron Wrangel Piotr Nikolaye-vitch, Russian general.

62. Nadezdha Osipovna Pushkina (1775-1836), mother of Pushkin.
By Xavier de Mestre.

63. Sergey Lvovich Pushkin (1770-1848), father of Pushkin.

64. Pushkin as a child. Lithography by Heitmann.

65. Compare Pushkin with another Hanibal's descendant, Alexandre Serguéiévitch Neytkirkh, born in 1975!

66. Semion Hanibal, Nadejda Hanibal's cousin.

67. Lev Serguéiévitch Pushkin, the poet's brother.

68. Olga Serguéievna Pushkin. Pushkin's sister

Below: Pushkin's children by N. L. Lanskoy

69. Alexander Alexandrovitch Pushkin

70. Maria Alexandrovna Pushkin

71. Natalia Alexandrovna Pushkin

72. Gregory Alexandrovitch Pushkin

73. Pushkin, by Joëlle Esso, 2010.

EPILOGUE

On his death the black 'barine' left an enormous fortune to his children: numerous estates in Pskov and in the region near the capital, a house in St. Petersburg, (no. 29 in the street now known as Tchaikovsky Street), his well stocked library, his collection of mechanical tools and physics apparatus, 60,000 rubles in liquid assets (a great sum in his day) and no less than 1400 male serfs!

The death of the patriarch, possibly the oldest surviving member of Peter I's intimates, marked the end of an epoch. With him the last vestiges of the glorious era of the reforming Tsar disappeared. When he died at the age of nearly eighty-five the calm existence of the household at Suyda was immediately disrupted by Catherine II's 'unquiet century'. In the summer of 1783 the property was divided between the children in accordance with the law of 1731, in force in the state, and not according to the dead man's wishes. Ivan did not inherit the lands of Mikhailovskoe, though it appears that he received the house in St. Petersburg and other of his father's goods in compensation[202]. The estates at Pskov were divided between Hanibal's three other sons.

At the end of the century the fame of the Hanibals was still widespread in Russia thanks to the talent of the eminent General Ivan Hanibal. Catherine II asked him to leave Kherson in 1783 and return to the capital where she "had a special commission for him". In recognition of his services to the Crimea in the building of Kherson he was awarded a fourth honour, the Order of Saint Vladimir[203].

Peter Hanibal, a colonel since 1781, retired from the army on 19 November 1783 with the rank of Major General. Three months later

Ivan fell ill and he also retired aged 49. He was awarded the rank of general in chief of the Imperial Army and Catherine II accorded him the right to payment of his full salary for the rest of his life[204].

Ivan Hanibal was a confirmed bachelor. He never married and had no children. His irresponsible brother Osip was tried for bigamy, and Ivan supported the case of his former wife, Maria Alekseevna Hanibal and her young daughter, Nadezhda. Prince Dolgorukov writes: "He treated his sister-in-law and his niece with remarkable care and affection. They both found a loving and respectful welcome in his house and he made himself responsible for the education of his niece..."

Ivan Hannibal was particularly fond of Nadezhda. He made sure that Maria and the child were well provided for by withholding 10,000 roubles from Osip's inheritance for their use. He employed the "best governesses and tutors for her; she learnt French, dancing – in short the full education of a society lady..."

Nadezhda Osipovna Hanibal was a pretty young woman with a dark complexion which recalled her African heritage. "She was intelligent, lively and incredibly charming... in society she was known as 'the beautiful Creole'[205]. A young lieutenant captain, Sergey Lvovich Pushkin fell in love with her and asked for her hand. Her uncle Ivan, giving the family's assent to the marriage, justified his acceptance of the proposal by saying: "He isn't wealthy, but he's very well educated." The marriage took place in Suyda in the family church on 28 September 1796 and Ivan stood as their sponsor. The charming Nadezhda was twenty-one years old. A year later, on 20 December 1797, she gave birth to a daughter, Olga.

The century was a few months from its end when "the beautiful Creole" had a second child, a boy, born in Moscow on 27 May 1799 (6 June on the new calendar) and named him Alexander. He was destined to become, a few decades later, the greatest poet and literary genius in the history of Russia, and one of the greatest poets of all time: **Alexander Pushkin.**

ENDNOTES

Chapter 1: From Logone to Constantinople

1. Annie Lebeuf provides the information that "in the sixteenth century Giovanni Lorenzo Anania made the first toponomic and ethnic nomenclature of the region. It is of particular interest in that the principal capital cities of the Kotoko are included: *Macari* (Makari), *Uncusciuri* (Kussiri) ...*Lagane* (Lagon-Birni), *Calfe* (the Kanuri name for Goufeil)..." Lange (1972), p.302, and Lebeuf, *L'origine et la constitution des principautés kotoko (Cameroun Septentrional),* in "Contribution..." CNRS, Paris, p.211.

2. A. Lebeuf, *idem*. p. 212

3. Barth (1861) pp. 74-76.

4. Barth, (1861), p. 82. In his book Barth reports that the country of Logone "used to be made up, like that of the Musgu, of numerous little principalities. The most powerful of these was Honkel, that is until the Miara or Sultan Broua founded the town of Logone 150 years ago and took up residence there. This prince and his immediate successors were still pagans and there were very few Mohammedans in the town during those years..." For the name of the Miara at this time see also Rodinson, 1955, pp.75-82.

5. The question whether Hanibal was really of royal blood has been raised in the past. Pushkin was the subject of a satirical piece by one of his enemies (Bulgarin) which appeared in *"The Northern Bee"* No. 94, in 1830: "A multitude of poets and versifiers in many countries have been driven crazy by Lord Byron's extravagant aristocratic manners and ways

of thinking (God knows if he really thinks). Every one of them has set out to create for himself a lineage dating back at least 600 years. Good luck to them! May God grant that they do credit to their famous ancestors (who may or may not have existed); in any case noble lineage does not in itself confer fluency and intelligence on either prose or verse. It is no secret that a certain poet from Spanish America, another of Byron's imitators, offspring of a mulatto man or woman, I don't remember which, began to pretend that one of his ancestors was a Negro prince. In the town hall of the city it was discovered that long ago there was a lawsuit between the skipper of a ship and an assistant of his for this Negro, whom each of them wished to claim as his own, and that the skipper contended that he had bought the Negro for a bottle of rum. Who would have thought then that a versifier would acknowledge connection with that Negro? Vanitas vanitatum!"

Pushkin was very annoyed and at the end of his poem "My Genealogy" published a "Postscript" which is well-known in Russia:

> Bulgarin says he understands
> That my black grand-dad Hanibal
> Bought for a bottle of rum, once fell
> Into a drunk sea captain's hands.
> That glorious skipper set our state
> Upon its grand and mighty course
> And his great rudder took control
> Of the whole Empire by his force.
> My grandfather, so cheaply bought,
> The Tsar himself treated with trust
> And gave him welcome at his court.
> Black but never again a slave.*

*Translation into English from Elaine Feinstein, Pushkin, 1998, p.188

There was in fact very little documentary evidence of his ancestor's origins to justify Pushkin's claim that he was the son of an African prince. He was not deterred, however, from making it clear that he was proud of his African ancestry. Hanibal's own written testimony (1742) on his noble birth was sufficiently explicit. There is no reason to doubt him in view of the fact that he was well known to the Empress Elisabeth, the daughter of Peter I, to whom he addressed his request through the offices of the Senate. She would have been fully aware of his history. Another point to take into account – in the Ottoman seraglios, children of noble birth were as a priority assigned to the household of the Sultan (*endurun* in Turkish). Reports of the young Ibrahim's stay in Constantinople speak of him as a page in the household of Ahmed III. See the article "Where was Hanibal born?" in Appendix 1.

6. Pushkin, *Eugene Onegin* First Edition, 1825.

7. Rodinson, *idem.*

8. Decalo, (1987) pp. 185-186.

9. Lebeuf, p. 215.

10. UNESCO, vol.V, p. 502.

11. Kaké I.B., (1985) pp. 177-178.

12. Fisher A. and H., p. 13.

13. Kaké I.B., *idem.*

14. Lebeuf, p. 215.

15. UNESCO, vol. V, p. 129.

16. Kersnovski (1992) p. 13.

17. *Mercure de France*, June 1717, p. 93.

18. *Archeologia,* no.35, July-August 1970, p. 25.

19. *Ibid.*

20. *Encyclopaedia of Islam*, see dev<u>shirme</u>

21. Lapteva, *Historical Archives*, no.1 (1992), p. 183.

22. Lapteva, *Historical Archives*, no.1 (1992), p. 188.

23. *Ibid.*, p. 187.

Chapter 2: The black godson

24. In response to the question: "Why did Peter I so urgently require to have black children?" Eidelman writes: " Generally speaking it was very fashionable to have an 'Arap' (by which was meant a negro) or

a young black at Court. It gave an exotic flavour to European courtly life... but Peter's intention was not just to make an effect. When he sent secret instructions to procure some black children 'the best and the most intelligent' *he wanted to show that black children were no less gifted in science and the arts than the numerous self-willed Russian boys* (our italics). In other words his purpose was educational. It was of course a commonly held opinion at the time that black people were savages. The arrogance of the white colonisers knew no limits. As we can see Peter I had no time for old customs and prejudices; he judged a person's brain by his abilities, his hands by their skill and took no account of the colour of his skin..." Eidelman, (1991), p. 24. Note also that the Tsar had in his service three blacks whom he had recruited on contract in Amsterdam: one as a painter, one as a shipbuilder and one as the commander of a supply fleet at Vyborg. (Teletova, (1981) p. 133.

25. Teletova, (1978).

26. de Grunwald, (1953), p. 169.

27. Teletova, (1978) p. 273. The first writer to have identified this portrait as a probable representation of the Tsar with his black protégé.

28. De Grunwald, (1953) p. 169.

29. *Journal de campagne de Pierre I pour l'an 1714* ,(1854), p. 110.

30. Leets, (1984) p. 31.

31. Blagoi, (1937) pp. 75-76 Pushkin also recounts this anecdote.

32. Leets, p. 30.

33. The word 'arap' at the time was used in Russian to designate black people; at the Russian Court the young African was commonly referred to as Abraham arap, that is to say, Abraham the Black.

34. Golikov, (1843) vol. XV, pp. 156-157. Leets also quotes him on pages 29-30 of his book. Pushkin, however, refutes the story that Abraham was Peter I's valet. "Golikov," he writes, "says that he was first of all the Emperor's valet but that Peter, noticing that he was exceptionally gifted etc., etc...Golikov was wrong. Peter I did not have a personal valet; he was attended by his orderlies, among others by Orlov and Rumiantsev, – ancestors of our present illustrious families."

Chapter 3: In France

35. Feynberg, (1983) p. 45.

36. Chistiakov, p. 376.

37. Semievski, p. 505

38. Khmyrov, (1873) p. 9.

39. de Grunwald, p. 173

40. Leets, p. 32.

41. Contrary to the widely held opinion the word 'Moor', in frequent use in Europe in the past, was not used exclusively to refer to North Africans. In German, (Mohr), French, (more or maure), Russian, (mavr) and English, to cite only four languages, the word is used to designate black Africans as well. Shakespeare's *Othello, the Moor of Venice*, was a black African. See also the interesting article, *"The Moor: Light of Europe's Dark Age"*, by Wayne B. Chandler, in the book *African Presence in Early Europe*, edited by Ivan Van Sertima, 6 edition, 1993. For the French usage of the word, see for example, *Vocabulaire Historique du Moyen-Age*, by François Olivier Touati, Paris, *"La Boutique de l'Histoire Editions"*, 1995, p.136.

42. Leets, (1984) pp. 38-39.

43. *Ibid.* p. 39.

44. de Grunwald, pp. .258-261.

45. Leets, p. 40

46. *Ibid.* p. 28.

47. This quotation has been taken from a typewritten script entitled "La Fère, Garnison Traditionelle de l'Artillerie" and " Historique du Quartier Drouot" kindly placed at our disposition by the Town Hall, La Fère, France

48. Anna Hannibal, pp. 208-209.

49. Leets, p. 43.

50. *Ibid.* p. 45.

51. Mercury, (1976) pp.75-79

52. Kersnovski, *History of the Russian Army* (1992) p. 48.

53. Pekarski, vol.1 p. 42.

54. Leets, p. 49.

Chapter 4: Return to Russia

55. From 1722 Menshikov had been President of the College of War in the Russian Senate.

56. Pushkin's celebrated expression for the ultra-faithful of Peter the Great's followers.

57. The name given by Peter I to his new capital, St. Petersburg.

58. Eidelman, (1991). Pp. 28-29.

59. De Grunwald, p. 173.

60. Vegner, pp. 33-34

61. *"Literaturnyïa rossia"* Russian Literary Journal, issue of 10 September, 1976.

62. Vegner, (1937) p.34.

63. Luppov, p. 245.

64. According to Luppov's classification , the collection of the Tsar's black godson would be placed eighth, after those of Prince Golitsyn (2765 volumes), the Tsar's doctor, Arkesin (2527volumes), Peter I (1621), Senator Bruce (1579), the boyard Mateev (1301), the Metropolitan Yavorski (609), and the Director of the Printsetters of Moscow, the editor Polikarpov (581). See Luppov, Table 13.

65. *Ibid..* pp. 246-247.

66. The name of the Russian dynasty of the Tsars.

67. The Tsarevich Alexis had married the Austrian Emperor's sister-in-law, Princess Charlotte of Hanover-Wolfenbüttel.

68. Leets, p. 42.

69. Khmyrov, (1867) p. 124.

70. Choubinski,(1904) p. 931.

71. de Grunwald, p. 245.

72. Extract from the preface to Hannibal's book, *"The Slave Route"*.

73. Feinberg, p. 25.

Chapter 5 : Exile

74. Peter I had first met the young and lovely Martha Skavronskaya at Menshikov's house. Certain writers suggest that she was at that time Menshikov's mistress, but that the Tsar, struck by the young woman's beauty and intelligence, persuaded his general to relinquish her. He had her rebaptised as Catherine Alexeevna and made her his favourite.

75. Choubinski, p. 933.

76. *Ibid.* p. 934.

77. *Ibid.* p. 936.

78. *Ibid.* p. 936.

79. Leets, p. 59.

80. Khmyrov, p. 19.

81. Prince Menshikov

82. There is no identification of the person using this pseudonym

83. Pachkov's pseudonym

84. Mikhail Bestuzhev's pseudonym

85. Alexis Bestuzhev's pseudonym

86. Choubinski, p. 949.

87. Vegner, p. 55.

88. The anthropologist Anuchin, in accordance with his theory of Hanibal's Ethiopian origins, suggested that Hanibal might be a corruption of the place-name, Addi Balo (an area in the north of Ethiopia). The hypothesis is not tenable since it is now certain that Hanibal came from a quite different region of Africa. Another suggestion is that Peter I had given this name to his black protégé. This is also unlikely as there is no trace in the archives of Peter I of the name ever being used for

Abraham Petrov. Another indication is that Abraham always wrote the name with one 'n'. Most Russian writers spell it as 'Hannibal' as the reader will have noticed in all the quotations. For our part we have chosen to retain the spelling 'Hanibal' as it appears in all eighteenth century documents in the archives.

89. Choubinski, pp. 962-963.

90. Vegner.

Chapter 6 : Marriage

91. Teletova, (1981) p. 145.

92. Malevanov, p. 159.

93. Khmyrov, pp. 162-163.

94. Feinberg, p. 78.

95. The commonly accepted version in Russian literature is that Hanibal was Ethiopian by origin, and Feinberg accepted that he was Ethiopian. Logone, Abraham's birthplace, as we have demonstrated, was a town in the north of present day Cameroon on the frontier with Chad.

96. Ley, (1959) p .8.

97. Sergev (1989), p. 81.

98. Khmyrov, p. 30.

99. Opatovich, (1877) vol. XVIII, p .71.

100. Optaovich, (1877).

Chapter 7 : New life

101. Leets, pp. 94-95.

102. An article relating to this question appeared in the Swedish paper *Stockholm Dagblad,* 11 June, 1899, and was kindly translated and made available to me by Ms. Fransesca Quartey. I wish to express my thanks to her at this point.

103. Leets, p. 84. According to this writer the interior of the Preobazhensky Cathedral (its present name) has been preserved unaltered from the eighteenth century, the time of Hanibal's marriage.

104. Opatovich, p. 73.

105. Leets, p. 85.

106. *Ibid.* p .86.

107. Russian writers of the nineteenth century like Anuchin and Annenkov (a celebrated Russian literary critic) were imbued with racial prejudice against Africans. They accepted without question Opatovich's information (on Eudoxia Hanibal's accusations) although it had never been verified, and in their publications described such cruel behaviour as "natural" to Africans! They were the source of similar negative clichés about Africans in much of Russian literature and Hanibal was depicted as a cruel and violent man...It is not impossible that Hanibal, who was deeply hurt by his wife's disloyalty and her attempt to poison him, may have been violent towards her; but it is ridiculous to suggest that any violence was due to his "African nature". Anna S. Hanibal, one of the black general's direct descendants, replies as follows to such accusations: "Writers on the Hanibal family are in the habit of attributing their so-called cruelty to their African roots. The accusation is unjust; one has only to read the chronicles of the ancient Russian families and the notes and memoirs relative to serfdom – from the first half of the eighteenth century and also into the nineteenth – to see that cruelty was a feature of the period and not confined to Africans. Despite his origins Abraham was a real Russian. He had been educated by the great Peter, lived many years at close quarters to him and could not be anything but Russian; if Russians had not been so consistently cruel and ruthless towards their families, their subordinates and their serfs it is unlikely that Hanibal would have resorted to violence in these circumstances." Vegner makes the same point: "One can not blame the African character for actions which have nothing to do with Africa."

108. Leets, p .96.

109. Sergev, p. 85.

110. Eidelman, p. 41.

111. Leets, p. 103.

112. *Ibid.* p. 103.

113. Malevanov, p. 161.

114. Lets, p. 102.

115. *Ibid.* p. 103.

116. For further information on Prince von Hesse-Homburg see Chapter 8.

117. Gastfreynd, (1903).

Chapter 8 : General

118. Khmyrov, p. 137.

119. Eidelman (1991) p. 53.

120. Old Russian word for a rural district.

121. Tsarevna means daughter of the Tsar, as Tsarevich means son of the Tsar.

122. This document was preserved in the USSR Central Historical Archives, Reference f.1329, op.1,d.66,1.129.

123. Chubinski, p. 965.

124. *Ibid*. p. 965.

125. *Russian Archives,*(1882) Book 1, p. 210.

126. In Tsarist Russia serfs were de facto slaves who belonged to the nobles in charge of the land. Only adult men, mostly heads of families, were included in the registers of the administration. Thus a property of five hundred and thirty-nine serfs in fact amounted to more than a thousand individuals.

127. It would appear that the elephant symbolised Africa and the eagle Russia. The elephant also refers to Hannibal of Carthage who fought on elephant back.

128. According to Eidelman the Latin FVMMO means "I am a cannon" and the cannons, cannon balls and standards included in the coat of arms signify the prowess of the Hanibals in battle. See Eidelman, (1983) p. 87.

129. The single storey house with a garden still stands in Tallinn, the capital of Estonia, at no. 1, Toompea Street.

130. Russia was at war with Sweden.

131. Anna Hanibal, p. 241.

132. Letter of 29 July, 1742, from Hanibal to Cherkasov, see Gastfreynd (1904) p. 30.

133. Peter the Great conquered Reval in 1710.

134. Gastfreynd, p. 31.

135. Malevanov, p. 165.

136. The negotiations between Russia and Sweden, which would eventually lead to the Treaty of Abo, had been under way for many months.

137. Leets, p. 144.

138. *Ibid.*

139. *Ibid.*

140. Troyat, (1977) p. 14.

141. Gastfreynd, p. 61.

142. Malevanov, p. 1165, Leets, p. 142

143. Leets, p. 142

144. *Ibid.* pp. 146-147

145. Khmyrov, p. 56

146. *Ibid.* p. 56

147. Teletova, (1981) p. 154.

148. *Ibid.* p. 154.

149. Teletova, (1981) p. 278.

150. Opatovich p. 76

151. *Ibid.* p. 75.

152. *Ibid.* p. 76

153. Granovskaya, (1992) pp. 70-77.

154. Prianichikov, (1981)

Chapter 9 : Chief engineer 1752-1762

155. Leets, p. 149.

156. Malevanov, p. 165 and Leets, p. 152.

157. Opatovich, p. 78.

158. Malevanov, p. 165.

159. Leets, p. 153.

160. Malevanov, p. 166.

161. Leets, pp. 153-154.

162. *Ibid.* pp. 153-154

163. Ivan Shuvalov was the President of the Academy of Fine Arts.

164. Blanchard, (1979).

165. Marc-Pierre d'Argenson was Secretary of State for War in the French government from 1743-1759, in Blanchard, (1979).

166. The Seven Years War was between the Anglo-Prussian Alliance and the Austrian-French-Russian Coalition. It lasted from 1756 to 1763.

167. Leets, pp. 155-156.

168. Central Military State Archives of the Russian Navy f235 op1, d.283,1.265.

169. Blanchard, p. 218.

170. 6 Leets, p. 157.

171. Troyat, p. 161

172. Ibid. p. 162.

173. Khmyrov, p. 63.

174. *Ibid.* p. 64.

171. Troyat, p. 168.

172. Teletova, (1981) p. 146 and Leets, p. 162.

173. Leets, p. 163.

174. Troyat, pp. 47-48.

175. Paina, p. 413 and Leets, p. 162.

176. Troyat, p. 205.

177. Leets, p.162.

Chapter 10 : The black lord

178. The original of this Imperial message can be seen in the Museum of History and Art in the Russian town of Pskov.

179. Gastfreynd, pp. 12-13.

180. Pushkin, 1825, in the first edition of *Eugene Onegin.* See also the "German Biography" of Rotkirkh.

181. Dictionary of Russian Biography (1914), Vol. Gaag, p. 217.

182. *Ibid.* p. 217.

183. Leets, p. 170.

184. *Ibid.* p. 179.

185. The hetman Oguinsky was the leader of a revolt in Lithuania.

186. Granovskaya, (1992) pp. 82-83.

187. *Ibid.* p. 83.

188. Teletova, (1981) p. 154.

189. *Ibid.* p. 154.

190. Joseph – in Russian this is Yosif or Osip (diminutive). He was Hanibal's third son who married Maria Alekseevna Pushkin in 1773.

191. Sophie Hanibal, born in 1759, was Hanibal's youngest child. She was 17 in 1776.

192. Teletova, (1981) p. 154. The original manuscript of Hanibal's will is in the Central Russian Historical Archives. reference f.1405, op.1, d.5168. 1-12-13.

193. Teletova, (1981) p. 155.

194. Tsarskoe Selo was the Imperial residence in the St. Petersburg region.

195. The original of this document is on display at the Museum of History and Art, Pskov (Russia).

196. Leets, p. 171.

197. For Osip's second marriage see Granovkaya, (1992) p. 87.

198. Teletova, (1981) p. 156.

199. Teletova, *Ibid.,* see also Lyublinski in *"Literary Archives"* vol. 1 (1938) p. 87.

200. Dolgorukov, (1867).

201. In September 1971 Gatchina District Council authorised the architect M. Meysel to erect a new monument, a funerary column in granite, on the site. Cf. Leets, p. 168 and also the newspapers *Smena* of 22 December 1991 and *Constable* (special edition of the *Gatchina Pravda*) of 23 June 1991 no. 81.

202. Teletova ,(1981) p. 156.

203. A bust of Ivan Hanibal was erected at the entrance to Kherson in recognition of his work as founder of the town.

204. Leets, p. 171.

205. Granovskaya, (1992)

APPENDIX 1

WHERE WAS IBRAHAM HANIBAL'S BIRTHPLACE?

It is common knowledge that Peter the Great's godson, Abraham Petrovich Hanibal, was an African in eighteenth century Russia who rose to be general in the Russian army, as well as being an eminent mathematician and a leading fortifications engineer. It was not, however, known which part of Africa he came from. There is no historical documentation available. It had been generally accepted that he was of "Abyssinian" origin, a theory advanced in 1899 by D. N. Anuchin, an academician, anthropologist and geographer who was highly regarded in his time. Let us examine Anuchin's theory concerning Hanibal's origins.

In the archives there is a single, very precious testimony from Hanibal himself: "I am originally from Africa, of illustrious noble lineage. I was born in the town of Logone, in the territory of my father, who also ruled over two other cities." These words were written by Hanibal in 1742 in a request to the Senate to grant him a coat of arms. There is no mention of which part of Africa he came from. His son, Peter, is not clear on the matter either. He wrote: "My father...was a negro, the son of a King." Pushkin wrote of his African ancestor: "My great-grandfather, Annibal, was kidnapped on the shores of Africa at the age of eight and taken to Constantinople." Pushkin also recounts how Hanibal's sister, Lagane, swam after the boat that was taking her brother away into slavery. Pushkin never names Hanibal's country, only saying that his great-grandfather "was a negro, the son of a reigning Prince." Abyssinia is never mentioned until the appearance of "The German Biography" of Hanibal, written after his death by his German son-in-law, Rotkirkh. Neither Peter Hanibal (who preserved "The German Biography") nor Pushkin, who translated it, seem to have attached any importance to the mention of Abyssinia, or for that matter to the other fanciful suggestions in the biography, such as the ties of blood with Hannibal of Carthage. The only serious testimony comes from Hanibal himself, when he speaks of Africa and his native city, Lagon or Logone. Serious research, I should like to suggest, should therefore be based on Hanibal's own words. Anuchin, however took "The German Biography" as his point of departure. The mention of Abyssinia led him to look for Hanibal's homeland in the area known as Abyssinia in the nineteenth century, not at all the same place as the Abyssinia of the period of Hanibal's birth. The *General History of Africa,* published by UNESCO, is precise on the term "Habesistan" or "Abyssinia" as used in Ottoman sources of the sixteenth to eighteenth century. "It comprised all the territory south of Egypt as far as Zanzibar island or Mozambique in eastern Africa." The author of "The German Biography" like most of his contemporaries, knowing little or nothing about Africa, probably thought of Abyssinia as the vast Empire whose frontiers reached "the Kingdom of the Kongo and the river Niger to the west and the natural barrier of "The Mountains of the Moon" to the south." Anuchin had only to study old maps to see that formerly Abyssinia or Ethiopia was the name given to almost all of Africa south of Egypt. Strangely, however, he limited his research to the territory known in his own time as Ethiopia.

There are two key words one must know to understand Anuchin's article: one is **Arap** (black, negro, from the Turkish) in old Russian and **Abyssin** (Ethiopian, the oldest Russian word for black people, from the Greek). Both words have been used in Russian to designate the black-skinned people of Africa. Anuchin made a fundamental distinction between the two terms. "The black race is inferior to the white on the intellectual and cultural level." He thought that the Abyssinians were a different race, a mix of Blacks and Semites and thus "capable of creating a much more advanced culture." Like other European anthropologists of his time Anuchin ranked the Abyssinians with the "Hamites", a white race which was thought to have civilised the African continent. (The theory of the Hamites is "one of history's greatest mysteries", cf. UNESCO publications.)

Anuchin was convinced "that it was a matter of doubt that a pure-bred negro...would have been able to reach the intellectual heights of Abraham Hannibal...or that in the course of time the great-grandson of that negro, A. S. Pushkin, would have been the genius who ushered in the new era of a European nation's literary and artistic development." The academician would have found it humiliating to admit that Pushkin had negro antecedents. Thus Anuchin ignored the fact that Hanibal himself claimed to be a black African and that his contemporaries saw him as such; he ignored Pushkin's claims and those of Hanibal's other descendants, and in spite of all the evidence came to the conclusion accepted as authoritative for the past hundred years in all studies of Pushkin. Admittedly Maria Tsvetayeva (the famous Russian poetess) wrote that "before the birth of racism Pushkin, by his very birth, proved it nonsense." Vladimir Nabokov (winner of the Nobel Prize for Literature) described Anuchin's article as "a composition which merits nothing but criticism from every point of view, historical, ethnographical and geographical."

.Nabokov was of course right. There are many facts which disprove the "Hamitic-Abyssinian" version, both historically and geographically. Anuchin claimed among other things to have located the region of Logone in Abyssinia, in the province of Hammassien, but he did not provide a map of that region. He also imagined that Hanibal's father was the ruler of the region, with the capital at Debaroa (Dobarva). According to him this town *"might well been known as Logon after the region in which it was situated.."*(our italics). N. Khokhlov, a contemporary researcher, travelled to the areas Anuchin described and found no trace of Logon. He did find a little village by the name of Logo, a few kilometres from Debaroa. Historians and specialists in the cartography of the region assured him that apart from Logo, no other locality had a name anything like Logone and that there had never been a town of that name in the country. The proper name Lagane is unknown in local nomenclature. In his disappointment at having found nothing to support his theory in Northern Ethiopia, Khokhlov accused Pushkin of "having too much imagination"! It would have been more logical to conclude that one should look elsewhere, since no town by the name of Logone existed in Ethiopia, and the name Lagane was unknown there.

Having made a systematic study of the history and toponymy of Africa in the sixteenth to eighteenth century, I have discovered that there was only one town called Logone in the whole continent. It was not in "Abyssinia" but in central Africa, south of Lake Chad, in the northernmost part of the modern state of Cameroon. This area of Africa was formerly known as Central Sudan. The city of Logone was mentioned by European travellers from the sixteenth century onwards as one of the region's capital cities. It was an ancient fortified town and the capital of the principality of Logone. Hanibal must have been well aware in his request to the Senate that the name of the town was sufficient without specifying the country of his birth. His father's kingdom had the same name as the town where he was born! The history of Logone at the end of the sixteenth century shows that the principality was subject to frequent attacks from its powerful neighbours, in particular from the Sultanate of Bagirmi which had trade links with the Ottoman Empire. Ibrahim, the son of the prince of Logone, might well have been taken prisoner in the course of one of the battles and then sent to Constantinople. The ruler of Logone at the time was Miara (a princely title) Broua. In the history of Logone he is remembered as the builder of the capital city with its massive fortifications. Many a European traveller noted them with amazement right until the nineteenth century. One might wonder whether Hanibal's talents in fortification were inherited!

There are other indications. The Prince of Logone had three important towns under his jurisdiction at the end of the seventeenth century, as Hanibal claimed in his statement to the Senate. What is more the town of Logone was situated on the banks of a long navigable river (one cannot help but think of Hanibal's account of being kidnapped and taken on board ship). The word "Lagane" is used in the local language to mean the river and the inhabitants of Logone were the "Lagane or Lagwane". Thus, the only two words of his native African language which Hanibal retained and passed on to his family – the name of his birthplace and the name of his sister – were words which existed in the language of the principality. In view of these discoveries it seems to me that one can make a convincing case for the town of Logone in the Lake Chad region to be the very one that Hanibal knew as his home. There is no other town of that name to be found in Africa and the seventeenth century history of this African city corresponds closely to all we know of Hanibal's childhood. Pushkin was not after all mistaken about his great-grandfather's negro African origins. Logone, a town in the heart of Africa, on the banks of the river Logone, the capital of the principality of Logone, should in future appear on Pushkin's African map in place of the tiny Ethiopian village of Logo.

APPENDIX 2

REPORT BY IRINA YURIEVA

Principal secretary to the Pushkin Society of Russia. A report on the paper presented by Dieudonné Gnammankou on 28/08/95 to the International Conference *"Pushkin Studies outside Russia"* in Moscow, entitled "New Research on Pushkin's Africa".

Dieudonné Gnammankou's research has been guided by the current interest in the African homeland of Pushkin's ancestors. Dieudonné Gnammankou is the first to make a firm identification of the town of Logone or Lagon (claimed by Abraham Petrovich Hanibal as his birthplace). He has assembled a large body of evidence on the history of Logone and has interpreted it in the light of facts which were familiar but had not been scientifically analysed.

He has made a critical study of all previous writing on the theme and based his research on the lines suggested by Vladimir Nabakov. He rejects the generally accepted version that Pushkin's ancestors were from Ethiopia, as proposed by the academician Dimitri Anuchin in 1899. He dismisses D. Anuchin's work as pseudo-scientific, both from the point of view of the ideology which informed his theory and also through mistaken perspectives on the history and geography of Africa. Dimitri Anuchin looked for Hanibal's birthplace within the boundaries of Abyssinia as it was in the late nineteenth century. It was not the same area as the Abyssinia of the seventeenth and eighteenth centuries. This was the Abyssinia of Hanibal's time and of the period of the "German

Biography", the only document where Abyssinia is mentioned in the whole archive relating to Hanibal's birthplace.

Toponymy was not a science that existed at the turn of the nineteenth century, which may explain why Anuchin made such an arbitrary decision in equating the town of Logone with the Abyssinian village of Logo Chova. It is a matter of regret that no later researchers, with the exception of Nabokov, attempted to challenge Anuchin's conclusions. Dieudonné Gnammankou is the first to demonstrate Anuchin's mistakes in the area of toponymic research. He is also the first to make a scientific analysis of the results of historical investigations in the region we know today as Abyssinia. He proves that in the territory investigated by Anuchin there was never at any time a town called Logone, the word Lagane is quite unknown in the region, and the history of the area (in the late seventeenth and early eighteenth century) does not fit in with the little we know of Hanibal's childhood and the circumstances of his abduction to Istanbul.

Dieudonné Gnammankou's research is based on the recent work by UNESCO on the history of Africa and makes use of modern scientific concepts of toponymy. The study of proper names has proved a major factor in understanding the historical relationship between language and geography. Hanibal himself provided us and his descendants, including Pushkin, with the vital information that is central to the research, and Dieudonné

Gnammankou has made a brilliant exposition of the whole issue.

He provides definitive evidence that there is only one town in Africa named Logone (also known as Logone-Birni). It is situated in the region of Lake Chad, in the north of the modern state of Cameroon. In the 16th-18th centuries it was the capital of the kingdom of Logone. A study of the history of Logone has shed light on many areas of doubt and contradiction in the history of Pushkin's ancestry:

1. It is now possible to put a correct interpretation on the claims made by Hanibal himself, namely that he was born "in his father's territory", "in the town of Logone" . It would probably have seemed unnecessary to name his father's kingdom as well as the capital, as they were the same: Logone.

2. It gives credence to Pushkin's version of the family legend concerning Hanibal's sister, Lagane, who threw herself into the water in pursuit of the boat taking her brother into slavery and was drowned in the attempt. The town of Logone is situated on the banks of a navigable river, the Logone. Another interesting point is that the local word for "river" is *lagane* and the people of the area are the Lagane or Lagwane.

3. Hanibal's first name, Abraham / Ibrahim / Abram is reminiscent of Broua, the name of the ruler of Logone in the late seventeenth century.

The linguistic evidence is irrefutable. The place names Logone/ Lagon, the ethnic names Lagane / Lagwane, the geographical feature Lagane, all support Dieudonné Gnammankou's hypothesis that the town of Logone was Hanibal's birthplace. Furthermore the history of Logone at the end of the seventeenth century confirms the information we have on Hanibal's childhood. The evidence is convincing: there were wars with the neighbouring Moslem states who traded with the Ottoman Empire, sending prisoners and slaves taken in battle; the accounts of European travellers (from the sixteenth to the nineteenth centuries) correspond to Hanibal's recollections; and the rebuilding of Logone with massive fortifications by Prince Broua in the seventeenth century (a fact that suggests that Hanibal's talents in fortification could have been inherited from his father) and so on.

Having identified the town of Logone in the heart of Africa as the birthplace of Hanibal we can return to Pushkin. He claimed to be the "descendant of negroes", that his great-grandfather was an "arap", a Russian word which to him clearly meant "black African". His negroid features are evident in his self portraits and the portraits of Hanibal we find among his manuscripts. Previous writers, relying on Anuchin's theory, have been obliged to discount all Pushkin wrote on his African ancestors as a flight of fancy. Dieudonné Gnammankou's work confirms the accuracy of Pushkin's accounts and provides a rich background for specialists in the work of the great poet and his frequent allusions to Hanibal and his African ancestors.

Dieudonné Gnammankou's paper, presented at the International Scientific Conference in Moscow, aroused enormous and well deserved interest among the specialists involved in the discussions. The mass media also took it up, especially the television chains "Ostankino", RTR and NTV, who presented the research of Dieudonné Gnammankou as one of the main news stories of the day.

Dr. es-Lettres Irina Yurieva
Principal secretary of the Assembly
of the Pushkin Society of Russia.

APPENDIX 3

AUTOBIOGRAPHICAL NOTE BY HANIBAL'S SON,
PETER ABRAMOVICH HANIBAL (1742-1826)

My father served in the Russian army, was promoted several times and was awarded the rank of General in Chief with the Orders of Saint Anne and Saint Alexander Nevsky. He was a negro, his father was of noble lineage, a ruling prince, and my father was taken hostage. He was abducted from the Court of Constantinople and sent to our sovereign, Peter I.

HIS MILITARY CAREER AND HIS EDUCATION

He was educated at court by our sovereign of glorious and eternal memory, Peter the Great, in person; he was present at all the battles and military campaigns in which the sovereign himself took part. The sovereign showed him great kindness and he was baptised in the town of Grodno[206] during the sovereign's visit to Poland. The sovereign was his godfather and the Queen of Poland his godmother[207]. He was given the name Peter, but during his childhood he wept when he was called by this name, and the Tsar ordered that he should be called by the old name from before the baptism, Abraham. In 1716 the Tsar sent him to France where he served in the French army and reached the rank of captain of Artillery. In 1723 he returned to Russia, following a ukase from his Majesty; he was made lieutenant bombardier in the company of Bombardiers of the Preobrazhensky Regiment of the Imperial Guard and ordered to teach the sciences of engineering and artillery – the subjects he had studied – to a company made up of young men.

Shortly before the death of our sovereign, Peter I, my father was sent on a mission to Riga to inspect and restore the fortifications there. When he returned at the end of the mission the Tsar was no longer of this world. He presented himself to the sovereign, Catherine I, who received him kindly, and he continued to live in the palace as he had previously. In 1730, on the ukase of the ex-Supreme Secret Council, he was posted to the garrison at Tobolsk with the rank of major, and on 25September of the same year he was transferred to the Engineering Corps as captain on a decree from Her Imperial Majesty. In 1723[208] , on an ukase from Her Majesty in response to his request, he was retired from the army for reasons of health. He was married in Pernov[209] to a Lutheran woman, Christina Matveevna, née Sjöberg, and bought a farm...made up of several villages, in the town where he was living[210]. He had separated from his first wife, a Greek woman, but had kept her daughter, Polixena[211]. In 1740, on the decision of the benevolent Empress, Elizabeth I[212], he returned to service and was promoted to the rank of Lieutenant Colonel in the Artillery. On 12 January 1742, on a decree of Her Imperial Majesty, he was promoted to Major General in the army and Chief Commander of Reval. On 25 April, 1752, he was transferred by Imperial decree to the Engineering Corps, retaining his rank. Later he was appointed General Engineer, then General in Chief, and put in charge of the construction of the canals at Ladoga, Kronstadt and Rogervik[213].

In 1760[214] he was retired from the army by the Emperor Peter III. He died on 21April 1781. My mother had died in the previous February. After his retirement they lived in the countryside on the property my father had bought at Suyda, 55 versts from St. Petersburg, in Ingria. They were buried in the village church at Voskresenskoe.

At his death his children were as follows: Ivan (Lieutenant General) Peter (Colonel in the Artillery), Joseph [Osip] (Captain of second rank in the Naval Artillery), Isaac (Captain of the third rank in the Naval Artillery) and the daughters – Elizabeth, married to Pushkin and a widow, Anna, the wife of General Neelov, and Sophie, the wife of Rotkirkh. By the Divine Will all my brothers and sisters and brothers-in-law have died with the passing years. I am the only one still living and the oldest of the Hanibals.

I will now recount the story of my own birth, my military career and the events of my life. I was born on 21 June, 1742, at 10pm, at Reval, the town where my father was Commander in Chief. The Empress Elizabeth Petrovna, of eternal memory, and her illustrious successor, Peter III, were my godparents by default. At the time my father had received the grant of land at Mikhailovskoe with five hundred serfs [569 to be exact], in the district of Opotchesk under the governor of Pskov. My father was baptised in Grodno in Poland and his godparents were the sovereign Peter the Great and the Queen of Poland[215].

APPENDIX 4

THE FIRST PART OF ALEXANDER PUSHKIN'S AUTOBIOGRAPHY

Our family is descended from a Prussian immigrant, *radchi* or *ratchi,* man of honouraccordingto our chronicler, that is a noble or a notable man), who arrived in Russia in the days of the rule of Saint Alexander Yaroslavich Nevski. His descendants are the Musins,the Boborichevs, the Miatlevs, the Povodovs, the Kamenskis, the Buturlins, the Kologrivovs, the Sherifedinovs and the Tovarkovs. My ancestors' names appear in every phase of Russian history. Few families of note survived unscathed in the appalling slaughter of the reign of Tsar Ivan Vasileivich the Terrible, but historians note the name of Pushkin among them. Gregory Gavrilovich Pushkin was one of the most remarkable characters of the Age of the Usurpers. In the Inter-regnum, according to Karamzin, another Pushkin, alone with Izmayilov at the head of an army that had been cut off *accomplished his task honourably.* Four Pushkins signed the charter electing the Romanovs to the throne, and one of them, the Okol'nichi, Matthew Stepanovich, signed the act of the council abolishing the code of pre-eminence (which does not do his character much credit). Under Peter I, his son, the official spokesman, Feydor Mateevich, was convicted of plotting against the sovereign and executed at the same time as Tsykler and Sokovnin. My great-grandfather, Alexander Petrovich, was married to the youngest daughter of Count Golovin, of the first regiment of the Andreevski Cavalry. He died young, having murdered his young wife in an attack of madness as she was giving birth to their child. His only son, Leon

Alexandrovich, served in the artillery and remained loyal to Peter III in the revolt of 1762. He was imprisoned in the fortress and set free two years later. He did not return to the service but from then on lived either in Moscow or on his country estates.

My grandfather was a fiery-tempered and cruel man. His first wife, born Voyeykova, died on a bed of straw in the cell to which he had confined her. She had been accused, falsely or otherwise, of a liaison with a Frenchman, her sons' former tutor, whom he had sentenced to be hanged, feudal fashion, in the servants' courtyard. His second wife, born Chicherina, led a terrible life with him. One day he ordered her to dress and accompany him on a visit to some place or other. My grandmother was on the point of giving birth and felt unwell but dared not refuse. Her pains began while they were on the road. My grandfather ordered the coachman to stop and the child was born then and there – it could have been my father. The new mother was taken home half dead and put to bed in all her finery, still wearing her diamonds. I do not know the whole story. My father never spoke of my grandfather's eccentricities and the old servants are dead long since.

My mother's family history is even more extraordinary. Her grandfather was a negro, the son of a minor ruling prince. The Russian ambassador to Constantinople somehow succeeded in abducting him from the seraglio where he was being held hostage and sent him to Peter I with two other young black boys. The sovereign had little Ibrahim baptised at Vilna in 1707 with the Queen of Poland, the wife of Augustus, and gave him the surname Hanibal. On baptism he was given the name Peter, but as he would burst into tears in dislike at being called by the new name, he was known as Abraham throughout his life. His elder brother appeared in Petersburg, offering to pay a ransom for his release, but Peter was not willing to part with his godson. Hanibal was his constant companion until 1716. He was then sent to Paris where he spent some time at the Military School, joined the French army, and was wounded in the head during the Spanish War, "in a battle underwater" (as it is described in the manuscript of his biography). He returned to Paris where he lived for a long time amid the distractions of high society. Peter I sent for him more than once, but Hanibal was in no hurry to return and stayed on under various pretexts. Finally the sovereign wrote to him that he had no intention of forcing him to return against his will, that he would leave it to him to decide whether to stay in France or go back to Russia, and that whatever the case he would never desert his former protégé. Hanibal was very moved by this letter and immediately set off for Petersburg. The sovereign came to meet him and gave him the icon of Peter and Paul, which his sons preserved but which I have been unable to trace. The Sovereign conferred on him the rank of Lieutenant Captain in the company of Bombardiers in the Preobrazhensky regiment. Peter himself was its captain, as is well known. That was in 1722.

His fortunes changed after the death of Peter the Great. Menshikov feared his influence over the Emperor Peter II and found a means of distancing him from the Court. Hanibal was made a major at the garrison of Tobolsk and then sent to Siberia to measure the Great Wall of China. Hanibal remained there some time in considerable boredom and then on his own initiative returned to Petersburg, having heard that Menshikov had been disgraced. He hoped for the protection of the Dolgoruky princes with whom he had connections. The fate of the Dolgorukys is well known but Münnich saved Hanibal by sending him in secret to a country estate in the Reval region, where he lived for ten years in a state of constant anxiety. For the rest of his life he could not hear the sound of a bell without trembling. On the accession of the Empress Elizabeth Hanibal wrote to her with the words of the Evangelist: "Remember me when you come into your kingdom". Elizabeth quickly brought him to court, made him first Brigadier and shortly afterwards Major General and General in Chief, granted him several villages in the regions of Pskov and Petersburg, Zuevo, Bor, Petrovskoe and others in the former region, Kobrino, Suyda and Taytsy in the latter. He was also presented with the village of Ragola near Reval, where he was for a period Commander in Chief of the place. He retired in the reign of Peter III and died a philosopher (so says his German biographer) at the age of 93. He had written his memoirs in French, but in an attack of panic, to which he was subject, he had them and other precious papers burnt in his presence. His family life was as unfortunate as that of my other great-grandfather, Pushkin. His first wife, a beautiful Greek woman, gave him a white daughter. He divorced her and forced her to take the veil in the convent of Tikhvin, but kept her daughter, Polixena, with him, gave her a good education and a rich dowry, but never allowed her into his presence. His second wife, Christina-Regina von Sjöberg, married him while he was Commander in Chief at Revel and gave him a large number of black children of both sexes.

His eldest son, Ivan Abramovich, is as worthy of note as his father. He went into the army against the wishes of his father, served with distinction, and only obtained his mother's pardon by begging for it on his knees. At Chesme he was in command of the fire ships and was one of those who escaped from a ship when it burst into flames. In 1770 he took Navarino; in 1779 he was responsible for the building of Kherson. To this day his edicts are in force in southern Russia. In 1821 I met old men there who retained vivid memories of him. He quarrelled with Potemkin, but the sovereign supported him and awarded him the Order of Saint Alexander. He left the service and thereafter spent most of his time at Suyda, highly respected by all the eminent men of that glorious epoch. Suvorov himself refrained from his pranks in his presence, and was received without any veiling of mirrors or any such formality.

My grandfather was Osip Abramovich (his real name was Yanuarl, but my great-grandmother refused to use it, as she found it difficult to pronounce with her Germanic accent. She used to say in strongly accented Russian: "The black tevil gives me black children and then they have tevilish names". – My grandfather served in the navy and married Maria Alexeevna Pushkina, the daughter of the voyvode of Tambov, my father's grandfather's brother (the second cousin of my mother). It was another unhappy marriage. The wife was jealous and the husband unfaithful. They were miserable, quarrelled incessantly and finally divorced. My grandfather's character was typically African; he was passionate by nature but his behaviour was frighteningly rash. He made amazing mistakes. He married another woman, having presented the authorities with a forged death certificate for his first wife. My grandmother was obliged to appeal to the Empress who took a personal interest in the affair. My grandfather's second marriage was declared illegal, my grandmother regained custody of her three-year-old daughter, and my grandfather was sent to join his fleet in the Black Sea. They lived apart for thirty years. My grandfather died in 1807, on his estate in the province of Pskov, from the effects of a dissolute life. My grandmother died eleven years later on the same estate. They were reunited in death and lie side by side in the monastery of Sviatogorsk.

APPENDIX 5

CHRONOLOGY

Year	Events in Russia	Hanibal
1696	Miarré Brouha reigning in Logone	Birth at Logone (West Africa)
1703	The principality of Logone was attacked by Sultan Abd el Kader of Baghirmi (up to 1707)	Victim of the slave trade and taken to the Ottoman Empire
	Events in the Ottoman Empire	
1703	Accession of Sultan Ahmed III	Page boy in the Sultan's seraglio in Constantinople
	Events in Russia	
1704	Narva captured by the Russian army	At Peter I's palace
1705		Baptised at Vilnius, 13 July.
1706	Charles XII of Sweden's victory at Grodno	Drummer in the Preobrazhensky Regiment
1708	Peter I's victory at Lesnaya	
1709	Poltava: the Russian army crushes the Swedish army	Abraham's 13th birthday
1710	Reval taken by Peter I	
1711	Battle of Pruth River Creation of the Russian Senate Marriage of Peter I to Catherine	
1714	Naval battle of Hangö	Tsar's orderly and private secretary
1717	Peter I tours Europe	Peter I's warrant officer

Year	Events in Russia	Hanibal
	Events in France	
	Peter I visits Paris	Studying mathematics in Paris
	John Law's reforms	
1717	War with Spain begins	Lieutenant in the French army
		Wounded at Fontarabie
1720	Artillery School at La Fère founded	Student engineer at La Fère
	Bélidor publishes his « *Sommaire d'un cours d'architecture militaire, civile et Hydraulique* »	
1723		Captain the French army
		Gains engineering diploma
	Return to Russia	
1724		Peter I's appoints him Lieutenant in the Preobrazhensky regiment and Professor of Mathematics and Military Engineering Translator in chief at the Palace
1725	Death of Peter I	Mathematics tutor
	Accession of Catherine I	to the future Tsar Peter II
1726		Presents Catherine I with his two volume manuscript, "Practical Geometry" and "Fortification"
1727	Death of Catherine I	
	Accession of Peter II	
	Menshikov becomes	Exile in Siberia.
	« Generalissimo »	Takes the name « Hanibal »
1730	Death of Peter II	Exile ended
	Anna Ivanovna becomes Empress	Appointed Major at Tobolsk
		Captain Engineer at Pernov
1731		Married Eudoxia Andréevna Dioper
		Professor of Military Engineering at Pernov
		Birth of Eudoxia Hanibal's white baby
1732		Demands divorce. Poison affair

Year	Events in Russia	Hanibal
1733	War of Polish Succession 1733- 1735	Purchases Kariakula estate (Estonia) Retires to the country Meets Christina Regina von Sjöberg
1735		Ivan Abramovich Hanibal born 5 June
1736	War with Turkey until 1739	Marries Swedish Christina Regina von Sjöberg at Reval
1737		Birth of Elisabeth Abramovna Hanibal
1740	Death of Anna Ivanovna The baby Ivan VI, Tsar Biron becomes Regent Palace revolution, Biron arrested, Anna Leopoldovna becomes Regent Münnich, Prime Minister	
1741	Sweden declares war on Russia. Lassi named army chief. Another palace revolution: Accession of Elisabeth Petrovna	Recalled to service Lieutenant-Colonel at Reval Birth of Anna Abramovna Hanibal, his second daughter
1742		Major-General and First Commander at Reval Elisabeth Petrovna gives him the Mikhailovskoe estate
	Coronation of Elisabeth Petrovna	The young Alexander Suvorov joins the army
	Russian army occupies Finland Sweden capitulates	Acting Governor of Reval Birth of Peter Abramovich Hanibal
1743	Peace with Sweden	
1744		Birth of Ossip Abramovich Hanibal
1745		Head of Russian commission to fix frontiers with Sweden at Stockfors (Finland)
1747		Birth of Isaac Abramovich Hanibal Buillds home at Petrovskoe
1748		Knight of the Order of St.Anna

Year	Events in Russia	Hanibal
1752		Major-General in charge of the fortifications at St.Petersburg Head of the Engineering Corps of the Imperial Army, in charge of training of engineers Directs fortification work in NW and W Russia : Kronstadt, Riga, Pernov, Peter and Paul Fortress in St.Petersburg
1753		In charge of fortifications under construction in western Siberia (Tobolsk-Itchimsk) State Mission to Finland The Holy Synod decrees divorce with Eudoxia Dioper
1754		Fortifications in southern Russia: Novosserbsk, Slavianoserbsk, Elisabethgrad Introduces teaching of civil architecture civile in the Engineering Schools Fortifications in Ukraine (Kiev-Petshersk)
1755		Responsible for construction and maintenance of the Kronstadt canal Creates hospital for workers at Kronstadt. Member of the commission for the works at Rogervik on the Baltic, the Canals at Kronstadt and Lake Ladoga. Lieutenant-General of the Army Head of the Engineering Corps Appointed Governor of Vyborg
1756	Seven Years War 1756-1763	The Senate decides to keep him in the post of Head of the Engineering Corps – he becomes the chief military engineer of the Russian Imperial Army. Opens a school for workers' children and apprentices in Kronstadt

Year	Events in Russia	Hanibal
1757	Field Marshal Apraxin replaced as head of army by General Fermor	Vice President of the commission studying the state of Russia's fortresses
1758		In charge of programmes at the Schools of Artillery and Engineering
1759		Birth of Sophia Abramovna Hanibal Director-General of the works on the Lake Ladoga canal and the works at Kronstadt and Rogervik. Purchases thel achète le domaine de Suyda (St. Petersburg).
1760		Awarded the cordon rouge of the Order of St Alexander Nevsky
1761	Death of Elisabeth Petrovna (24 December) Accession of Peter III	
1762		Peter III retires him after 57 years' service to Russia (.9 June)
	Assassination of Peter III Accession of Catherine II	Retirement at Suyda Life of a rich landlord and philosopher
1765	Catherine II writes to Hanibal regarding the Moscow – St. Petersburg canal project	Regular visits by the Suvorovs to Suyda
1770	Naval battle of Chesme	
1775		Birth of Nadezhda Ossipovna Hanibal
1776		80th birthday. Birth of Paul, son of Isaac Abramovich Hanibal Hanibal's writes his will
1780		Birth of Benjamin Petrovich Hanibal, son of Peter Abramovich Hanibal New house at St.Petersburg

Year	Events in Russia	Hanibal
1781		Death of Christina, his Swedish wife after 48 years together. Death of Hanibal (20 April)
1796		Nadezhda Hanibal, the "beautiful Creole", marries Sergey Pushkin
1799		Birth of the poet Alexander Pushkin, Great grandson of General Abraham Hanibal

APPENDIX 6

GENEALOGY OF THE HANIBAL FAMILY
(1696-1906)

Abraham Petrovich Hanibal (1696-20 IV 1781)	Christina Regina von Sjöberg (17..?-II 1781)
SECOND GENERATION: CHILDREN (7)	
1. Ivan Abramovich Hanibal (1735-1801)	2. Elisabeth Abramovna Hanibal (1737-?) m. to Andrei Pavlovich Pushkin
3. Anna Abramovna Hanibal (1741-1788) m. to Semion S. Neyelov, d. en 1786	4. Peter Abramovich Hanibal (21 VII 1742-3 VI 1826) m. 1777 to Olga Grigorievna von Dannenstern (5 VI 1742-18 VI 1817)
5. Ossip Abramovich Hanibal Grandfather of the poet Pushkin (20 I 1744-12 XI 1806) m. to Maria Alexeyevna Pushkina[1] (20 I 1745-27 VI 1818)	6.Isaac Abramovich Hanibal (1747-1803) 7. Sophia Abramovna Hanibal (1759-1802) m. to Adam Karpovich Rotkirkh (1746-1797)

---

1. Pushkin had two daughters, Maria and Natalia, and two sons, Alexander and Gregory. They gave him 19 grandchildren. Today he has descendants living in Russia and all over the world. For example, his great granddaughter, Nadezhda Mikhailovna de Torbi who married in 1916 the German prince, Georg Battenberg (Mountbatten) after moving to London became Nada, Marchioness of Milford Haven. Georg's brother, Louis Mountbatten was the last Viceroy of British India and their sister, Alice von Battenberg was the mother of Prince Philip of Greece who became Duke of Edinburgh after his marriage to the future Queen Elizabeth II of England.

(Roussakov V.M. Potomki Pouchkina St.Pbg, Lenizdat 1992)

THIRD GENERATION: GRANDCHILDREN (12 identified)	
1. Benjamin Petrovich Hanibal, son of Peter Hanibal (1780- 23 XII 1839) **2. Nadezhda Ossipovna Hanibal, son of Ossip Abramovich Hanibal, mother of the poet 21 VI 1775- 29 III 1836)** 3. Christina Semionovna Neyelova, daughter of Anna Hanibal 4. Paul Isaakovich Hanibal, son of Isdaac Hanibal (1776-1841) m. to Barbara Tikhonova Langay (?-21 VI 1866) 5. Semion Isaakovich Hanibal, son of Isaac Hanibal (?-1853) 6. Jacob Isaakovich anibal, son of Isaac Hanibal (?-1840) m. to Elisabeth Alexandrovna Vyndomskaya, sister of P.A.Ossipova	7. Dmitri Isaakovich Hanibal, son of Isaac Hanibal (?-1837) 8. Cathetrine Isaakovna Hanibal, daughter of Isaac Hanibal m. to Swedish Ivan Karlovich Melander 9. Alexandra Isaakovna Hanibal, daughter of Isaac Hanibal 10. Ivan Adamovich Rotkirkh, son of Sophia Hanibal (Rotkirkh) 11. Nadezhda Adamovna Rotkirkh, daughter of Sophia Hanibal (1782-1856) m. to Col. Paul Leontievich Chemiot (1769-1859) 12. Lyubov Adamovna Rotkirkh, daughter of Sophia Hanibal (7 X 1785-11 II 1855) m. to assessor Bibikov
FOURTH GENERATION: GREAT GRANDCHILDREN (9 identified)	
1. Maria Benjaminovna Hanibal, daughter of Benjamin Petrovich Hanibal m. 1826 to Theodore Pavlovich Korotov 2. Olga Sergeyevna Pushkin, daughter of Nadezhda Hanibal (20 XII 1797-2 V 1868) m. 1828 to Nicolas Ivanovich Pavlitchev (6 V 1802-8 XII 1879) **3. Alexander Sergeyevich Pushkin, son of Nadezhda Hanibal and great grandson of Abraham Petrovitch Hanibal (6 VI 1799-10 II 1837) m. 1831 to Natalia Nicolayevna Gontcharova (27 VIII 1812-26 XI 1863)** 4. Leon Sergeyevich Pushkin, son of Nadezhda Hanibal (17 IV 1805-19 VII 1852) m. to E.A.Zagriayskaya 5. Alexander Yakovlevich Hanibal, son of Jacon Isaakovich Hanibal (27 IX 1797-III 1834)	6. Vladimir Ivanovich Rotkirkh, son of Ivan Rotkirkh, grandson of Sophia Hanibal (20 VI 1809-11 II 1889) m. to Rosalia Versman (1809-1906) 7. Semion Pavlovich Neyelov, grandson of Anna Hanibal 8. Sophia Pavlovna Chemiot, daughter of Nadezhda A.Rotkirkh, granddaughter of Sophia Hanibal (1798-1827) m. to Alexander F. Veyman (1791-1882) 9. Olga Pavlovna Chemiot , sister of Sophia Pavlovna Chemiot (1802-1879) m. to Alexander F.Veyman after the death of Sophia Chemiot, his first wife

244

APPENDIX 7

GENEALOGICAL TREE: ABRAHAM HANIBAL TO PUSHKIN

Abraham Petrovich Hanibal **1696-1781**	**Christina-Regina von Sjöberg** **17..-1781**

Ivan Abramovich Hanibal 1735-1801	Elisabeth Abramovna Hanibal 1737- ?	Anna Abramovna Hanibal 1741-1788	Peter Abramovitch Hanibal 1742-1826

Osip (Joseph) Abramovich Hanibal **1744-1806** Married to Maria Alexeyevna Pushkina* 1745-1818	Isaac Abramovitch Hanibal 1747-1803	Sophia Abramovna Hanibal 1759-1803

Nadezhda Osipovna **Hanibal** **1775-1836**	Sergey Lvovich Pushkin 1770-1848

Alexander Sergeyevich Pushkin **1799-1837**

APPENDIX 8

LIST OF EMPERORS OF RUSSIA IN THE XVIIIth CENTURY

Life	Name	Reign
1672-1725	PETER I THE GREAT	1689-1725
1684-1727	CATHERINE I	1725-1727
1715-1730	PETER II	1727-1730
1693-1740	ANNA IVANOVNA	1730-1740
1740-1741	IVAN VI	1740-1741
	ANNA LEOPOLDOVNA (Regent)	
1709-1761	ELIZABETH PETROVNA	1741-1761
1728-1762	PETER III	1761-1762
1729-1796	CATHERINE II	1762-1796

* Maria Alexeyevna Pushkina was the daughter of the voévode of Tambov (in the centre of Russia), Alexis Feodorovich Pushkin. The latter was the brother of Alexander Petrovich Pushkin, grandfather of Sergey Lvovitch Pushkin, te father of the poet.

APPENDIX 9

INVENTORY* OF HANIBAL'S BOOKS

Classification	Nos.	Titles
H.Hispan.	50. 93-94.	Histoire de la vie du Cardinal Ximenes.1704 Histoire des Iconoclastes. Paris. 1683. 2 vols.
H.Ecclès.	106-120. 138. 139.	Histoire des Juifs : Basnage. 1716. Vol. I-XV Moeurs des Chrétiens : Fleury. 1712 Moeurs des Israélites : Fleury. 1712.
H..German.	83-86 104. 39-41. 47-48.	Histoire de l'Empire Vols. 1-4. 1715 La Vie de l'Empereur Charles V. Amsterdsam. 1704 Voyages de Lucas. 1741. Vols. 1-3. Voyages de Lahontant. 2 vols. 1718.
E. Exotica.	49-50. 72-81. 115.	Histoire de la conquête du Mexique. Paris. 1714. 2 vols. Voyages de Chardin en Perse. Vols. 1-9. 1711 Voyages de Struys en Moscovie. Vol.1. 1719.
Epistolog.	110. 196. 202. 205.	Lettres de Rabutin C. de Bussy. 2 vols. Lettres de Fontenelle. 1718. Lettres d'amour d'une Religieuse Portugaise. 1701 Mercure Galant.
Lexicogr.	110. 201	Veneroni, Maître Italien. 1713 Veneroni, De la prononciation de la langue franç. 1703..

247

Classification	Nos.	Titles
Mathémat.	7. 43-44. 24-28. 49. 88. 140. 200.	Dictionnaire Mathématique by Ozanam. 1691. 4.º Ozanam, Recréations mathématiques. 1694. 2 vols. Ozanam, Cours de Mathématiques. 1693. 3 Vols. Ozanam, Nouvelle Géometrie pratique. 1693. Les Eléments d'Euclide. Paris.1709 Les Eléments de Géométrie : Mess. de Port Royal. Pratique d'Arithmétique: Claire Combe. 1702
Archit. Mil.	7. 24. 50. 74. 81.	L'art universel des Fortifications : Bitainvieu. 4º Ingénieur François. 1696. Pratique de la guerre : Malthus. 1681. L'expérience de l'architecture militaire. 1685. L'Art de la guerre. 1672
Politici	75. 142. 174. 221 289 81 96-101.	Le Prince: Machiavelli. 1714 L'Homme de Cour: Gracian. 1710 Le Testament Politique: Colbert.. 1694. Le Testament Politique: Louvois. 1706 Nouveaux Intérêts des Princes de l'Europe. 1686 Apophtegmes des Anciens. 1664. L'Espion dans les Cours des Princes Chrétiens. Vols 1-6.
Amour	271. 347. 354.	Les Galanteries Angloises. 1700 Les devoirs de la Vie domestique. Les caractères du faux et du véritable amour. 1716
Critici	132-35 164-166. 281-89. 201-202 348-50..	Le Spectateur. 1722.Vols. I-IV. Explication des fables: Banier. Vols. 1-3. Mémoires des Hommes illustres: Brantôme. 9 Vols. Œuvres de Cyrano de Bergerac. 1709. 2 vols. Lucein in the translation by Mr. D'Ablancourt. 3 vols.
hys.	40-41.	Rohault, Traité de la Physique. Vols. I.-II. 1705.
Philosoph.	209-210.	Malebranche, De la recherche de la Vérité. 1721. Vols. 1-4.
H.Univers.	79-80. 81-82 83-87	Bossuet, Histoire Universelle. 2 Vols. 1707 Pratique de la Mémoire universelle 17192 Vols. Géographie universelle by de la Croix. Vols. 1-5.

Classification	Nos.	Titles
H. Graeca	31-33.	Histoire de la guerre de Péloponnèse Vols.1-3. 1714.
	67.	Histoire d'Alexandre le Grand: Q. Curce. 1709. 2 vols.
H. Romana	57.	Histoire Romaine depuis la fondation. 1716.
	58.	Histoire des deux Triumvirats. Amsterdam. 1715.
H.Galliae	38.	Le Sacre et le Couronnement du Roi de France. 1620
H.M.Britan.	68-70.	Histoire des révolutions d'Angleterre: le P. d'Orleans. 3 vols.
	79.	Histoire de Cromwell. Utrecht. 1692.
H.Belgii	12-14.	Histoire de la guerre de Flandres: StradaVols. 1-3
	22-23	Histoire de la Hollande.
Archit. Mil.	7.	L'art universel des Fortifications:. Bitainvieu. 4º
	24.	Ingénieur François. 1696.
	50.	Pratique de la guerre: Malthus. 1681.
	74.	L'expérience de l'architecture militaire. 1685.
	81.	L'Art de la guerre. 1672
Politici	75.	Le Prince: Machiavelli. 1714
	142.	L'Homme de Cour: Gracian. 1710
	174.	Le Testament Politique: Colbert.. 1694.
	221	Le Testament Politique: Louvois. 1706
	289	Nouveaux Intérêts des Princes de l'Europe. 1686
		Apophtegmes des Anciens. 1664.
	81	L'Espion dans les Cours des Princes Chrétiens.
	96-101.	Vols 1-6.
Amour	271.	Les Galanteries Angloises. 1700
	347.	Les devoirs de la Vie domestique.
	354.	Les caractères du faux et du véritable amour. 1716
Critici	132-35	Le Spectateur. 1722.Vols. I-IV.
	164-166.	Explication des fables: Banier. Vols. 1-3.
	281-89.	Mémoires des Hommes illustres: Brantôme. 9 Vols.
	201-202	Œuvres de Cyrano de Bergerac. 1709. 2 vols.
	348-50..	Lucein in the translation by Mr. D'Ablancourt. 3 vols.
hys.	40-41.	Rohault, Traité de la Physique. Vols. I.-II. 1705.
Philosoph.	209-210.	Malebranche, De la recherche de la Vérité. 1721. Vols. 1-4.

Classification	Nos.	Titles
H.Univers.	79-80.	Bossuet, Histoire Universelle. 2 Vols. 1707
	81-82	Pratique de la Mémoire universelle 1719 2 Vols.
	83-87	Géographie universelle by de la Croix Vols. 1-5.
H. Graeca	31-33.	Histoire de la guerre de Péloponnèse Vols.1-3. 1714.
	67.	Histoire d'Alexandre le Grand: Q. Curce. 1709. 2 vols.
H. Romana	57.	Histoire Romaine depuis la fondation. 1716.
	58.	Histoire des deux Triumvirats. Amsterdam. 1715.
H.Galliae	38.	Le Sacre et le Couronnement du Roi de France. 1620
H.M.Britan.	68-70.	Histoire des révolutions d'Angleterre: le P. d'Orleans. 3 vols.
	79.	Histoire de Cromwell. Utrecht. 1692.
H.Belgii	12-14.	Histoire de la guerre de Flandres: Strada Vols. 1-3
	22-23	Histoire de Hollande.

Note

Extract from an article by Anna S. Hannibal, "Les Hannibal" in *Pushkin and his contemporaries*, St. Petersburg, 1913, with minor amendments.

BIBLIOGRAPHY

Books in French and English

ABREGE de l'Histoire du Czar Pierre Alexievits avec une relation de l'Etatprésent de la Moscovie, *de ce qui s'est passe de plus considérable depuisson arrivée en France, jusqu'a ce jour,* Mercure de France, Paris, 1717.

ALLAINVAL (L), *Anecdotes du règne de Pierre 1er,* Ière et I^{ème} parties,Paris, 1745.

ARCHEOLOGIA, Juillet-Août 1970, n°35.

AUGOYAT (col.), *Aperçu historique sur les fortifications, les ingénieurs et* sur *le Corps du génie en France,* Tome II, Paris, 1862**.**

BARTH (H),*Voyages et découvertes dans l'Afrique septentrionale et centralependant les années 1849 à 1855,* Tome III, Paris, 1861.

BLANCHARD (A), *Les ingénieurs du «Roy» de Louis XIV à Louis XVI. Etudedu Corps des Fortifications,* 1979.

BLANCHARD (A), *Dictionnaire des ingénieurs militaires 1691-1791,*

Montpellier.

BOBLAYE (Th. le P.), *Esquisse historique sur les Ecoles d'Artillerie,* Metz.

Archives militaires du Service Historique de 1'Armée de Terre (SHAT) auVieux Fort de Vincennes. Cote : 34523.

DEC ALO (S), *Historical dictionary of Chad,* London, 1987.

DOLCOROUKOV (prince P), Mémoires, Genève, 1867.

DUMAS (A), *En Russie,* Paris, François Bourin, 1989.

GENERAL HISTORY OF AFRICA, vol. 5, Unesco, 1992.

GNAMMANKOU (D), « La traite des Noirs en direction de la Russie ».Communication présentée au Colloque Unesco, « *La Route de l'Esclave* » à Ouidah, sept. 1994, à paraitre dans Actes du Colloque « La Route del'Esclave », Unesco.

GRUNWALD (C. de), *La Russie de Pierre le Grand,* Hachette, 1953.

GUICHEN (vicomte de), *Pierre le Grand et le premier Traité franco-russe,*1682 à 1717, Park, 1908.

HELBIG (H), *Russische Guntlinge,* Tubingen, 1809.

HISTOIRE GENERALS DEL'AFRIQUE, vol. 1, Unesco, 1980.

KAKE (I. B). «La traite négrière et le mouvement de populations entre1»Afrique Noire, 1'Afrique du Nord et le Moyen-Orient », *La traite négrièredu XVIe au XIXe siècle,* Unesco, 1985.

LEBEUF (A), «L›origine et la constitution des principautés Kotoko».*Contribution de la recherche ethnologique à l'histoire des civilisations duCorneroun,* Paris, CNRS.

LEY (F), *Le maréchal de Munich et la Russie au XVIIIe siècle,* Paris,Librairie Plon, 1959.

LORTHOLARY (A), *Le mirage russe en France au XVIIIe siècle,* Paris, Editions Contemporaines, 1951.

MASSIE (R K.), *Pierre le Grand,* Paris, Fayard, 1985.

MERCURE DE FRANCE, N° d›avril, mai et juin 1717 aux Archives de laBibliothèque Nationale de France, Cote : microfilm – m – 238.

MERCURY (F), «Le secret *de* Law», in *Les Grandes Enigmes du temps jadis* par Bernard Michal, Ed. Famot, Genève, 1976.

NACHTIGAL (G), *Sahara and Sudan,* III, London, 1987.

PETITFILS (J.-Chr.), *Le Régent,* Paris, Fayard, 1992.

ORHONLU (Cengiz), *Habesh Eyaleti,* Istanbul, Edebiyat Fakultesi Matbasi, 1974.

POUCHKINE (A), *Œuvres complètes,* t.I, Lausanne, L'Age d'homme, 1973.

POUCHKINE(A),*CEuvres completes,* t.III (autobiographie, critique, correspondance), Lausanne, L'Age d'homme, 1977.

POUCHKINE (A), *Poésies,* Paris, Gallimard, 1994.

POUCHKINE (A), *La dame de pique et autres textes,* Paris, La Collection P.OJ.Nota Bene : le lecteur intéressé y trouvera le texte français du romaninachevé de Pouchkine, *Le Nègre de Pierre le Grand,* traduit par RostiskHofman.

RODINSON (M), «Généalogie royale de Logone-Birni (Cameroun)» in *EtudesCamerounaises,* tome III, mars-juin 1950, n°29-30, IFAN, pp.75-82.

ROUSSET de MISSY (J), *Mémoire du règne de Pierre le Grand, Empereur de Russie,* en 4 volumes, La Haye, 1725-1726.

SAINT-SIMON, *Mémoires,* Paris, 1826.

SAINT-SIMON, *Mémoires complets et authentiques du duc de Saint – Simonsur le siècle de Louis XIV et la Régence,* Paris, 1829.

SCHTCHERBATOW (M), *Journal de l' empereur Pierre le Grand depuis1698 jusqu'àlapaixde Nystadt en 1721,* publié par J.H.S. Fon, 1773-1774.

STOCKHOLM DAGBLAD, numéro du 11/06/1899.

TRIMINGHAM, *Islam in Ethiopia,* Oxford University Press, 1952.

TROYAT (H), *Pouchkine* (1946), Paris, Plon, 1953.

TROYAT (H), *Catherine la Grande,* Paris, Flammarion, 1977.

TROYAT (H), *Pierre le Grand,* Paris, Flammarion, 1979.

URVOY, *Histoire de l'empire du Bornou,* 1949.

UZUNCARSILI (I), *Kapukulu Ocaklari, I* et II, Istanbul, 1988.

VAUDAL (A), *LouisXVet Elisabeth de Russie,* Paris, Plon, 1882.

VOLTAIRE, *Histoire de l'empire de Russie sous Pierre le Grand.*

EYS (E), *Esclavage et guerre sainte. Consultation adressée aux gens duTouatpar un érudit nègre, cadi de Tombouctou,* 1900.

ZOUBER (M. A.), *Ahmad Baba de Tombouctou (1556-1627) Sa vie et sonœuvre,* Paris, G.-P. Maisonneuve et Larose, 1977.

Books in Russian

АННЕНКОВ, (Annenkov) А.С. Пушкин в александровскую эпоху: 1799- 1826. (A.S.Pouchkine à l'époque alexandrine : 1799-1826) СП6, 1874

АНУШИНД. Н. **(Anoutchine)** *А. С. Пушкин : Антропологическийэскиз.* **(A.S. Pouchkine : Esquisse anthropologique) М. : Рус. Ве**домости**, 1899**

*АЗАНЧЕВСКИЙ (Azancevski) История*Преображенского*Полка* (Histoire du régiment Preobrajenski) 1859 [History of the Preobrazheski Regiment]

*БАНТ*ЫШ-КАМЕНСКИЙД*. Н.* **(Bantych-Kamenski)** *Словарьдостопамятныхлюдейрус скойземли.* (Dictionnaire des gens illustres de la Russie) M., 1836 [Dictionary of Famous people of Russia]

БЛАГОЙД. Д. **(Blagoi)**АбрамПетровичГаннибал – АрапТетраВеликого. (A. P. Hannibal – le Negre de Pierre le Grand) Мол. Гвардия, 1937. N°3

БЛАГОЙД. Д. **(Blagoi)** ТворческийпутъПушкина. (L'itinéraire littéraire de Pouchkine) М.: Ид-во АН СССР. 1967 [The literary Path pf Pushkin, Moskwa, Edition of the Academy of Science, USSR, 1967]

БОЗЫРЕВ В. **C.** (Bozyriev) Музей-Заповедник А. С, Пушкина. СII6.,1970

ВАЛИШЕВСКИЙ К. (Valisczewski) Дочъ Петра Великого. (La fille de Pierre le Grand) М.-Минск, Издание А. С. Суворина, 1990

ВЕГНЕР М. **(Vegner)** Предки Пушкина. (Les ancêtres de Pouchkine) М.:Советский писатель, 1937

ВИНОГРАДОВИ. **(Vinogradov)** Здесърождалисъволшебныестроки(Pouchkine composa ici des vers magiques) // Правда от 05.06.1977

ГАННИБАЛА. П. **(Hanibal)**(ПрактическаягеометрияифортификацияGéométrie pratique et Fortification.T.1-2 1725-726

ГАННИБАЛ*А. С.* **(HannibalAnna)** ....

Ганниалы : новые данные для их биографиии

(Nouveaux documents pour la biographie des Hannibal) : // Пушкини ero совремнники. Пг., 1914. вып. XIX – XX

ГАСТФРЕЙНДН.__(Gastfreynd)__ПисьмаАбрамаГаннибала (Lettresd'AbrahamHannibal) // Всемирныйвестник, 1903, N°l

*ГЕЙЧЕНКО*С. (Gueytchenko) БиблиотекаГаннибала (Labibliothequed'Hannibal) // ЛиературнаяРоссии, 1976

ГЕЛЬБИг **(Helbig)** Руссие избранникиислучайныелюди (Les favoris des tsars de Russie) // Русскаястарина 1963 *N°4*

*ГНАММАН*КУД. (Gnarnmankou) *Где Fue родилсяИбрагиГанибф? (Ou est né Ibrahim Hannibal?)* // Россискиевести. 1995, N°101

ГНАММАНКУД. **(Gnammankou***) ТакгдежеродинаГанибал ?(Recherches sur les véritables engines africaines d'Ibrahim Hanibal) //*

Вестник АН, (Messager de 1'Academie des Sciences de Russie) 1995, N° 12

ГОЛИКОВ (Golikov) Дополнения к деяниям Петра ВеликогоСПб 1794

ГОЛИКОВ (Golikov) Деяния Петра великого, (Oeuvres de Pierre leGrand) T.XV// Русский архив, 1877, //

ГОРДИН **А. М. (Gordine)** *А Всё-такиГаннибал (Le portrait d'Hannibal) //*

Временник пушкинской коммисси Л, 1993

ГРАНОВСКАЯ Н. И. (Granovskaia) « Если ехатъ вам случится...». Л.: Лениэдат, 1989

ГРАНОВСКАЯ Н. Н. (Granovskala) «Род Пушкиных мятежнный СПб. 1992

КЕРСНОВСКИЙ (Kersnovski) Истоия руской арми, В 4х томах.T.I, 1992

КОЗЛОВ В. (Kozlov) Когда родился прадед А. С. Пушкина // Неделя1969, N°44

КОСТОМАРОВ Н. И. (Kostamarov) Очерк домашней жизни и нравов великорусского народа в XVI В XVII столетнях. М.: Республика 1992

ЛАСКОВСКИЙ Ф. (Laskovski) Материалы для истории инженерного искусства, М.

ЛОНГИНОВМ.Н.(Longuinov)АбрамПетровичГанибал(AbrahamPetrovitchHannibal) // Русскийархив, 1864, N°2

*ЛУППОВ С. П. (****Louppov****) Гнига в России в первой чертверти XVIII века, Л. 1973*

МАЛЕВАНОВ Н. А. (Malevanov) К БИОГРАФИИ А. П. Ганнибала (Pourune biographie d'Hannibal) // Пушкин: Исследования и материалыМ.- Л. Изд-во АН СССР, 1962 T.IV

МАЛЕВАНОВН. А. **(Malevanov)**Прадедпоэта (Lebisaïeuldupoète) //Звезда, 1974. N°6

МОДЗАЛЕВСКИЙБ. Л. **(Modzalevski)** РодПушкина (LagenealogiedePouchkine). 1907

НАБОКОВ В.В. (Nabokov V.) Пушкин и Ганибал (Pushkin and Cannibal) // Encounter, 1962) // Легенды и мифы о Пушкине, СП6., Гуманитарое Агенство «Академический Проект», 1995

НЕСТЕРЧУК (Nestertchouk) Предки А. С. Пушкина — инженеры идеятили водного хозяйства // Речной транспорт, 1962

ОПАТОВИЧ С. И. (Opatovitch) Евдокия Андреевна Ганнибал (Eudoxie Hannibal) // Русская старина, T. XVIII, 1877

ПАИНА 3. С. (Paina) Об обстроятельствах отставки А. П. Ганнибала (Aproposdudépart à laretraitedʼHannibal) // Пушкин: Исследования и материалы. м. — Л.: Изд-во АНСССР, 1962. T.IV

ПАВЛЕНКО Н. И. Птенцы гнезда Петрова М.: Мысль. 1989

ПАВЛИЩЕВ Л. Н. (Paviischev) Из семейной хронии М., 1890

ПЕКАРСКИЙ П. П. (Pekarski) История императорской Академии Наук в Петербурге. СП6, 1870. Т. I

ПЕКАРСКИЙ П. П. (Pekarski)Введение в истоию просвещения в России XVIII столетия СП6., 1862. Т. I

ПЕКАРСКИЙ П. П. (Pekarski) Наука и литератра в России при Петре Великом. СП6., 1862

ПУШКИН А. С. (Pouchkine) Полное обрание сочинений В 16 Т. М.:Изд-во АН СССР. 1937-1949

САВЕЛЬЕВ А. Н. (Saveliev) Исторический очерк инженерного управления в России. СП6, 1879

СЕРГЕЕВ М. (Sergueiev) Сибирские злолючения Арапа Петра великого (Les m&aventures du Negre de Pierre le Grand en Sibérie) // Алмавах «Ангара». Иркутск. 1970

СЕМЕВСКИЙ М. И. (Semeski) Тайная служба Петра I, Минск.: «Беларусъ», 1993

СОЛОВЬЕВ С. М. (Soloviev S. M) История России с древнейших времён. кн. II, Т. 17, 18, М., 1963

СОНДОЕВСКИЙ Г. И. (Sondoevski) Сборник трудов членов Псковсого Археологическогообщеста, Псков. П.А.О., 1896

*СТАССОВ В. В. (**Stassov**) Арап Петра Великого в калмых Екатарины I.СП6., 1861*

255

СТРУКОВ Д. П. (Strukov) Главное Артиллерийское управление, частъпервая, книга I, СП6., 1902

ТЕЛОТОВА Н. К. (Teletova) Ганибалы – предки Пушкина (Les Hannibal: aieux de Pouchkine) // «Белые ночи», Л.,1978

ТЕЛОТОВА Н. К. (To1etova) Забытые родственные связи А. С. Пушкина. Л., Наука, 1981

ТЕЛОТОВА Н. К. (To1etova)О мнимом и одлинном изображении А. П. Ганнибала // Легенды и мифы о Пушине. СП6., Гуманитарное Агенства «Академический проект», 1995

ФАБРИЦИУС И. Г. (Fabricius) Главное инженерное управление,частъ I, СП6., 1902

ФЕЙНБЕРГ И (Feynberg) Абрам Петрович Ганнибал – прадец Пушкина (Abraham Petrovitch Hannibal, l'arrière-grand-p**è**re dePouchkine) М.: Наука, 1983

ХМЫРОВ М. Д. (Khmyrov) Абрам Петрович Ганнибал (Abraham Petrovitch Hanniba)//**//Историческиестатьи, СП6., 1873**

ЧЕРЕЙСКИЙ Л. А. (Chereyski)Пушкин и его окружение. л.: Наука, 1988

ЧИСТЯКОВ Й. С. (Tchistiakov) История Петра Велиого. М.: буклет, 1992

СЛИЯПКИН Н. А. (Shliapkin) Из неизданных бумаг Пушкина, СП6, 1903

ШТЕЛИНГ Я (Chteling) Подлинные анекдоты собранные... в 4х томах, М. 1830

ШУБИНСКИЙ С. Н. (Choubinski) Княгиня Волконская и её друзья (La princesse Volkonskaia et ses amis) // Исторический вестник,Т.98, 1904

ЭЙДЕЛМАН Н. Я. (Eydelman N.) Твой 18-й век. Прекрасен наш союз. Мыслъ, 1991

ЭЙДЕЛМАН Н. Я. (Eydelman N.) Ганниибалов колольчик // Наука и жизнъ N° 10, 1983 стр. 86-93

Бракоразводное дело Ганнибала, Архив Духовной Консистории N° 2. 466, СП6.

Историчесий обзор фондов Рукописного отела БАН, вып.I, XVII век. 1956

Кабинетные дела II, N° 38, л.82, 83, 84,86, 93

Кабинетные дела II, N° 42, л.71

Карты и планы XV-XVIIIв. М. Galaxy Publishers, 1992

Материалы для истории руссого флота, частъ IX, СП6. 1882

Материалы ерховного тайного совета и кабинета министров, Русское Историчесое общество, Т. 79, 84, 101, 106, 130

Письма русских госуарей и других ооб царского семейства. ГИМ.1861

Походный журнал за 1714 год, СП6.,1854

Россия в период реформ Петра I, М., 1973

Русский архив, книга I, 1881

Русскй биографический словарь, 1914

Русский энциклопедический словарь Ф. А. Броктауз и И. А., 1892

Сборник выписок из архивых бумаг о Петре Великом, частъ II, СП6, 1872

Сенатский архив, **T.V, СП6., 1892**

Временник пушкинской коммиссии АН СССР, **N°** 21, Л. 1984

Временник пушкинской коммиссии АН СССР, **N°** 23, Л. 1987

Гатчинская Правда, **N°** 81 **о**т 23/05/1991

Исторический архив, **N° I, М., Изд-во ЛИТ, 1992 СТР. 182-188**

Литературная Россия от 10/09/1976

Нева, **N°** 12, 1970

Пушкинский край, **о**т 20/08/1977

Слов**о**,N° 7, 1992

LIST OF CAPTIONS

1. Portrait presumed to be of Abraham Hanibal.

2. Trade routes linking Borno with North Africa and the Nile Valley.

3. The Principality of Logone and neighbouring states in the 16th to 18th centuries.

4. Sign in present day Logone celebrating the birth of Pushkin's ancestor.

5. Map of the Kotoko country in northern Cameroon.

6. Ancient Manuscripts in Arabic and in the local Kotoko language.

7. The royal genealogoy of the Logone-Birni kingdom. According to this document the first Miarré ruler of Logone was Mra Amana.

8. Abraham Petrov aged 12, drummer boy at the battle of Lesnaya (1708).

9. Detail of cover picture.

10. Compare the detail of the drummer boy and the present Sultan of Logone-Birni photographed in 1956.

11. Mahamat Bahar Maruf, Sultan of Logone-Birni (2014).

12. Sultan Mahamat Bahar (reigned 1900-1914).

13. Drawing of the *gudu* (tower) of the ancient Kotoko city of Gulfeil.

14. Sultan of Baghirmi. (19th c)

15. A 19th Century view of the fortifications of Logone, seen from the Logone river.

16. The Logone river in 2010.

17/18. The Sultan's palace at Logone (1940).

19/20/21. Inauguration of the plaque commemorating Hanibal's stay in La Fère, France. 2010.

22. Mahamat Bahar Maruf, Sultan of Logone-Birni since 1965.

23. The Queen of Logone, mother of the young Brouha (the future Hanibal).

24. Peter the Great as a young man in 1697.

25. Tsar Peter with the black child.

26. Allegorical portrait of Peter I, conqueror of the Turks at Azov and of the Swedes at Poltava, and of his black godson Abraham Petrov.

27. Catherine I (1684-1727) Empress of Russia.

28. Anna Ivanovna (1693-1740) Empress of Russia, niece of Peter I, who brought Hanibal back from exile.

29. Elisabeth Petrovna (1709-61), Empress of Russia, daughter of Peter I and sister of Hanibal by adoption.

30. Peter I and Hanibal.

31. Abraham Hanibal's signature in a geometry book given to him by Peter the Great in 1711.

32. Another signature by Hanibal.

33. Abrhaham Hanibal's two volumes on geometry and fortifications, 1726-1726.

34-38. Extracts from Abraham Hanibal's two volumes on geometry and fortifications.

39. Empress Elisabeth's ukase nominating Hanibal as Major-General.

40-41. Hanibal's park and land in his Petrovskoe and Mikhailovskoe estates, near Pskov.

42. View of Reval (Talinn) in the 18th century. Military costumes of the period.

43-44. The commandant's house at Reval (Talinn) where Hanibal lived as Major-General and military commandant of the Estonian province.

45. Hanibal's house (now museum) at Petrovskoe.

46. Bust of Hanibal at Petrovskoe.

47-48. Hanibal's study.

49-50. The Order of Saint Anne and the Order of Saint Alexander Nevsky.

51. Hanibal's mansion in St.Petersburg.

52. Hanibal's Coat of Arms.

53. Bust of Hanibal by Chevchenko.

54. Alexander Pushkin by Kipriensky.

55-56. Lauritz Galtung (c. 1615-1661), a Norwegian nobleman of the Galtung family, admiral of the Dano-Norwegian fleet and his wife Barbara Grabo. They are the great grandparents of Abraham Hanibal's wife, Christina Regina von Schöberg.

57. Lauritz Galtung and Barbara Grabo's children. Their eldest daughter, Klara Maria is Christina Regina's grandmother.

58. General and Admiral Ivan Hanibal. Abraham's eldest son, Russian war hero, builder of Crimean city and port of Khirson.

59. Peter the Great waiting for his godson to return from France.

60. General and admiral Ivan Hanibal, Abraham Hanibal's eldest son. Russian war hero, builder of Crimea city and port of Khirson.

61. Baron Wrangel Piotr Nikolayevich.

62. Nadezhda Osipovna Pushkina (1775-1836), mother of Pushkin.

63. Sergey Lvovich Pushkin (1770-1848), father of Pushkin.

64. Pushkin as a child.

65. Compare Pushkin with another of Hanibal's descendants, Alexander Sergeyevich Neytkirkh, born in 1975!

66. Semion Hanibal, Nadezhda Hanibal's cousin.

67. Lev Sergeyevich Pushkin, the poet's brother.

68. Olga Sergeyevich Pushkin's sister.

69-72. Pushkin's children.

73. Pushkin, by Joëlle Esso.

INDEX

A

Abbeville 23

Abd-al-Aziz ben Yacoub 23

Abd el Kader (Sultan) 237

Abdul 43, 44

Abo (Turku) 153, 161, 216

Abraham, Abraham Petrov (see Hanibal) 47, 49, 50, 51, 52, 53, 56, 58, 59, 60, 64, 65, 68, 69, 72, 78, 80, 82, 84, 86, 90, 95, 96, 101, 102, 103, 104, 109, 110, 126, 141, 189, 190, 213

Abramovna, Elizabeth 184, 239

Abumov 170

Abyssinia 1, 220, 221, 222, 223, 225, 226

Academy of Sciences 82, 91, 103, 145, 151, 170, 179, 185

Ahmed III (Sultan) 26, 27, 28, 208, 237

Albedil 127

Alexandrovskoe 191

Alexis Petrovitch, Grand Duke 46, 67, 142

Alexis Petrovitch, Grand Duke (Tsarevich) 94, 101, 211

Ali Gaji 23

Amo, William Anthony 15, 167

Amsterdam 58, 60, 61, 105, 209, 249, 250

Anania, Giovanni 21

Aniaba, Captain 65

Abramovna, Anna 184, 239

Anna Ivanovna 101, 103, 104, 127, 132, 238, 239

Anna Leopoldovna 132, 140, 141, 239

Anna Petrovna 98, 100, 101, 138, 157

Anna Semionovna 66

Anthès, Georges d' 18

Antwerp 61

Anuchin 19, 212, 214, 220, 221, 222, 225, 226, 227

Apraksin, Count 45

Argenson 217

Assechka Ivanovna 88

Astrabad 77

Astrakhan 103, 106, 142

Azov 27, 51

B

Baba, Ahmed 24

Bachmakov 171

Bagirmi 21, 23, 223

Baku 77

Baltaci Pasha, Grand Vizier 52

Barth, Heinrich 21

Baumann, Ivan von 188, 190

Baumgarten, Jacob 166

Beaumont 62

Beauvais 62

Benghazi 25

Bélidor, Bernard Forest de 72

Berwick 64, 69

Bestuzhev-Riumin brothers 142

Bibikov 168

Biren 107, 110, 132, 140, 181

Bitka 53

Blanchard, Anne 70, 175

Blumenstrot 85, 145

Bodlov 85

Bohemia 58

Bolotov, A. 82

Bornu 23

Borzov, Theodore 178

Bossuet, Cardinal 101, 248, 250

Boulogne 62

Bozhinski, Gregory V. 100

Brouha (Miara) or Brouwa 22, 23, 24, 47, 237

Brouha (Miara) or Brouwa 22, 23, 24, 47, 237

Bruges 61

Bulgarin 206, 207

C

Caliph 23

Cameroon 1, 2, 14, 16, 19, 21, 213, 223, 226

Catherine I Alekseevna, Empress of Russia 14, 79, 85, 87, 90, 92, 140, 142, 174, 180, 230, 238

Catherine II 18, 157, 181, 182, 184, 185, 186, 188, 191, 192, 204, 205, 241

Chad 1, 2, 11, 21, 213, 223, 226, 251

Charles XII, King of Sweden 43, 48, 49, 50, 51, 52, 85, 237

Charlotte of Brunswick 58

Chelpanov, Savva 188, 190

Cherkasov, Ivan 87, 93, 152

Chesme 187, 235, 241

Chétardie 140

Chichkov, Jacob 108

Chistiakov 59, 210

Choubinski 87, 211, 212, 213, 256

College of War 83, 85, 93, 95, 98, 101, 103, 105, 109, 111, 132, 142, 149, 153, 159, 160, 168, 174, 175, 211

Constantinople 14, 18, 21, 25, 26, 27, 28, 44, 45, 46, 49, 52, 68,

102, 144, 163, 206, 208, 220, 223, 229, 233, 237

Conti, Princess 70

Corneille 14, 84

Cossacks 50

Courland 107, 132

Court of St. James 81

Crimea 191, 204

Cromwell 84, 249, 250

D

Daria Yakovlevna, Princess 88

De Brevern 151

Debrigny 135, 136, 137, 138

Denham 21

Derbent 77

Dimitriev, Roman Dioper, Captain Andrew 178

Dioper, Eudoxia 105, 106, 128, 240

Dnieper river 191

Dobroe 50, 109

Dolgorukov, Prince Mikhail Vladimirovich 101

Dolgorukov, Prince Sergey 101

Dolgoruky, Prince Basil 53

Dombes, Prince of 63, 90

Dorpat 44, 49

Drouot 72, 210

Dunkirk 61

E

Edirne 27

Eidelman, Nathan 19

Ekaterinburg 81

Eleanora, Queen of Sweden 85

Elitsy 189

Elizabeth Petrovna, Empress of Russia 130, 141, 144, 157, 231

Elliott, George 72

Engineering, School of 82, 109

Erastfehr, battle of 49

Eremeev, Semion 178

Erenchild 53

Esko Yann 155

Estonia 52, 86, 103, 106, 126, 128, 130, 132, 153, 154, 170, 181, 216, 239

Ethiopia (Abyssinia) 1, 2, 16, 19, 26, 212, 221, 222, 225, 253

F

Farquharson 44

Feinberg 16, 19, 91, 107, 212, 213

Fermor, general 176, 177, 241

Fezzan 23

Finland 13, 149, 153, 161, 162, 170, 188, 239, 240

Fortifications, Department of 168, 174

Fraustadt 48

G

Galata Sarai 27

Gastfreynd 134, 215, 216, 218, 254

Geyshenko, S. 82

Grocius, G. 84

Gibraltar 72

Glebov 179

Golitsyn 86, 101, 211

Golovin, Count 27, 43, 232

Golovkin 80

Goulfeil 23

Great Northern War 48, 49, 50, 51, 52, 69, 85

Grunwald, Constantin de 50, 89

H

Halle, University of 15, 166, 167

Ham, malediction of, Hamites 24

Hangö, Cape 53

Hanibal (also Hannibal, Annibal) 20, 82

Hanibal, Isaac Abramovich 239, 241

Hanibal, Ivan Abramovich 239

Hanibal, Nadezhda Osipovna (Nadine) 205

Hanibal, Osip Abramovich 187, 192, 235

Hanibal, Peter Abramovich 17, 184, 239, 241

Hannibal of Carthage 101, 102, 215, 221

Heebourg, M. 72

Helsingfors (Helsinki) 53, 153

Henning, Helarius 166

Hesse-Homburg, Prince von 137, 158, 215

Holmer, Major 134, 135, 137, 157, 158, 160

Holstein-Bek, Prince von 157

Holstein-Gottorp, Duke of 98

Homer 84

Horn 85

Hungary 26

I

Ibalaghuan 22, 23

Ignatiev, M. 159

Ilin, Peter 128, 166

Ingria 161, 182, 189, 230

Irkutsk 102, 126

Istanbul (see Constantinople) 26, 226, 252

Italy 65, 69

Ivan VI, Tsar Ivan Antonovich 132, 239

J

Johnson 56, 83

K

Kalm, Johann 60

Kanuri 22, 206

Karelia 82

Kariakula 126, 127, 130, 131, 132, 133, 155, 162, 239

Karlsbad (Karlovy Vary) 58

Karnak Loggon 22

Kayserov 105, 106, 111, 170

Kazan 95, 96, 97, 98

Keksholm 52

Keyzerling 107

Kherson 14, 191, 192, 204, 219, 235

Khmyrov 18, 19, 69, 107, 210, 211, 212, 213, 215, 216, 217

Kiev 27, 51, 60, 171, 240

Kiev-Petchersk fort 171

Kizlar Aghâsi (the Grand Eunuch) 26

Korovin, Stefan 77

Kotoko 2, 21, 23, 206, 252

Kramer, Anna 100

Kronstadt 80, 81, 85, 88, 89, 105, 169, 172, 173, 174, 177, 178, 179, 180, 230, 240, 241

Kuliabka, Archbishop 165

Kuriakin, Prince Alexander 77

Kussiri 23, 206

Kutuzov, Timothy 103

Kuzminski, Gabriel 110

L

Lachinsky 77

Lacosta 61

Ladoga, Lake 49, 52, 161, 180, 240, 241

La Fère 71, 72, 77, 78, 169, 174, 179, 210, 238

Lagane, Hanibal's sister 11, 12, 22, 23, 186, 206, 220, 222, 223, 226, 227

Laganie (Lagwanie) 12, 21

Lagon Birni 21

Larmessin, Nicolas de 50

Lassy, Field Marshal 153

Law, John 76, 238

Leets, G. 87

Leibnitz 58

Lesnaya 50, 109, 237

Lestocq 56, 83, 101, 181

Leszczynski, Stanislas 50

Levenvold 100, 107

Liudvig 168

Livonia 86

Loewendal, Baron von 134, 149, 152, 153

Logone (Lagan, Lagone) 2, 3, 11, 19, 21, 22, 23, 24, 25, 27, 47, 144, 172, 176, 186, 192, 206, 213, 220, 221, 222, 223, 224, 225, 226, 227, 237, 252

Lomonosov 173

Lopukhin 100

Louis XIV 9, 63, 64, 65, 70, 101, 102, 251

Louis XV 60, 63, 71, 78, 90, 153, 175

Löwenhaupt 50

Luppov, S. 91

M

Maine, Duc de 63, 65, 70, 90

Makarov 60, 66, 67, 68, 73, 74, 76, 77, 93

Malevanov 53, 161, 168, 172, 177, 213, 215, 216, 217, 255

Manisa 27

Manstein, General 105

Maria Alekseevna 187, 192, 205, 218

Marouf (Miara) 22

Martin, Pierre Denis 50

Maurin, Semion 87, 93, 98, 99, 103

Mazarin, Duc de 72

Mecca 23, 26

Medina 26

Mengdel 107

Menshikov, Prince 50, 81, 86, 98, 100, 212

Michukov, Vice Admiral 153

Mikhailovskoe 141, 144, 162, 183, 189, 193, 204, 231, 239

Mitawa 47

Mitshurin 77

Mohammed 84

Moldavia 27, 28

Molière 9, 84

Montreuil 62

Moroccans 23

Moscow 2, 12, 15, 16, 18, 27, 28, 43, 44, 45, 46, 58, 67, 79, 80, 94, 97, 98, 100, 102, 128, 144, 150, 159, 169, 173, 184, 185, 205, 211, 225, 227, 233, 241

Münnich, von 81, 85, 104, 105, 107, 109, 110, 111, 127, 132, 133, 181

Musin-Pushkin, Count 45, 76

Mustapha II (Sultan) 26

Nathalie Alexeevna, Grand Duchess 101

Navarino 18, 186, 235

Neelov, Semion 184, 230

Neledinsky, Senator Yuri 103

Nepluev 81

Nevsky, Order of Saint Alexander 192

Nienschantz 49

Nöteburg 49

Novoserbsk 169

Nutto Hendrik 155

Nystadt, Peace of 48, 85

O

Oguinsky 218

Opatovich 129, 130, 213, 214, 216, 217

Oranienbaum canal 180

Orenburg 165

Orleans, Duke of 63

Orlov 55, 209

Osipova, Madame P. 17

Ottoman Empire (see also Turkey) 23, 25, 26, 44, 45, 48, 223, 227, 237

Ovsianikov 61

Ozanam 84, 248

N

Nachtigal 21

Narva 44, 48, 49, 134, 135, 137, 153, 157, 237

P

Pachkov, Major-General 98

Paris 1, 61, 62, 63, 64, 65, 66, 67, 68, 69, 70, 72, 73, 74, 75, 76, 77, 80,

84, 101, 102, 153, 206, 210, 233, 238, 247, 248, 251, 252, 253

Pas de Calais 61

Pekarski 66, 211, 255

Pernov 52, 53, 106, 107, 108, 109, 110, 129, 169, 170, 238, 240

Persian literature 27

Persia, Persian campaign 77, 79

Peter Alexeevitch, Prince 85, 86, 87, 90, 93, 94

Peterhof 85, 96

Peter I (Tsar Peter the Great) 9, 10, 19, 44, 45, 46, 48, 49, 50, 51, 52, 53, 55, 56, 58, 61, 63, 64, 67, 69, 73, 79, 81, 82, 85, 86, 87, 89, 91, 92, 93, 94, 96, 98, 101, 102, 103, 105, 107, 126, 127, 130, 132, 137, 138, 144, 158, 159, 163, 172, 176, 181, 184, 191, 204, 207, 208, 209, 211, 212, 229, 230, 232, 233, 237, 238

Petersburg, St. Petersburg 12, 14, 21, 49, 52, 53, 72, 73, 75, 76, 77, 80, 81, 88, 94, 95, 96, 97, 98, 102, 103, 105, 107, 110, 128, 129, 131, 132, 135, 139, 141, 142, 145, 146, 147, 150, 151, 153, 157, 159, 160, 163, 165, 168, 169, 170, 171, 174, 179, 180, 183, 184, 185, 188, 192, 193, 204, 211, 218, 230, 233, 234, 240, 241, 250

Petrovskoe 84, 162, 234, 239

Petyer Feodorovich, Grand Duke 157

Philipievna 88

Philosphov, Major General Mikhail 138

Poland 25, 52, 58, 101, 187, 229, 231, 233

Polotsk 46

Poltava 14, 48, 50, 51, 69, 109, 237

Potemkin 191, 235

Preobrazhensky Regiment 95, 101, 139, 140, 229, 237

Prokopovich, Theophane 51

Pruth River 52, 58, 86, 102, 109, 237

Pskov 14, 141, 183, 189, 191, 192, 204, 218, 219, 231, 234, 235

Pushkin, Alexander 1, 9, 10, 13, 14, 205, 242

Pushkin, Col.André 184

Pushkin, Sergey Lvovich 205

R

Rabutin, Count 94, 102, 103

Racine 14, 84

Ragola 132, 141, 154, 155, 156, 162, 234

Raguzinski, Savva 27, 28, 43, 44, 49, 68, 100, 102

Ranenburg 98

Reding, General 141

Repnin 85, 86, 159, 161

Resanov, Gabriel 77

Reval (Talinn) 13, 14, 52, 53, 56, 58, 126, 127, 128, 132, 133, 134, 135, 137, 138, 139, 140,

141, 144, 145, 146, 147, 148, 149, 150, 151, 152, 154, 155, 156, 157, 158, 159, 160, 161, 162, 163, 166, 181, 191, 216, 230, 231, 234, 237, 239

Riga 52, 86, 127, 141, 151, 169, 230, 240

Rode, Georg Reynhold 148

Rogervik 172, 177, 180, 240, 241

Romanov, Sergei 188, 190

Roos, General 50

Rotkirkh 218, 221, 230

Rumiantsev 55, 209

Runovo 183, 189

Russia 1, 2, 9, 10, 11, 14, 15, 16, 17, 18, 19, 20, 25, 28, 44, 45, 46, 48, 49, 50, 51, 52, 53, 55, 57, 58, 59, 61, 64, 65, 67, 68, 70, 72, 74, 77, 78, 79, 82, 84, 86, 87, 89, 90, 91, 92, 100, 105, 106, 107, 109, 110, 127, 132, 134, 139, 142, 143, 144, 149, 151, 153, 154, 161, 162, 168, 169, 170, 171, 172, 175, 176, 177, 179, 180, 181, 186, 188, 192, 193, 204, 205, 207, 211, 215, 216, 219, 220, 225, 228, 229, 232, 234, 235, 237, 238, 239, 240, 241, 253

Russian Navy 105, 178, 188, 217

Russian Senate 21, 22, 104, 152, 172, 211, 237

Ruysch, Professor 61

S

Saint Denis 62

Salih V (Miara) 21, 22

San Sebastian 69

Schlüsselburg 169

Schoenebeck 46

Schumacher, Johann-David 145

Selenginsk 102, 103, 109

Shapirov, Peter 80

Sheremetev, Boris 49

Shevakinsky 171

Shuvalov, Count Peter 175, 179, 180

Siberia 96, 97, 100, 101, 104, 107, 110, 126, 142, 145, 169, 234, 238, 240

Siniavin 53

Sjöberg, Christina Regina Matveevna 128

Sjöberg, Christina Regina Matveevna von 128, 130, 170

Sjöberg Georg-Karl 127, 156, 162, 163

Sjöberg Georg-Karl von 156

Sjöberg, Georg-Karl von 162, 163

Sjöberg, Matthias Johann von 127, 147

Slavianoserbsk 169, 240

Slavonic-Greek-Latin Academy 44

Spiritov, Admiral 186

Staroladhozhky convent 170

Stockfors 161, 170, 239

Stockholm 15, 127, 213

Sublime Porte (see Ottoman Empire) 44, 52

Sudan 19, 23, 24, 25, 223, 252

Sumarokov, Peter 98, 101

Suvorov, Alexander 143, 187, 239

Suvorov, Vasili 142

Suyda 183, 187, 188, 189, 190, 192, 193, 204, 205, 230, 234, 235, 241

Sweden 48, 49, 52, 85, 132, 136, 151, 161, 170, 216, 237, 239

T

Talysin 102

Tatischev 59

Taytsy 183, 189, 234

Tchaikovsky Street 204

Teplov, Gregory 185

Tessé, Marshal de 62

Tikhvin 103, 234

Timbuktu 24

Timofeev, Maxim 178

Tobol-Ichimsk 169

Tobolsk 95, 96, 97, 98, 102, 103, 104, 109, 230, 234, 238, 240

Tolstoya, Ustina 192

Tolstoy, Peter 27, 94

Tondibi 23

Torgau 58

Touat 24

Toulouse, Comte de 70

Trezzini 171

Tripoli 25

Troyat, Henri 157, 180

Trubetskoy, Prince Nikita 180

Tsarskoe Selo 184, 191, 218

Tuffereau 78

Turenne 64

Turkey (see also Ottoman Empire) 20, 23, 25, 45, 51, 52, 186, 239

Tuvolkov 74

U

Ukraine 14, 25, 28, 171, 240

V

Vallières 72

Vasilevskiy Island 170

Vasiliev, Andre Vauban 43

Vegmas river 82

Vegner 16, 19, 130, 168, 211, 212, 213, 214, 253

Vendôme 64

Venetians 26

Veselovsky 142

Veyman, General 187

Villiard 64

Vilnius 14, 43, 46, 47, 49, 55, 90, 237

Volkonskaya, Princess Petrovna 87, 92, 93, 94, 95, 97, 98, 99, 100, 101, 102, 103, 107, 110, 142

Von Anhalt-Zerbst 157, 181

Von Pilhau, Pilar 156

Von Taneev 159

Von Tiren, Joachim 154, 155, 156, 162

Von Voberzer, Alexander 188, 190

Voronezh 45

Vsevolovsky 103

Vyborg 52, 159, 169, 173, 174, 209, 240

W

White Sea 82

Bartjens, Willem 58

Wittenberg, University of 15, 167

Y

Yanov, Constantin 43

Yurov 64, 66, 67, 68, 76, 77

Yusuf 21

Z

Zenan, King of Assini 101

Zotov, Konon 66, 82